Walking with God
52 Weeks of the Year

May 30, 2012

Congratulations Blake on your
High School graduation!

Love, DeeDee

! See especially pp. 46, 105, 113, 142, 152,
192, 286, 324, 227,

DD

Walking with God 52 Weeks of the Year

INCLUDING WALKING WITH
GOD AND FAMILY LIVING

Love from
Cynthia Shoemaker

Cynthia C. J. Shoemaker

To order additional copies of this book, contact:
Xlibris Corporation
1-888-795-4274
www.Xlibris.com
Orders@Xlibris.com
46304

DEDICATION

"This book is dedicated to my four children and to their children and to all who have helped me over the years."

PREFACE

These meditations, written over a 14 to 25 year period, began with a goal of 365 days but became *Walking with God 52 Weeks of the Year* and 300 days to allow for a weekend day and holidays. Prayers that are appropriate for individuals, workplace concerns, world events, child raising, family living, and children as they reach young adulthood are here. Each single day and meditation or essay is meant to stand alone. The author's years of research and graduate teaching in the fields of early childhood education, child development, family types, ages and stages including the importance of parent involvement enhance the second part of the book captioned "Walking with God and Family Living." Child development is the same in every culture so some pictures of children growing up in Africa, taken by a dear friend, are included at the end of the book. So many families today are enmeshed in work and family life that some insights into ages and stages through which children naturally progress, seemed helpful to include in a book of daily devotions. My daily quiet time of prayer and Bible study began 44 years ago, and continues to this day, and has inspired this book. Some additional insights into ages and stages were late additions to this work:

Walking with God is . . . enjoying nature at any age.

"The earth is the Lord's and all that is in it, the world and those who live in it." ((Ps 24:1 NRSV)

When I was seven and in second grade I walked to school every day in Winter Park, Florida. My friend and I walked through the arch covered walkways of Rollins College there. On the way home often low branches of fruit trees would be hanging right over the sidewalk and we could pick a tangerine and eat it as we were walking home.

Later in fifth grade my awareness of nature was expanded by Miss Rice, our fifth grade teacher. She thought our learning should include learning about wild flowers and the song birds around the Arlington, Virginia area where we now lived. Everyday we learned about one or two new birds or flowers.

Still later as a 13-year-old going to Girl Scout Camp in the mountains near Cloudcroft and Ruidoso, New Mexico, I loved the views of mountains from our cabins and on the hikes. Even now, as a grandmother I enjoy the fields and woods along my commute to work.

God's provision of creation can be noticed and enjoyed at any age, starting very early with touch and smell of flowers and green leaves.

Lord, help us build an awareness of nature with children.

Walking with God and family living means . . . respecting diversity early and learning about new things.

"There is no longer Jew or Greek, there is no longer slave or free, there is no longer male or female; for all of you are one in Jesus Christ." (Gal 3:28 NRSV)

As a young teen grows up, more independence as appropriate and safe, is in order. When I was 13 years old in the early 1950's we lived in El Paso, Texas. My friends and brother and I rode the bus a long way to school, so it seemed natural to take the same public bus transportation with a friend downtown to look at the department stores.

As teenagers we always liked to sit in the back of the bus on the bench seat. We noticed the little sign and arrow that said "colored section" above it but we thought it was graffiti! Someone finally reproached us for sitting there although I don't recall if we moved or not. Looking back I now can recall other symbols of segregation which are mostly gone now. Today all diversity is much more welcome by race, ethnicity, gender or appearance. If someone comes to fix your computer, you don't care what they look like if only they can make it work right! Even if they have green skin and two heads, if they are able to fix the computer it's okay. Talent and competence triumph old prejudices in the modern day.

At thirteen and fourteen I was allowed to go to a horseback riding "trail camp" in the mountains of New Mexico. I even learned to rope (lasso) a calf from a moving horse! Later, still a teen, I took a long trip by train from St. Louis to visit friends in El Paso. This did not seem odd for, as a five-year-old, my mother and two brothers and I had taken two or three long train trips back and forth from Florida to Massachusetts and Connecticut to live with one or another of her two older sisters. Taking a train to go to college did not seem new or overwhelming when that made sense for a family with three more children at home and only one car. These train trips might be airplane trips today.

Lord, let us let our children branch out as they are growing up. Help them to notice the culture in which they find themselves for once they see two cultures they will see there are more than two.

ACKNOWLEDGEMENTS

Many thanks are given to contributing author Rev. Allison Jones Lundeen, who is in active ministry in the Presbyterian Church today and has given many insightful and well-thought-out sermons. Also many thanks are given to those with photo credits listed at the end of the book under #300 who have helped bring these words to life.

Cynthia C. J. Shoemaker, Ph.D.
June, 2010

TABLE OF CONTENTS

#1

Walking with God is . . .   finding new opportunities in the midst of any challenge.

"If any want to become my followers, let them deny themselves and take up their cross daily and follow me." (Luke:23 NRSV)

We can see the power of God to bring about change and transformation in a rainbow. A majestic rainbow arching across the sky is an inspiring sight. We all have "rainbow experiences" in which opportunities come out of challenges, and something better, sometimes far more abundantly than all we ask or think (Eph 3:20 RSV), comes about. When we praise the Lord for all things that happen as part of His will for our lives and learning, new insights emerge. If we look beyond appearances for the potential for good that is in every experience even though it may be hidden, God's creativity boosts us forward. Is there something I've done or written that needs a fresh look to be updated? God's call to you may appear humanly impossible, but as we move into the information age, many new things are possible. And we know that with God all things are possible.

The apostle Paul said "it is by Grace you have been saved, through faith—and this is not of your own doing, it is the gift of God" (Eph 2:8 NRSV). God doesn't require us to be perfect. God asks us for honest effort, perseverance, humility, and repentance if we make a mistake. If we are to find new opportunities in the midst of challenges, know that the power of God is behind us, encouraging us and giving us guidance. As you build, develop, write, launch, and establish new projects and programs that help people in need, God will guide you to follow the path he has created for you. Our opportunity for transformation awaits us.

Lord, help us see the opportunities you provide.

#2

Walking with God is . . .   knowing God is my provider and opens a world of opportunity to me.

"The one who endures to the end will be saved." (Matt 10:22 NRSV)

Knowing that God is the one source of all our blessings, material or spiritual, means that I know that God is my provider and can open a world of opportunities to me. Because I am aware of the presence of God, I accept each opportunity, or as many as possible, and move forward with them. Often this requires endurance _and_ creative thinking. Should I climb _over_ this obstacle? _around_ it? _under_ it? _through_ it? Or simply stay put and turn the obstacle into a new invention and a source of prosperity?

The thinkers Isaac Newton, Daniel Bernoulli, and Michael Farrady thought and thought about ordinary things and discovered wonderful insights into the natural world (gravity, the principles of fluid and thrust that allow an airplane to fly, and electromagnetism and the electric motor). When we learn how little was known about these things in their day and age (1665 to 1831), we realize how big an obstacle these discoveries must have presented to these fairly ordinary, but bright people, some of whom were working-class people. Their stories and others like them encourage us to persevere and "enhance to the end" the opportunities we are given. God has many blessings awaiting us and for others who will be blessed by our perseverance and endurance.

Remember: God is "able to provide you with every blessing in abundance, so that by always having enough of everything, you may abundantly share in every good work" (2 Cor 9:8 NRSV). Whether these are times of waiting or times of moving ahead, we can pray for direction, and trust God to guide us—He is our provider and opens a world of opportunity to us.

Lord, help us to follow the guidance you give.

#3

Walking with God is . . .   understanding the difference between
commitment and surrender. Commitment is
about doing; surrender is about being.

"To all who received him, who believed in his name, he gave power to become children of God." (John 1:12)

If we surrender to God and focus on *being* a child of God, then we are able to commit to *doing* for God. *Surrender* is a positive word with Christ. Our culture tells us surrender is weak and negative. Paul told us in 2 Corinthians 12:9 (RSV) that the Lord told him that "my grace is sufficient for you for my power is made perfect in weakness . . . for whenever I am weak, then I am strong." Walking with God is about surrender. It's not about being a "better" or "stronger" Christian. It's about following.

"Follow me and I will make you fishers of men" is not a commitment command from Jesus . . . it's a surrender command. Remember the song you learned as a child . . . " Jesus loves me this I know, for the Bible tells me so . . . little ones to him belong . . . . they are weak but he is strong." In weakness there is strength. Write in a Journal about your weaknesses . . . give them to God and ask God to be your strength.

Lord, help me to surrender the control.
Rev. Allison Jones Lundeen

#4

Walking with God is . . .   not settling for plain life but expecting and looking for life-abundant.

"I have come that they may have life and have it abundantly."
(John 10:10 NRSV)

Christ does not want us to settle for less. Are you or I scared to part with mediocrity because you or I aren't sure of our Lord? Ask him to "help my unbelief" (Mark 9:24) and give him your whole life. God is waiting to bless us with unimaginable abundance but is unable to do so if we are holding on to "good enough." Even Jabez prayed, "Lord, bless me indeed, enlarge my horizons with your hand upon me" (1 Chron 4:9-10). You were created in the image of God; you are an heir of the Kingdom. You and I are not expected to *not* want the best. Think about what you think of as the best and what God thinks of as the best for you. Read Isaiah 55, "For my ways are not your ways . . . . neither are my thoughts your thoughts, says the Lord." Let go of the security blanket of your life—a job? a relationship? an addiction? an anger?—and watch God fill you with life abundant. God will give you an unbelievable deal on your trade-in. Settle for more. Write in a Journal about how you would like your life to look that is different, two months from now. What do you really WANT in life?

Lord, help me to know what I really want in life.
Rev. Allison Jones Lundeen

#5

Walking with God is . . .   choosing for yourself what is better.

"Mary has chosen the better way, which will not be taken away from her." (Luke 10:38-42 NRSV)

Jesus's rebuke of Martha is not for being helpful and productive around the house. It is because she has submitted to the cultural expectation for herself, rather than choosing for herself in the moment what was better. Jesus affirms Mary because she drew on her God-given power to choose—to sit at his feet regardless of the cultural and gender expectations. God has gifted you with His power. We are granted gifts and abilities and interests and passions. Choose for yourself what is better. What is it that you WANT in life? God wants you to use your gifts and your desires to honor him and to honor others. You will not know peace if you are giving up your power to someone else's wants for your life. Practice the presence and awareness of God. Be in prayer throughout your day . . . and be in tune with when to sit at Jesus's feet and when to serve Jesus.

Lord, help me to be in tune with you.
Rev. Allison Jones Lundeen

#6

Walking with God is . . .   recognizing God's answer to my prayers
with a grateful heart.

"God is not a God of disorder but a God of peace." (1 Cor 14:33 NRSV)

God has given me a way to proclaim good news of his love in many ways, both simple and complex. Simply welcoming a child or a stranger might be one of these. When I accept daily events with a grateful heart, I am given the grace to recognize God's answer to prayer, so every day is a fresh new start for me. I take new thoughts, experiences, and insights with me into each day. God is within me and within all others. God is helping me to make a fresh start in a goal, a relationship, or in life. Divine order is not disorder.

I know that in gardening, plants need nourishment and watering to help them have strong roots to support them in the years to come. I remember now, that I can have deep spiritual roots, rooted in the rich soil of God's divine love and peace. This love and peace nourishes me and all my relationships, so I remember to take time to water and nourish my spiritual roots, to praise the Lord, for everything that happens to me has part of his divine plan for my life, and to try to see things from a new perspective—God's higher perspective. God's divine order will emerge more clearly to me as I do this. Remember, "It is not you that supports the root, but the root that supports you" (Rom 11:18 NRSV).

Lord, remind me to let you support me.

#7

Walking with God is . . .   walking by faith, not by sight.

"If you know me you will know my Father, also." (John 14:7 NRSV)

John says that those who receive Christ are children of God (John 1:12). When we open our lives to God, we build a close relationship with God. To build this close relationship we communicate with Jesus, confide in Him, open our hearts to Him, and tell Him our feelings. He will show us the Father and the path we are to take. Through my daily experiences of acting on my faith in God, I do learn to let go of concerns and let God do what is best. He has brought me this far; He will be with me every step of the way into the future.

"Be strong and of good courage; be not frightened, neither be dismayed; for the Lord your God is with you wherever you go." Joshua 1:9 tells us (RSV). Knowing this, I give my whole attention to divine wisdom. I enjoy comfort and peace from just knowing God is in charge. By letting go and letting God, I cooperate with God's divine work and "walk by faith, not by sight."

Lord, help me to "let go and let God."

#8

Walking with God is . . .   listing dreams and the steps to reaching them.

"See, the former things have come to pass, and new things I now declare." (Is 42:9 NRSV)

Where God is, divine order will prevail. I relax and open my mind to new possibilities and creatively revisit past ideas for possibilities. Events that are planned or unplanned can bless me with new understanding and appreciation. Therefore "I will praise the name of God with a song," Psalm 69:30. Just widening one's peripheral vision allows this to happen sometimes.

God's presence motivates me to make the most of my talents and abilities that He has given me—perceived ones and unperceived ones—in order to reach the fulfillment of my dreams that are inspired by God.

"From there you will seek the Lord your God, and you will find him, if you search for him with all your heart and soul" (Deut 4:29).

List below the dream or dreams you would like to pursue and five first steps that are needed for each dream. List steps that take about five minutes to do. For example, call a travel agent or look on the Internet to find out the cost of a trip you want to take.

Lord, help me to trust in my dreams that are from you.

#9

Walking with God is . . .   seizing the opportunity to show God's love.

"Ask and it will be given to you, search and you will find; knock and the door will be opened for you." (Matt 7:7 NRSV)

Do words and actions show the love of God to others? You and I always have the opportunity to show others what the God of love looks like. With every step you and I take, the presence of the Lord God has gone before us, so you and I can step forward with confidence and faith (Jo 1:9, "Be strong and of good courage be not . . . dismayed; for the Lord your God is with you wherever you go.").

Even when you and I are doing something new or in unfamiliar surroundings, we are enfolded in God's love. You and I can have faith that God will guide us and our loved ones and keep our own and their way safe, as we seize the opportunity to show God's love whenever we can.

Relaxing and relying on the power of God to do "far more abundantly that all that I ask or think" enables you and I to step out with confidence and take positive action. Our goals are dreams inspired by God which are becoming a reality. You and I can keep our goals clearly in our minds and hearts, and God's presence motivates us to use our talents and abilities to reach the fulfillment of our dreams.

Lord, remind me that you can do far more
abundantly than all that I ask or think—even
though I ask and think a lot.

#10

Walking with God is . . .   committing your work to the Lord.

"Commit your work to the Lord, and your plans will be established."
(Prov 16:3 NRSV)

Water in motion in a busy pool or inlet, can be like a life—with many tiny subtleties that make up the whole—subtleties that are invisible to others perhaps. There is usually a shallow part—the puddles, like daily routine, a middle depth part, like one's work and social activities, and a deep end for deep problems, for expert divers and/or those with a firmly rooted faith.

If you and I could see the invisible activity of God's grace, we would see a constant swirl of love moving in and around us. As you and I thank God for the sometimes invisible blessings of his grace and love, we become more aware of it and perhaps of blessings of which we had been unaware. We can give thanks for all the ways God blesses us and commit our work to the Lord, that our plans might be established.

If you and I make a mistake, we "cast all our [my] anxiety on him for he cares about us [me]" (1 Peter 5:7) and know that if I make a mistake, grace is God's love and acceptance of me as I am right now. Grace moves in many ways to bless you and I and to guide us, to assure us that we can do better and to show us that we are not limited by what we thought we could do in the past.

Lord, help me remember that walking with You is committing my work to the Lord.

#11

Walking with God is . . .   trusting in the power of God.

"He looked up to heaven, and blessed and broke the loaves . . . and all ate and were filled." (Matt 14:19-20 NRSV)

Christ did not question that all would be fed from just five loaves and two fish, but instead offered a blessing for what he *did* hold in His hands. Often what we hold in our hands seems like so little, when a need seems so great. But trusting God to bless and prosper our efforts, to provide the growth and multiply the results, enables us to move forward actively and productively. If we are really blessed, we will even see or hear about the results. But trusting God to provide may also take twenty or thirty years or a lifetime, as some missionaries have found.

As we express our joy and thanksgiving for God's many gifts to us, we do whatever we can to bless others. Being God's partner in peace, in action among people, and believing that God will provide, helps us to follow Jesus's example and walk with God.

Remembering "Behold I am doing a new thing, now it springs forth; do you not perceive it? I will make a way in the wilderness" (Is 43:19 RSV) reminds us to drop preconceived notions as to what success or results might look like, and to be open to new ideas, pathways, and "ways in the wilderness."

Lord, help me to trust in your power.

#12

Walking with God is . . .   shining God's light on what is most important.

"For the Lord God will be their light." (Rev 22:5 NRSV)

When faith comes into your mind and heart, something wonderful happens. You gain greater understanding of any situation by putting it in God's light—and God takes your mind off any distractions and focuses your attention on what you need to know or do. The guidance of God is a light of love and understanding. As you focus, you persevere, you learn new things, you widen your horizons and scan for new solutions. You are strengthened day by day and year by year and live "fresh and green" throughout all your days (Ps 92:14 NIV).

Shining God's light on what is most important focuses us in such a way that we come away with greater understanding and appreciation of what is seen and heard. We are able to praise God, as this is His perfect plan for our lives.

Lord, help us to praise you for your perfect plan for our lives.

#13

Walking with God is . . .   knowing that God will help me find the right solution. He is the answer to every prayer.

"Call to me and I will answer you and tell you great and hidden things that you have not known." (Jer 33:3 NRSV)

Jeremiah 33:3 has been called "God's phone number" as you can "call" whenever you need to. Whenever you call to me, I will answer, God is saying, and we can know that His answer will be what is highest and best for us (His utmost and His highest for us as one book title says), even though it may be different than we expected.

God has promised to do "far more abundantly than all that we ask or think" (Eph 3:20 NRSV), and He can show you how to do more than you ever dreamed you could. He can take you beyond your greatest imaginings and bring untold blessings into your life. No dream is too great and no need is too small for Him to handle.

Like the streams of living water that flow out of the believer's heart (John 7:38 NRSV), Christ can pour unhindered out of your hearts to refresh and sustain a needy world. The "elevator of faith" will lift our spirits as we focus on God and God's love—just don't get off at the wrong floor or too soon. Then we can give the world the water of life that we receive from Christ, in Christ's name.

Our prayer is that the love of Christ renews
ourselves and our needy world.

#14

Walking with God is . . .   holding on to Jesus, the Bread of Life.

Jesus said to them, "I am the bread of life." (John 6:35 RSV)

A wonderful book is titled *Sleeping with Bread: Holding What Gives You Life* by Dennis, Sheila, and Matthew Linn. During the bombing raids of World War II, thousands of children were orphaned and left to starve. The fortunate ones were rescued and placed in refugee camps where they received food and good care. But many of these children, who had lost so much, could not sleep at night. They feared waking up at night to find themselves once again homeless and without food. Nothing seemed to reassure them. Finally someone hit upon the idea of giving each child a piece of bread to hold at bedtime. Holding their bread, these children could finally sleep in peace. All through the night the bread reminded them: "Today I ate, and I will eat again tomorrow."

The refugee children of World War II were only secure when they had bread to clutch through the night. Jesus is the bread of life. Security and new life come through Christ. In Christ we are reconciled to a loving and perfect relationship with our Father (and Mother) God. Regardless of the emotional bond or lack of bond that was developed for each of us early in life, we are re-parented in God through Jesus Christ, the bread of life. Our god is the ultimate attachment parent. God's discipline, rearing, and boundaries for us revolve around God's relationship with us through Jesus Christ, the bread of life. The baby of our soul is not left to cry it out. John 6 verse 35 tells us that with Jesus we will never be hungry or thirsty. Verse 37 tells us that anyone who comes to him will not be turned away. We are held and comforted and nurtured in the arms of God whenever we want, as children or as adults. Verse 39 tells us that he will lose none of us. He gives us himself to hold, to clutch . . . through the days, nights, wars, and peace times of our lives. This reconciled relationship, this re-parenting is possible through Jesus, the bread of life, who gave his life for us.

My prayer is that Lord you would help me and all of my friends and family sleep with bread, and hold what gives them life. You, Jesus, are my bread of life. Amen.
Rev. Allison Jones Lundeen

#15

Walking with God is . . .   letting go and letting God.

"Fear not for I am with you, be not dismayed for I am your God. I will strengthen you and I will help you. I will uphold you with my victorious right arm." (Is 41:10 RSV)

Trust in God is a choice to believe and to be guided by God. The apostle Peter chose to trust Jesus and stepped out of the boat when Jesus said "come." He did not start to sink until he looked down and "lost his nerve," as we say today. Jesus reached out a hand to him and saved him. This is a good example of why we should "keep our eyes on God and not on the problem." Letting go and letting God is a practical approach that allows us to relax and allows for time and perceptions to change. With trust in God I have peace of mind and can do my part in God's unfolding divine plan. Just thinking of God upholding me with his victorious right arm gives me added strength and clearness of thought. By letting go of worry and not being "dismayed" easily, I save a lot of time and energy.

Psalm 63:1, 6-8 (KJV) says and I pray: Lord,
"because You have been my help (in times past), my soul
follows close behind You . . . Your right hand upholds me."

#16

Walking with God is . . .   growing toward Christ.

"God has not given us a spirit of fear but of power, and love and of a sound mind." (2 Tim 1:7 KJV)

Christ's life of love was his sermon. As we show love, kindness, and compassion, we can be like a letter from Christ "to be known and read by all" (2 Cor 3:2 NRSV). The Bible could be known as the only book we'll ever read for which the author is present with us as we read it.

When you and I are down, we can pick up the Bible and read the verse for today and read the Psalms. Psalm 91 has been called "God's insurance policy." Psalm 37 tells us to "fret not yourself about the wicked . . . for they shall fade like the grass" (RSV). If you have seen this happen, and many have, your faith builds and you can see more clearly that it will happen again. Where is Hitler today? Stalin? Where is the Berlin wall? (All in rubble.) These are large examples, but small ones happen every day.

William Penn once said, "People who do God's work don't need praise and reward—they always get it in the end." As we grow toward Christ, we can claim a spirit of love and courage and self-control.

Lord, help us to rest in the shadow of your wings and draw upon your power and self-control.

#17

Walking with God is . . .   honoring diversity.

"Beloved, let us love one another." (1 John 4:7)

Albert Einstein once said, "In the middle of difficulty lies opportunity." He also characterized his work as "creative combinativity" meaning that he creatively combined elements in new ways. Energy, mass, and the speed of light existed before he wrote the famous equation "$E=MC^2$." He just combined them in a new way.

As we combine people in new ways and honor all people as they work together, tremendous new energy, power, and insights may also emerge. An atmosphere of listening, mutual understanding, and mutual respect builds the opportunity for new perspectives and even new markets in the business world. As we listen to and watch others, a tremendous appreciation of God's diverse world builds within us. What wonderful qualities has God given this person? Even an ostrich (known to be stupid—see Job 39:17) is a fast runner and has beautiful and useful plumes. When we build on strengths, and on our own strengths, and not on our weaknesses, wonderful abilities and facets emerge that help us develop new and loving approaches for the future.

Lord, help us to combine people and ideas creatively.

#18

Walking with God is . . .   waiting for the Lord.

"Trust in the Lord with all your heart and do not rely on your own insight; In all your ways acknowledge Him and He will make straight your paths." (Prov 3:5-6)

What helps us to trust in God as you and I wait for something? "You also must be patient. Strengthen your hearts," James tells us (chapter 5:8a NRSV). And Psalm 37 (3-5 RSV) says: "Trust in the Lord with all your heart . . . take delight in the Lord and he will give you the desires of your heart. Commit your way to the Lord, trust in Him and He will act." The verse from Proverbs above says, "Trust not in your own _understanding_" in the King James Version (KJV) and both "insight" and "understanding" remind us that a higher, wider perspective than our own may be operating. These verses have helped many people "wait for the Lord" whether for a new baby, a difficult divorce to be finished, or a troublesome illness to be over and healing to take place. These simple words remind us of what is always true: God is always with us, enfolding us in his love and assuring us that all is in divine order. This divine order is God's perfect plan for us. You and I experience serenity and peace in knowing that God's presence and God's wisdom is within us. God not only inspires you and me, but also shows us the ways in which our dreams can become a reality.

Lord, help us to be still and know that you are God.

#19

Walking with God is . . . knowing that with God all things are possible.

"For God all things are possible." (Mark 10:27 NRSV)

What may seem impossible for me alone may be entirely possible when I include God in my plans. If I have faith that God will inspire me in choosing my goals and activities and help me in achieving them, I can dream and stretch out beyond my limitations or the limited expectations of others or even of my own.

Now may be the time to step forward in faith. Now may be the time to accept the golden opportunities God is presenting to me. If I dream on one day and write down my ideas, do a reality check the next day, and withhold criticism until a third day, I can step out with confidence, knowing that God is supporting me. After all, He created my imagination, a great gift. Walt Disney always separated these three—dreamer, realist, and critic—on to separate days in order not to limit the dreams and creativity that are possible when new connections and combinations are made, without limiting them. Thomas Edison set himself a goal of a certain number of new ideas per week and came up with six ideas every ten days and one major idea every six months. To experience the blessings God has for me, it is important to remember that all things are possible with God.

Lord, open my mind to the divine ideas you have for me.

#20

Walking with God is . . .   asking and imagining receiving the answer.

"Whatever you ask for in prayer, believe you have received it, and it will be yours." (Mk 11:24)

"What you can conceive, you can achieve" is not simply a saying but a very real problem-solving approach. In order to conceptualize something, you have to think what it will look like and, how it will work. In fact to develop the best ideas, use all of the senses, for what it will sound like, smell like, feel like, and maybe even taste like. This last is not recommended for machinery, however.

For instance, do you want a happy home? What cooking would it smell like? taste like? Baking bread, even in a bread machine as Dad's or Mom's special project, makes a wonderful smell. What decor would contribute to each room? What would it *feel* like? Would people be loving and supportive of each other? What would it *look* like? (Otherwise, how would you know when you have found it, if you're looking for new furniture or a new home?) What would it *sound* like? music playing? preschoolers screaming? Maybe you need a new rule, "no screaming in the house" or "use your inside voices in the house."

God's grace moves in to bless us as we persevere and try to follow the path Christ laid out for us of peace, love, service to others, ignoring differences, and seeking mutual goals.

Ask God for faith, believe you have received it, and it will be yours.

#21

Walking with God is . . .   resting our confidence not on what we can see but on the goodness of God.

"Don't be afraid . . . those that are with us are greater than those who are with them." (2 Kings 6:16 NIV)

"The things that are seen are temporary but the things that are not seen are eternal." (2 Cor 4:18 NKJV)

The story in Kings about Elisha says that Elisha prayed, "Please open his eyes that he may see." So the Lord opened the eyes of the servant and he saw; the mountain was full of horses and chariots of fire all around Elisha (2 Kings 6:17 NRSV). Sometimes when you are working for the better way, whether in the workplace, at home, or in the community, for what is good and true, it seems as if those around you cannot see. Every now and then a time comes when their eyes may be opened and you will be allowed to see them "seeing." They may not acknowledge this to you or to others, or they may even claim credit for this "insight" for themselves, as sometimes happens in today's workplace. But your prayer that their eyes be opened and that the good work move forward has been answered.

No evil in the world can thwart God's purposes. God's holy forces of good surround us and are working on our behalf and on the behalf of the better way. Little things known as "taking the rocks out of your path" versus "putting the rocks in your path" may be all a coworker or colleague can do, but God's work can move forward. Elisha's resounding confidence still speaks assurance and comfort to us today. Know that there are more people backing you and supporting your position than you ever imagined.

Lord, like the first time riding a bike can open blessings,
I can hardly wait for the next blessing.

#22

Walking with God is . . .   moving mountains.

"If you say to this mountain 'be removed and cast into the sea' it will be done." (Matt 21:21 NKJV)

Verse 22 of Matthew goes on to say, "And whatever you ask in prayer, believing, you will receive. Living as children of the light" (Eph 5:8 NIV) can lead to mountains being moved. We are meant to be glowingly alive, full of life and of the light that we share. Verse 14 of Ephesians 5 says, "Sleepers awake, rise from the dead, and Christ will shine on you." Not being afraid to shine for Christ helps us to persevere in the better way, toward higher goals; for the world needs people who are willing to shine as God's children of light.

A spotlight on a stage focuses attention on what is most important. Shining God's light on a problem takes my mind off distractions and focuses my mind on what I need to know. Slowly, perhaps a teaspoonful or a tablespoonful at a time, a mountain *can* be moved. Whether it is a mountain of ignorance, disease, poverty, terrorism, or simply not knowing the stages and sequences of child development and what to expect next, God's light can help us think through, around, or under, and help us to move this mountain.

Dear Lord, give me the desire to shine and stand out for you.
Give me the creativity to share your light in new ways. Amen.

#23

Walking with God is . . .   thinking bigger.

"Where two or three are gathered in my name, I am there among them."
(Matt 18:20 NRSV)

Never underestimate the power of praying with other believers. As God "opens the eyes of our souls" to see the good in all people, we are able to think bigger, with more imagination and with fewer limitations. Sharing with others builds this synergy through the power of prayer.

Imagining what would be good twenty years from now and ten years from now, and thanking God for it as *if* it existed today, enables us to picture something in more detail and list the steps needed to get there. Then when we list the *gaps* that still exist, we begin to "know what we don't know" and have more focus for researching and praying about those questions. Perhaps answers do exist, but not in a practical way as yet. For practice, try imagining all the ways the information age can help to make the lives of children better. Interactive positive activities on a computer might be one example of an answer. Leaving an electronic message on another device might be another answer.

All the great scientists and artists trying something new for the first time felt the tremendous stretch needed to think bigger and in a different way. Education has always helped societies move from one age into another. God can dream a bigger dream for you than you can dream for yourself, and your role on earth is to attach yourself to that divine dream and release yourself to it. Then trust that the way will be provided. Use your faith to rise above negative thoughts and replace them with positive thoughts.

Lord, show me your dream for me.

#24

Walking with God is . . .   treasuring ourselves as God treasures us and looking to God for our identity.

"So that times of refreshing may come from the presence of the Lord." (Acts 3:12 KJV)

Letting each day bring you to a greater awareness of your oneness with God, the Holy Spirit, and the knowledge that the "the kingdom of God is within you," builds a true sense of self-identity. Each person is unique with an individual purpose and their own particular talents. The early brain research on babies shows that a baby is born with billions of brain cells and trillions of brain connections that are either reinforced by their parents and their surrounding environment, or not reinforced and carved away. Thus a truly unique individual is created, above and beyond the original heredity. God's magnificent creations, human beings, are great masterpieces. You are a great masterpiece. We are truly blessed to live in an environment created to sustain and nurture us and a world of people. The sun's warmth, water, vegetation, fields, and all living things are part of God's gifts to that amazing creation—you. When you feel low, remember your true identity as one of God's amazing creations and His beloved child.

Lord, thank you for your times of refreshing and for creating me just as I am.

#25

Walking with God is . . .   faith, hope, and love, knowing that the
greatest of these is love.

"Now I will show you a still more excellent way." (1 Cor 12:31 NRSV)

At a wedding, one of the scripture readers, being a trifle flustered finished reading 1 Corinthians chapter 13 by saying, "And so abide faith, hope and the greatest of love is these." With a hasty correction she reread "faith, hope and love, but the greatest of these is love." The interrelationship of these three is significant and may be a little different for different people. Love often *does* require faith and also hope. As we pray for God's help in reflecting love in our relationships with others, we can remember that the gift of love is the most excellent way of serving God.

With faith, we can say a prayer every day for our loved ones in our quiet times. With hope, we can hope for God's best for this person, as this person unfolds God's divine and unique plan for their lives. Having faith to encourage these people (or one's self) to attach their lives to God's divine plan for life, and to hope for God's loving step-by-step guidance for this plan, fills my heart with love and gratitude. God's plans and dreams for us are usually bigger than you and I can dream for ourselves, but He also can provide the step-by-step guidance needed if you and I but release ourselves to it, and treat each day as an opportunity to learn.

Lord, help me to love as you would have me love.

#26

Walking with God is . . .   filling my home with the sacred atmosphere of God's presence.

"O Lord, I love the house in which you dwell, and the place where your glory abides." (Ps 26:8 NRSV)

"God saw every thing that he had made, and indeed, it was very good." (Gen 1:31 NRSV)

The presence of God is everywhere. In my home I want to remember that God's presence is there to welcome me. Because God gave us life, we are called to honor it in ourselves and to nourish it in others—our family and our society. The spirit of God within me makes my home a holy place, for the presence of God resides within me and is a presence of peace, love, and understanding. My home can be a place of renewal, refreshment, and peace for all who enter into it, including myself.

When we are saved by faith, Christ redeems us—we are saved—forever! He holds us and never lets us go. He has promised to help order our lives, and this includes our homes as we pray about daily, weekly, monthly, and yearly tasks. Extra energy and strength is ours to claim, as we pray:

" . . . for thine is the kingdom, and the power and the glory forever." Amen

#27

Walking with God is . . .   passing through the waters.

"Thus says the Lord . . . who created you . . . . when you pass through the waters, I will be with you;" (Is 43:1 NRSV)

When crossing a stream, a loving hand reached out to me as my foot stretched for the next rock. This is just the help God offers us through life. He will help and won't let me fall. I trust Him and reach out for His help in my quiet times. God is there to help us as we cross life's raging rivers as well as life's quiet streams. Sometimes we need to open our eyes to see where God *is* helping us in our lives, however. Jeremiah 31:3 tells us, "I have loved you with an everlasting love; therefore with loving-kindness I have drawn you" (KJV).

Faith brings you and me to a moment when we realize that we are on solid, safe ground in Christ's loving embrace, as we cross streams and rivers. God has given you and me the precious gifts of joy and gratitude, to sing praise and give thanks for this wonderful promise and truth.

Lord, help us reach for your hand for the next steps.

#28

Walking with God is . . .   waiting for the Lord.

"I believe that I shall see the goodness of the Lord in the land of the living. Wait for the Lord; be strong, and let your heart take courage; wait for the Lord." (Ps 27:13-14 NRSV)

My son was at college and on a very demanding Navy scholarship when he seriously injured his knee during a basketball game, which had been injured before playing high school football. The Navy had been very understanding, but he had been thinking of relinquishing his scholarship anyway, and working out the expense of this Ivy League engineering school in other ways, such as with an internship. This injury plus an incident on his Navy cruise seemed to be a catalyst for his decision, and in my prayers as a single mother around this subject, Psalm 27 and the verses above came clearly to me. The Bible offers us reassurance. Those who wait on the Lord do "find their strength renewed . . . . they will run and not grow weary, they will walk and not be faint" (Is 40:31 NIV).

This son did withdraw from the Navy, managed his finances creatively (with some help), and has completed graduate school. He is well into a fine career. His younger brother did stay the four years for the scholarship in a different service, the Air Force, also with a successful result.

Lord, help us to wait for you and to be strong and of good courage.

#29

Walking with God is . . .   telling the next generation the glorious
deeds of the Lord.

"We will tell the coming generation the glorious deeds of the Lord, and his might, and the wonders that he has done." (Ps 78:4 NRSV)

Our children and grandchildren need to see and hear about our faith at home, and see faith in action in our everyday lives. God has done many wonderful things in our lives, and His grace overflows to us. By surrendering to God, you and I open our lives to blessing after blessing.

As we share a greater awareness of God with our children and grandchildren, we are answering the question "If not me, then who?" Your and my commitment to live and share our lives so that we bring sacredness to all that we do, by thinking, living, and moving by faith, opens an almost bottomless well of refreshing water.

Whether it is saying (or teaching) bedtime prayers to a two-, three-, or five year-old grandchild, posting Bible verses in big print where they (and you) can see them, these and other simple steps, like saying grace before meals, are easy to do. They can result in an "oh, of course" attitude on the part of the children that will later bring you joy and pleasure for decades and generations.

Lord, remind us to say prayers with children.

#30

Walking with God is . . .   allowing God to guide us even when we don't understand the larger plan.

"We walk by faith, not by sight." (2 Cor 5:7 NRSV)

Letting go and letting God, I cooperate with the divine work God is bringing about. Abram did this when he followed God's direction to pack up and go to a new land. "Go from your country and your kindred and your father's house, to the land that I will show you," the Lord said to Abram (Gen 12:1 NRSV). Abram trusted God to lead him. God promised that "in you all the families of the earth shall be blessed" (verse 13). Abram later became Abraham and has been remembered down through the ages. So also must we trust God to show us each step in the larger plan for us. Each day brings new possibilities and opportunities for us to listen, to learn, and to serve God, especially as we move into this new era, the information age.

We can have faith that God is guiding us along the path that He wants us to take. He also gives us the courage to follow His leading. As I let God work through me, I put aside any thought of my limitations that might get in the way of a solution. I give my attention wholly to divine insights as they come and even write them down, to review later and at regular intervals.

Lord, help us to remember that following your guidance can lead
to the blessing of many.

#31

Walking with God is . . .   setting my mind on the Spirit.

"To set the mind on the spirit is life and peace." (Rom 8:6 NRSV)

Walking with God, in this walk of faith, is allowing my mind and body to relax in the sacred presence of God's unconditional love. Hebrews 10:23 goes on to say, "For He who promised is faithful." As I begin to feel peaceful and at rest, writers on creativity know that this is a first step to opening the mind to its own—and God's—tremendous potential. Gently, quietly, God speaks to me, and I relax into the calm of love and peace. As new ideas come to me, I jot them down for review later. Modern writers call this and its results "out of the box" thinking. My trust in God is complete, and I know God will lead me to experiencing wholeness in my life and in my spirit. His energy and healing and forgiveness are mine to claim. As God blesses me with peace, I invite God's healing activity into my mind and heart. Barriers are broken down, and I accept loving relationships, health, and creative insights that are mine to enjoy.

Lord, teach us to accept your blessings as freely as they are given.

#32

Walking with God is . . .   planning with God.

"Trust in the Lord with all your heart and do not rely on your own insight. In all your ways acknowledge him and he will make straight your paths.' (Prov 3:5-6 RSV)

These two verses were very helpful to me when I was in the middle of a messy divorce and had four children in college. Rather than suffer any more broken bones (eight plus a ruptured disk was enough), I had chosen to set up a new life and somehow, through scholarships, loans, and an auto accident settlement, we found money for all four children to finish college and later graduate school. Today, eighteen years later, all have finished graduate school, are married, and have children. These are indeed "plans for welfare, a future and a hope" (Jer 29:11 RSV). Not relying on my own insight or "understanding" (KJV) was hard at times, but as I had worries, I would get up in the night if necessary and write them down. Then I'd write a Bible verse or two beside each one from some of those used in these devotionals. This simple procedure brought guidance from the Lord, and I was able to sleep. One year I wrote, "Have three lawyers check house contract" and the next year the problem was "slipcover blue chair," which shows an example of how large problems move on by, and are replaced with small problems. All can be solved with prayer and reliance on the Lord.

Lord, help us remember, "It came to pass, it didn't come to stay"
when things get difficult.

#33

Walking with God is . . .   allowing Him to set my feet on a rock.

"[The Lord] drew me out of the miry bog, and set my feet upon a rock, making my steps secure." (Ps 40:2 NRSV)

When I remember God's promises and use the gift of prayer, I receive release and peace. Whether finding and learning my way in the work world, complex finances, or personal relationships, I know the better way will come to me or be revealed to me. As I set my problems before the Lord and enunciate them, my peripheral vision throughout the next few days picks up clues and answers to my "miry bog." Or it may be my faith and perseverance allows three days to pass, and a person in the workplace gets over *their* trouble and cheers up. "Even Christ rose from the dead in three days" has become a phrase that means have faith and patience. When I reach the limits of my human resources, I discover again the unlimited resources of God.

Lord, thank you for being with me always, especially today.

#34

Walking with God is . . .   walking in the good works that God prepared beforehand.

"For we are his workmanship created in Christ Jesus for good works which God prepared beforehand that we should walk in them." (Eph 2:10 RSV)

Some translations of the Bible end this verse with "that we should live in them" or "to become our way of life" (NRSV). Anyway we view it, this verse is consoling when we find ourselves in 'over our head' in something that is essentially a "good work." Whether it is a Chairmanship or as an officer of a nonprofit organization or an Internet enterprise, spreading love and caring for God's children will always be a worthwhile endeavor—a good work. If God prepared it beforehand, maybe I'm not so crazy to have gotten involved in it!

With God as my inspiration, I try to live a life of love and understanding and bring this to my initiatives. Our efforts, while perhaps not expert, may be just enough to inspire or focus others who ARE experts, to rise to the occasion and help accomplish a goal or mission.

Lord, help me to remember that if You helped get me into this, You will help get me through it or out of it.

#35

Walking with God is . . .   praising the Lord and "forgetting not all his benefits."

"Bless the Lord, O my soul, and forget not all his benefits." (Ps 103:2 RSV)

While driving along, listening to classical music, I like to add words to familiar classical melodies. The words in the verse and title above lend themselves beautifully to many tunes, even to Beethoven's ninth Symphony's Third Movement or to the Mozart Clarinet Concerto in A minor, second movement. Doing this instantly lifts my spirits—but of course is done best alone in the car, or in the shower. Music experts would tell us that 4/4 time or 3/4 time will lend themselves to certain verses particularly. Any music in these times will do—country, popular, whatever is familiar. Another set of words that fits many melodies is "Love abides, God's love abides, in you and me forever," which fits 3/4 or the waltz tempo. Music soothes the soul, and setting words to familiar tunes helps the brain to recognize the melodies by name more quickly as an added benefit, because two kinds of intelligences are being used.

The act of praising the Lord, alone, refreshes one. Remembering His benefits, looking out over beautiful seasonal foliage or landscapes adds to the peace it is possible to feel, even while driving.

Lord, thank you for the gift and benefit of music.

#36

Walking with God is . . .   understanding the deepest source of your
identity is God.

"The Lord is the one who goes before you. He will be with you, He will not
leave you nor forsake you." (Deut 31:8 RSV)

   Understanding that the deepest source of my identity is God means that I am
a child of the Most High God, and anything is possible to me. I am special. As
I question everything I do and ask, "Is this what God wants me to be doing?" I
hold everything up to the light of God's reality and truth. "Teach us to number
our days aright that we may gain a heart of wisdom," the Psalmist tells us (Ps
90:12 NIV), and the heart of wisdom begins to be mine. I look ahead to where
God is guiding me—a place of wisdom, fulfillment, peace and order. There is
order in every change inspired by God, and in every ending there is a beginning.
God will uphold me with his victorious right arm (Is 41:10).
   "Forgetting those things which are behind, I press forward towards the goal
for the prize of the upward call of God in Christ Jesus" (Phil 3:13-14). As I
walk with God, looking forward and knowing God as the deepest source of my
identity, all things are possible to me whether it's moving an office, moving a
house, or moving a job, or some other new beginning.
   Whether decisions need to be made, or just problems (challenges) listed on
a "To Do" list with days and dates beside them, I move forward with confidence
and verve. A new beginning that is a grand adventure in which I will help create
my own world of life-enriching experiences await me.

Lord, help me to see this as a new beginning.

#37

Walking with God is . . .   finding the joy of the Lord is your strength.

"The joy of the Lord is your strength." (Neh 8:10 NKJV)

My prayer to God is one of thanksgiving: *God, thank you for life and for all the blessings that life includes*. The joy of the Lord is indeed my strength and as I look back on what may have looked like a mountain only yesterday, and is only a small hill that I can climb perhaps with rest stops, or have already climbed, today. Whether I am taking down the Christmas tree or putting one up or even just planting a tree, I have new strength. Each new day is a new day in which I am reborn—spiritually as well as physically. I am open to new guidance from the Lord, and the good news indeed is that a child was born at Christmas who would bring greater love and understanding to us all and to the world. "Fear not for I bring you good tidings of great joy, for unto you is born a savior who is Christ the Lord" (Lk 2:10 KJV) is a message for all peoples at all times of the year.

God is the love who lives through us and in us, and it is His love that brings great joy for all people. It is His child, the Way-Shower, who would show people the divine potential that lies within all of us. Human beings do have "the mind of Christ" as brain research is now showing with billions of brain cells and trillions of brain connections. As these are used in infancy, in early childhood, and most of them, throughout life, we become stronger and more able to choose from all the possibilities God has put before us. Furthermore, divine wisdom and understanding will always be available to us.

Lord, your joy is truly our strength.

#38

Walking with God is . . .   abiding in the shadow of the Almighty.

"You who live in the shelter of the Most High, who abide in the shadow of the Almighty, will say to the Lord, 'My refuge and my fortress; My God in whom I trust.'" (Ps 91:1-2 RSV)

Psalm 91 has been called "our insurance policy" as it tells of God spreading his wings (pinions in King James Version) and "under his wings you will find refuge" (91:4). Watching birds and recalling these images remind us of God's promise to be our refuge when we face danger. We have a clear picture of God as our faithful protector. Isaiah 43 tells us, "When you pass through the waters, I will be with you; and through the rivers, they shall not overwhelm you . . . . Thus says the Lord who makes a way in the sea and a path in the mighty waters" (43:2, 16 NRSV). Psalm 107 tells us, "He led them forth by the right way" (verse 7). God is committed to leading us always onward to new life. He gives us courage to swim or to wade in deeper waters, as He knows the waters well, and our skill is less important than our faith in Him to show us *how* to improve our skill, if that's what is necessary.

"The Lord will guide you continually, and satisfy you continually, and satisfy your soul in drought, and strengthen your bones; you shall be like a watered garden, and like a spring of water, whose waters do not fail" (Is 58:11). As we praise the Lord and turn to Him continually, the power that comes only from Him will produce results and multiply them "far more abundantly than all that we ask or think." And furthermore God's assurance is with us "because you have made the Lord your refuge, the Most High you dwelling place, no evil shall befall you." (Ps 91:9-10).

Lord, please guide me continually.

#39

Walking with God is . . .   is moving ahead even when it seems impossible.

"Peter . . . walked on the water." (Matt 14:29 RSV)

God will not call you beyond *His* ability to see you safely to the other side. The walk of faith may *seem* like walking on water because God always calls us beyond our abilities. One should believe, for the walk of faith says "it's possible!"

As I move forward in the walk of faith, my positive thoughts create positive responses. I remember that God is always with me and his divine order is always being established in my life (including in bad weather). Even as a tree appears dead in winter, but bursts into life in the spring, so a period of planning, nourishment, prayer, and quiet may precede a burst of more active scheduling of plans and activity.

Just as trees are beautiful in different ways in winter, spring, summer, and fall, so are we beautiful throughout our lives in God's sight. In winter, the dark branches of trees against a sunset sky are beautiful. Leafless branches in the woods, especially with snow on the ground, allow us to see more clearly. In spring, new foliage and even flowers on fruit trees burst into bloom, and in summer, they come to full foliage. In the fall, people go on long trips to see the beauty of fall tree colors; they are so varied and magnificent. God delights in us also, in every season of our lives, as each life stage brings its own particular beauty and insights.

Lord, help us to look up to Your outstretched hand
and enjoy the season of life we are in.

#40

Walking with God is . . .   welcoming a child.

"Whoever welcomes one such child in my name welcomes me, and whoever welcomes me welcomes not me but the One who sent me." (Mk 9:39 NRSV)

Those who work with children know the importance of welcoming children in a group program setting. Professionals in early childhood teach volunteers and aides to welcome each child as he or she comes in and to talk to the children by kneeling down or bending down to their eye-level. Now that the early brain research is coming out, we know that all babies and children are born with the "mind of Christ," large and well wired, and that the language they hear and learn in their early environment literally sculpts it to a unique pattern of being. The trillions of connections in the brain are either reinforced and developed, or not-reinforced, and fade away. The mind is a wonderful gift from God to all people. Researchers know, however, that half of the intellectual quotient (IQ) as measured at age eighteen, is developed by age four. The brain is 95 percent of adult size by age seven but the connections are not all in place. So whether one is a loving parent or grandparent, or a citizen voting for a bond issue to improve the schools, this valuable resource of our children's brains needs to be nurtured, encouraged, and preserved.

As we pray to a loving God, who gives us the assurance that He is always with us, ask for compassion for others so that we may dedicate ourselves to service in the name of Jesus Christ. Whether one is serving children, their parents, or their grandparents, we are all children of God and deserving of respect and kindness. As a bee is attracted to honey, the sweetest reward comes with a child's smile when someone at home, in group care, or in Sunday School does a simple learning activity with a child that helps build a sense of achievement, or a sense of trying new things and a feeling of competence. Children are the future of the world, and being treated with love and fairness helps them to grow up to treat others with love and fairness and respect. Memories of a model or mentor with integrity and character have helped to shape many of today's well-respected men and women. Jesus took a little child into his arms and blessed the child when he explained about welcoming a child. He will do the same for you.

Lord, bless us and help us bless the children.

#41

Walking with God is . . .   calling on God.

"Call to me and I will answer you." (Jer 33:3 NRSV)

There is a divine plan unfolding in your life and in my life, and you and I can trust God to show us how to cooperate with it. Interruptions were a common part of Jesus's life, but he always responded with patience and compassion. On the way to heal one person he took time to heal another person (Lk 8:40-56). Interruptions were important because people coming to Jesus were bringing Him their real and heartfelt needs. Jesus listened and gave them his undivided attention.

Interruptions are often blessings in disguise or an opportunity to give a blessing, often by listening. In counseling young people about the education that would improve their lives and take them where they want to go, parents, teachers, and adults hear their needs and goals and by listening bestow a wonderful blessing and often give guidance. With work and love, people can rediscover the beauty that God has created that lies beneath the surface in every human being and within ourselves. Any care that we give *one* member of God's family surely must honor God and the whole family of God. And the essence of a family is love and communication.

> *Lord, let thy beauty be upon us, and establish*
> *the work of our hands for us.*

#42

Walking with God is . . .   knowing that the Kingdom of God is within you.

"For indeed the Kingdom of God is within you." (Luke 17:21 KJV)

God has given us a wonderful gift of the grace to be able to *see* what a "Kingdom of God" vision for the answer to a problem would be like. That is if only we can look at it. With big problems this is easier because it is more abstract: a "kingdom of God" solution to world hunger would be for all to be fed, and for the homeless it would be for all to have a safe place to sleep. God trusts us to let our true potential come forth in addressing the challenges of life. As we trust God to support us through both the valleys and mountaintop experiences in life, God is willing to take our hands and lead us to experiences that will spark our enthusiasm and bring out our best. God's kingdom within leads to fulfillment of life and of all that we were created to be. "Trust in the Lord with all your heart," Proverbs 3:5 tells us.

For instance, the challenge for families and for schools in the twenty-first century and beyond will be to see the big picture. This means to choose the future they would like to see, make a plan, consider the steps, and write them down, and then take the first step. Even if parents, families, churches, and schools have to adapt along the way, they are much more likely to arrive at this goal or vision, or a closer approximation of it, than if they hadn't planned or taken steps.

Allowing God to direct us in the best way to be a blessing allows God to work through us to bless others. And it underscores the wisdom of the prophet: "Choose this day whom you will serve . . . . as for me and my household, we will serve the Lord" (Josh 24:15).

Lord, show us the solution to the problem you would have us work on next.

#43

Walking with God is . . .   knowing that "we are God's workmanship, created in Christ Jesus to do good works, which God created beforehand that we should walk in them." (Eph 2:10 RSV)

"Out of the believer's heart shall flow rivers of living water." (John 7:38 NRSV)

John knew the power of one believer's desire and prayers, and as one writer said, this person can have an enormous effect on the populace. By letting your faith and my faith be in God and letting it guide you and me in being open to all ways to receive guidance, assistance, seemingly impossible projects can be done, one step at a time. Whether planting seeds, writing a book, creating a Compact Disk or a painting, God speaks through human hearts and hands. Any work or effort that carries a positive uplifting force carries a message of God's love and caring. When we speak or act from the Spirit within, great things can happen and amazing results can follow. Nehemiah rebuilt the walls of Jerusalem in just fifty-two days from his strong desire, and with people organizing to rebuild each gate, and the walls in between (Neh 2).

Planning without God's involvement and vision is like going somewhere in a car without a map. The chances of getting where you want to go are greatly lessened. For example, in looking down a road, one can see cars and the road ahead and can see that at a distant point on the highway there is construction or an accident. One can then *anticipate* that it will be more advantageous to move into the better lane. This is in essence looking into a future time frame. Having a vision means looking ahead. People realize that in looking ahead in driving, they can change lanes when they note that in one lane far ahead, cars are moving more effectively and faster. They *anticipate* that it will be more advantageous for them to stop or to move over into the better lane. People can also look ahead and change lanes in life and work with the help of some knowledge of a project at hand. This perceiving of a future order and acting now to move toward it or away from it is what prayer (especially as children grow up) is all about. Out of a believer's heart truly flow rivers of living water as we ask:

Lord, what are your plans and purposes for me?

#44

Walking with God is . . .   seizing the moment.

"If you seek me with all your heart, I will let you find me, says the Lord."
(Jer 29:13-14 NRSV)

Each day is a new opportunity to look for and find blessings. As I seek God with all my heart, to seek God's spirit within other people, and God's presence in all situations, I am ready and willing to recognize and savor blessings and to see clearly what a "kingdom of God" solution might look like for problems. What would be the better way for children? for the elderly? for the sick? for my church?

As we record these thoughts, gather the proper tools, enlist help as needed, and seek to leave the world a better place, we reflect God's spirit as we travel through each day. Seizing the moment of beauty or joy in a sunset, a bird's song or flight, a rose unfolding, renews one's energy and helps us to use our opportunities to reflect God's love to those whose paths we cross. "You will find me, if you seek me with all your heart."

Lord, help us to seek you in all situations and in all people.

#45

Walking with God is . . .   releasing the power of God within me.

"If you had faith the size of a mustard seed, you could say to this mulberry tree, 'Be uprooted and planted in the sea,' and it would be obey you." (Luke 17:6 NRSV)

There is incredible power in just a little faith—if it is in a great God. If Jesus said the faith could be as small as a mustard seed—which is pretty small, for this is the smallest of seeds. Your faith can remind yourself to *release* the power of God that is within you and is His spirit, to love, to encourage, to think clearly, to heal, to comfort, to prosper, or to do whatever you are called to do. The possibilities are unlimited and your talents, whether perceived or unperceived, can be trained and enabled to help you. Your faith helps you to know that this is true for you and for others.

Lord, show me how to release Your power in my efforts to serve You.

#46

Walking with God is . . .   being transformed by the renewing of your
mind.

"But be transformed by the renewing of your minds, so that you may discern
what the will of God is—what is good and acceptable and perfect." (Rom 12:2
NRSV)

If you are unhappy with your behavior, examine your feelings . . . behind
your negative emotions there is some skewed thinking. Our thinking is the key.
God wants to transform us by setting our thinking straight. Steep yourself in the
Word of God and you will come to understand God's thinking and God's intention
for humanity's thought. Read and pray about your creation and the dignity given
you in Genesis chapter 1. Read and pray about the Lord's familiarity with your
brokenness and sin and yet his love remains. Read and pray about the Lord's
answer to your brokenness and sin in the Gospel accounts. God knows you.
God's love is not about accomplishment or good deeds, it comes from grace.
Study and meditate on creation, your fall, the cross, and your salvation. Ask
Christ to set straight your thinking and you will be transformed. The "patterns
of this world" to which we are tempted to conform (Rom 12:2) would tell us
that our worth is based on effectiveness, success, obedience, good works, or
value to society. But Paul says, "No . . . be transformed by the renewal of your
mind." Remind yourself of the truth of Christ. It runs contrary to those truths
of the world. Next, write in a Journal about what your self statements are that
you live by, even if unconsciously? Are they of Christ?

Lord, transform me by the renewing of my mind.
Rev. Allison Jones Lundeen

#47

Walking with God is . . .   responding to God.

"In this is love, not that we loved God but that he loved us and sent his Son to be the atoning sacrifice for our sins." (1 John 4:7-12, verse 10 NRSV)

We are not required to take the initiative. God has done so. We love because he first loved us. It is as we ourselves are filled up with his love, and with gratitude for it, that we are able to love God back and love our neighbor. God did not give the Israelites a list of ten do's and don'ts just to be the almighty policeman in the sky. The preface to the Decalogue says this: "I am the Lord your God, who has brought you out of the land of Egypt, out of the house of slavery." Christ is the Lord who has brought us out of the land of enslavement to sin and brokenness. It is because of what he has done for us that we are told to have no other Gods before him. He has earned his place as king. None of Christ's requests of us are unthinkable when we begin to fathom his inestimable, unfathomable love for us first. We have been delivered out of the land of brokenness into the land of hope, the land of joy, the land of reconciliation with our Creator. Our journey to that land is not of our doing . . . we were delivered. Your redeemed life is a Promised land of milk and honey! Our part in this life is easy . . . we are responders. Write in your Journal what God has done for you. What is God now asking of you?

Lord, thank you for all you have done for me.
Rev. Allison Jones Lundeen

#48

Walking with God is . . .   clinging to Christ.

"She came up behind him, and touched the fringe of his clothes, and immediately her hemorrhage stopped." (Luke 8:44 NRSV)

The hemorrhaging woman grabbed on to Christ's robe in the midst of suffering and persecution. She had faith when we would expect her to have despair. In the moment of her faith, she was filled with his power. When we believe, his power is released in us. Then Jesus can say to us, "Go in peace." It was risky but look at the return on her investment! We are sure those around her who laughed at her and scorned her did not leave the encounter "in peace." They left still haggled or even tormented by their own problems, issues, and brokenness. God does not need us to have the answers or to have faith bigger than a mustard seed. All that is required is a grasp for the cloak. God is honored by a heart that believes more in Him than in present circumstances or in societal responses. Clench that cloak with all your might. Christ is the only one worth grabbing at.

Lord, give me faith when I am hopeless. Thank you that you are faithful even when I am faithless. Help my unbelief. Help me cling to you in bad times and in good times. Amen.
Rev. Allison Jones Lundeen

#49

Walking with God is . . .   considering the source of all life.

"Out of the ground the Lord God made to grow every tree that is pleasant to the sight and good for food." (Gen 2:9a *NRSV*)

God is the source of life. Every leaf on every branch on every tree in every yard, in every acre, in every forest, on every hill gains its life from God. No living thing exists without the source of its life, the creator. God is able. God grows trillions of trees and billions of human beings all at the same time. Our God is a master of management. This One wrote the book on Total Quality. We resent death because we take life for granted. Life, each breath, each cell, each leaf, is a gift. All of life is a freebie. Get the most out of your freebie. Take advantage of the too-good-to-be-true offer. And don't put limits on the giver. Or resent it when the ride is over. It's a gift. All of God's energy is yours. Through Christ you have been reconciled to your Creator. This creator formed you, birthed you, and nurtures you. Enjoy Him.

Look out the window, any window or drive down the road or walk down the street—find a tree . . . start to count the leaves . . . consider their Source. Consider that each leaf is alive . . . growing and thriving thanks be to God. How big is your God? How small?

As in Psalm 100, we pray that we make a joyful noise to the Lord, and in all the earth. Teach us to worship the Lord with gladness; to come into his presence with singing. Help us know that you Lord are God. It is you that made us, and we are yours. Amen.
Rev. Allison Jones Lundeen

#50

Walking with God is . . .   welcoming the Light into your darkness.

"Jesus said I am the light of the world. Whoever follows me will not walk in darkness but will have light of life." (John 8:12 NRSV)

The only time in the history of the world that the skies lit up when they should have been dark was when Jesus was born. The only time in the history of the world that the skies darkened when it should have been daylight was when Jesus died. Luke 23:45 tells us that the sun's light *failed* . . . how often does that happen? Jesus really is the light of the world. Consider your life without electricity. Consider living by candlelight all the time. Sooner or later the candle is consumed. John 1 tells us that the light shines in the darkness and the darkness did not overcome it. Verse 9 tells us that Jesus is the true light that enlightens everyone. It takes a lot of darkness to make a bright room dark, but only a little bit of light to brighten it back up. Invite that little bit of light into your heart, into your worry, into your family, your relationships, into your soul . . . and watch THE Light of the World shine in all His glory.

Lord, come into my life and heart and light my darkness. Amen.
Rev. Allison Jones Lundeen

#51

Walking with God is . . .   realizing God meets us where we are.

"But as it is, God arranged the members in the body, each one of them, as he chose. If all were a single member, where would the body be?" (Cor 12:18-19)

"Then God said, 'Let *us* make humankind in *our* image, according to *our* likeness;'" (Gen 1:26a NRSV)

Many nonbelievers say that Christianity is fractured because there are so many different denominations. One bumper sticker seen on a college campus said, "My karma ran over your dogma." True . . . dogma differences that result in unloving spirits are not part of Christ. Or dogma at all is not part of Christ. But perhaps we underestimate God when we judge another's dogma, theology, liturgy, or worship style. Perhaps God is the author or coauthor of denominationalism. Our God is a community of three. We are created in God's image. As individuals and as communities we represent the diversity of God. Perhaps God grows up all kinds of different leaders and traditions for His/Her name's sake for the purpose of reaching all different kinds of followers with the good news of Jesus Christ. Some of us are formal, casual, mental, emotional, active, passive, and so forth. Our God meets us where we are . . . heart and soul.

Try this: Worship this Sunday at a church most unlike yours. See God at work. See the creativity and the largeness of God.

Lord, help us to see the truth, power, and love in the Gospel for all people.
                                        Rev. Allison Jones Lundeen

#52

Walking with God is . . .   letting God mother you.

"Can a woman forget her nursing child, or show no compassion for the child of her womb? Even these may forget, yet I will not forget you. See, I have inscribed you on the palms of my hands." (Is 49:15-16a NRSV)

There is a parenting philosophy called "Attachment Parenting" that focuses on the idea that for babies and toddlers, attachment begets security and independence and not dependence. That the more parents allow the babies to be attached by holding, nursing, or comforting . . . the more the children will feel secure in the bond and therefore bold to venture out and explore and grow up. God is our attachment parent. Be cradled each day in the arms of God. Do not turn away that embrace. Feel the love of God and you will feel more secure in the world. God is father as stereotyped . . . encourager, provider, protector, teacher, but also in the scripture, God is mother as stereotyped . . . . nurturer, comforter, feeder, warm caregiver. (See verse above.)

Today: Practice visual prayer. Feel the arms of God around you. Hear the voice of a mother or a father singing you to sleep.

Lord, help us to feel secure and cared for in your arms. Amen.
Rev. Allison Jones Lundeen

#53

Walking with God is . . .   being a fool for Christ.

"For since, in the wisdom of god, the world did not know God through wisdom, God decided, through the foolishness of our proclamation, to save those who believe." (1 Cor 1:21 NRSV)

God tried to reach us through regular wisdom, but it didn't work, so he used "foolishness" instead. For the Jews of Corinth, the cross was a huge stumbling block in their religion . . . the long-awaited Messiah was certainly not supposed to be cursed of God on a tree. And for the Greeks of Corinth, the cross was foolishness . . . for everyone then "knew" that God doesn't feel because that in their minds would mean God was affect-able and change-able and less than God. Certainly god in Christ "felt" at Gethsemane and again while hanging on the cross, slowly suffocating to death. But God knew that we were only reachable through foolishness. Jesus was the ultimate "fool" by our world's standards. He stood up in front of throngs of people and told his friends to feed them all with just a few loaves of bread and some fish. Later he told some of these same friends to cast their fishing nets on what everyone knew was the wrong side of the boat. And then during his final week, he came riding into Jerusalem on a jackass. But the most "foolish" was how he was always hanging out with losers, like the adulterous woman and the unclean woman, and Zaccheus and Levi, the crook. We are all called to be fools. People you and I know and don't know will come into a personal relationship with Christ once you and I are willing to be foolish in the world's eyes, like giving away money or loving someone otherwise unlovable or taking the rap for something you didn't do, or hanging out as a teen with a "loser." Find an obnoxious and rude person to love . . . chances are their rudeness will melt just like the Wicked Witch of the West when you love them with the love of Christ.

Lord, show me how I may be wise in you today, even if it is foolish to the world. Direct me to some "foolishness" for your name's sake. Amen.
                                                              Rev. Allison Jones Lundeen

#54

Walking with God is . . .   is keeping your eyes on God—not on the problem.

"Ask anything in my name and I will do it." (John 14:14 NKJV)

After the September 11, 2001, attack on the World Trade Center towers and Pentagon, many people prayed, "Heavenly Father, we pray that there will be no more terrorists' attacks." The united spirit of problem solving that emerged to make flying and airports safer, to make public buildings and Federal office buildings safer, and to truly honor the Firemen and Policemen who worked so hard in the rescue efforts, was highly impressive. Perhaps it might become possible that the angry people, many representing "have not" countries of the world, would not cause any more terrorist attacks. Even when people _think_ there is a good reason to hate, love can overcome.

To drive by the Pentagon one week after 9/11 and smell the burned electrical wiring smell really brought the disaster there home to us, residents of a nearby area. As one man said, who worked near the World Trade Center, looking out the window and seeing the first tower and then the second go down: "Good cow! Let's get out of here!" He remembered running across the bridge. "We just wanted to get to the other side" he said.

Lord, help us "get to the other side" of negative feelings, and we pray there will be no more terrorist attacks.

#55

Walking with God is . . .   abiding in Him and letting His words abide in you.

"If you abide in Me, and My words abide in you, ask whatever you will and it shall be done for you." (John 15:7 RSV)

God knows and will show me what is best for me, and for me to do, as I let His words abide in me. By letting go and letting God show me what to do, I open my horizons and my peripheral vision to take in all that God might be showing me. As I collect information and pray about choices, I feel clearness as God guides me.

Sometimes God is opening new doors that lead me to helpful solutions and fulfilling experiences. God is able to bless me in expected and in unexpected ways. My prayer had been for increased parent involvement with their children. Children that feel loved, valued, and attended to, thrive and do well in life according to the best research and to God's guidance. Watching parent information, activities, and advice go out over the Internet and being read by people in many countries is an example of this—a result "far more abundant" than I could ask or think. (See www.homelearning.org/) Another example of such abundance is www.cbsinterntational.org/ that stands for Community Bible Study International and carries prayers and study opportunities for the Word of God around the world.

My prayer had been for increased parent involvement with their children, and it is being answered. "And whatever things you ask in prayer, believing, you will receive" (Matt 21:22 NKJV).

Lord, help us to be involved with our children.

#56

Walking with God is . . .   serving the Lord.

"As for me and my house, we will serve the Lord." (Josh 24:15 RSV)

When my son was driving north in Florida, a hurricane was behind him as he left Miami. He was going to his home, which was more inland. Driving through the Everglades, he said the wind and the rain were fierce, but suddenly, the sun came out, and it was quiet. All around the edges, the horizon was dark—just the reverse of a dark, cloudy rainy day with light at the edges. He said he felt as if this was like God watching over him. As a Mom I replied, "God has always been watching over you." We later figured out that he must have driven through the "eye" of the hurricane—as his car was moving faster than the storm—and as he drove, the fierce wind and rain began again.

This is the last of my four children to tell me of having a true and deep understanding of God's love and protection for him. When the children were young, I read, "You shall write them on the doorposts of your house" (Deut 6:9 RSV). I decided to print a variety of meaningful scripture verses on poster board and place them over the door and over the sink in the bathroom. Later, my daughter, when she had a home of her own, kept a typed list of verses over her sink—to read while washing dishes or other household chores. My other sons also married girls who had strong church upbringings and those years ago when I read, "As for me and my household, we will serve the Lord," have born much fruit in these four Christian families, and their twelve children. Serving the Lord *is* a conscious choice and can permeate a household with the fragrant joy of God's good news.

Lord, help us to remember that your words can carry through the generations.

#57

Walking with God is . . .   serenity and peace.

"I have loved you with an everlasting love; therefore with loving kindness I have drawn you." (Jer 31:3 NKJV)

One of the most beautiful funerals I have ever attended was for the wife from a Korean couple who died suddenly of a massive stroke. The service for her was given by her ministers from the Korean Presbyterian Church. In this moving Christian Memorial service, one of the ministers spoke the words, "The author and creator of our life has called his daughter to eternal peacefulness." What reassurance this is that we rest our eternal soul on the heart of Christ and feel eternal spiritual security.

As a young child rests his or her head on the heart of an adult carrying or sitting and holding the child, so can we rest secure in the knowledge of God's kingdom.

In our garden at home, we have given different parts of the garden Chinese names, such as "Garden of heavenly peace," 'Garden of earthly peace," and "Garden of restful peace." I had never thought of these beautiful images, taken from the garden names of old Peking, in conjunction with a beautiful Christian memorial service, but that was the theme of this Korean service. What richness the blending of these two cultures brought to this life experience. God has indeed loved us with an everlasting love.

Lord, thank you for your serenity and peace.

#58

Walking with God is . . .   having a faith like the centurion's—
believing it will be done.

"And to the centurion Jesus said, 'Go; let it be done for you according to your faith'." (Matt 8:13 NRSV)

The centurion explained to Jesus that in the military if the leader *said* "Go and do it" it was as good as done. In the military this is necessary as in wartime there often isn't time for explanations. The centurion took it a step further by saying "(you don't) have to come there, but only speak the word and my servant will be healed." Jesus's response in the verse above has celebrated the centurion's faith down through the centuries. "And the servant was healed in that hour" ends verse 13.

Ask yourself to take one minute for each goal and write out some goals you have for your life, for the next year and for the next five years. Now write a goal for the next six months and for this week, in one more minute (for each). Now take a minute to pick three goals from *all* these lists. Look at each one and write a task (or tasks) that would take only three to five minutes that would help each goal. Don't comment on whether these goals or tasks mention certain tasks or not at this point. These goals should then be put on a calendar perhaps doing this with a copy of this month's calendar at hand. Each week or at least monthly or quarterly, look at the goals and update them.

All we need to say is "Yes, God, I am willing," and when my will is a reflection of God's will, whatever willingness I am able to express will be multiplied and returned to me as God upholds me in doing my best and being my best. Our eyes and ears become opened to solutions, information, and possibilities all around us that lead to freedom and ability to accomplish God's will.

Lord, I believe. Help my unbelief.

#59

Walking with God is . . .   realizing the wonder of God's grace.

"And now I commend you to God and to the message of his grace, a message that is able to build you up and give you the inheritance among all who are sanctified." (Acts 20:30 NRSV)

The assurance of God's love and grace is truly an amazing wonder as I listen to God in my quiet prayer time and realize God's unconditional love for me. God builds me up and directs me in living a life that loves and accepts and blesses others and myself. The further promise of the inheritance among all who are sanctified reminds me that all believers are saints of God. The amazing beauty and generosity of God's grace helps me to have a greater consciousness and awareness of God's presence and grace, as I go about daily life.

Lord, help me to have a vision and a consciousness of awareness of you.

#60

Walking with God is . . .   praying for God's help in solving conflicts between nations.

"Nothing is impossible with God." (Luke 1:37 NKJV)

For thousands of years, as long as there have been nations, there has been conflict between them, more or less. As weapons and information technology increase in range and scope, reasoning together and understanding the historical, geographical, *and* cultural differences behind conflicts becomes even more important. As we understand other peoples, and the sometimes generations of unfairness and injustices that have existed between them, we become less judgmental and more able to think clearly and pray for healing for those involved. Praying for the humanity of each individual and for a decrease in dehumanizing phrases, cultures, and points of view, we remember "nothing is impossible with God."

Jesus's ministry two thousand years ago began the globalization of God's healing grace. As we pray for healing for those we know, love, or empathize with, we pray for inner peace and protection as the U.S. rebuilds the nation after the September 11, 2001, attacks.

Lord, we pray for Your help in solving conflicts between nations.

#61

Walking with God is . . .   praying for God's protection as we rebuild
our nation.

"Your godliness will lead you forward and the Glory of the Lord will protect
you from behind. Your healing will come quickly." (Is 58:8 NKJV)

The verse in Job 1:10 (RSV) that says the Lord will "hedge you both before
and behind" always made me feel protected in situations of personal danger. As
citizens pray for protection while rebuilding in any country, their godliness will
lead them forward to rebuilding in the right way and being protected from behind.
The Lord has promised healing that "comes quickly" or "rises up speedily"
depending on the translation of the Bible you are using. This may occur in our
timing as people strive to "get things back to normal" after September 11, 2001,
or it may occur in God's timing that is not ours to really know.

Patience with slow healing is something that diabetics and the elderly learn
to develop. Prayer, the beauties of nature, and clear thinking, the same things
that help rebuild a nation, also help individuals to regain healing and confidence
that they will be all right, and perhaps even better than before.

Lord, we pray for your healing.

#62

Walking with God is . . .   seeing all that is right and good and true, even when it's painful.

"Live as children of the light . . . (seeking) all that is right and good and true." (Eph 5:8-9 NRSV)

A friend of mine and her husband lived next door to the husband's dear old army buddy, whose health began deteriorating over what were to be his last months. The couple I knew helped him, even with calls at 2:00 a.m. and made his last days comfortable. His son and daughter lived far away, and the father had refused to call them.

After he died, the daughter came and berated the couple fiercely because she couldn't find some of his tools, that she thought would be in his shed and that she thought they had stolen. The son, on the other hand, wrote a nice letter thanking my friends for all they had done. In discussing this disappointing and surprising turn of events with her Bible study group, the wife said, "I *like* to help other people—but I don't like to be accused of having ulterior motives." I have since learned that in processing and mourning a death of a loved one, people often accuse other people of other losses that are hard to explain. Processing a loss is hard.

The Bible Study group discussed the costs and promises of serving the Lord in helping other people. The costs, of course, include time, energy, and resources, plus deferring one's own plans on occasion. The promises—inherent in serving the Lord, which build reliability, responsibility, and trust—build character over a lifetime. The reward is not of this world. It helps us to remember that Jesus was crucified for his good deeds and paid the ultimate cost. The prayer at the end of this page helped my friend to be cheerful and neutral when the daughter called up later, in a more pleasant frame of mind.

Lord, help this not to matter so much—and to remember it is sharing your sufferings and even an experience of the cross.

#63

Walking with God is . . .   walking into the light.

"The light shines in the darkness and the darkness has not overcome it." (John 1:5)

While teaching five-and-six-year-old Sunday School, a friend of mine found the children, eleven boys and two girls, were really "bouncing off the walls" after a rainy week. She began to wonder why she was teaching Sunday School again. The project for that day was to build an Ark of the Covenant using the blocks that were in the room and gold foil that she had brought in. As the children got engrossed in their project, a quiet calm cover settled over the room.

Suddenly the sun broke through the clouds and a sunbeam shone in the window, making its way around the room, lighting on the little heads so busily at work. It even reflected and shined on the teacher. She felt a great peace about her teaching of Sunday School, after all.

In a culture that has many attractive but hurtful things, seeking the right and good and true is not always easy. We're reminded "but there's more" to a good life than just obeying the law and avoiding pain. We are reminded that God's love and light are shining on us and supporting us. We can reflect it anyway, as the life of a Christian has a vision and a focus, leading us into the light.

Dear Lord, enfold us in Your love and light. Help us to reflect it to others.

#64

Walking with God is . . .   like seeing a light in the window.

"I will love you, O Lord my strength . . . . The Lord is my rock and my fortress and my deliverer; my God, my strength, in whom I will trust; my shield . . . . and my stronghold." (Ps 18:1-2 NKJV)

When traveling or returning home after dark, seeing a light shining from a window of my home, welcomes me home. No matter how gloomy outward circumstances appear, the same "welcome home" feeling comes from my relationship with God. The light of God's spirit shines in my quiet prayer times, and I can remain focused, and list steps, for that on which I need to be focused. The feeling of peace from being embraced in the love of God pervades me. My mind clears, and problems are enunciated, and solutions begin to appear.

Since a problem identified is a problem half solved, I make notes of various ways to define a challenge or a problem, and note the different definitions this might engender: I can write these by date and revisit it later if necessary. God's gracious light shines in my mind, and his Wisdom becomes available to me as I take a longer and higher perspective.

Lord, help me to reflect Your light as the moon reflects the sun and to acknowledge You as my creator. Thank you for being my strength, my rock, and my redeemer.

#65

Walking with God is . . .   knowing that Jesus doesn't need a calm sea.

"Peace! Be still . . . . Why are you afraid?" [Don't you know that I am in the boat with you?] (Mk 4:39-40 NRSV)

My family grew up boating on the Chesapeake Bay, so there were times on a long sailboat trip that the water was rough and we were several hours from shore. This verse has always spoken to me because, not only did Jesus *sleep* through the storm, when he awoke, he reminded the disciples that he was with them. He calmed the sea with a few words. He knew and trusted that God would get him to the other side.

How often in rough waters do we focus on the storm and the smallness of the boat we are in. Focusing on God, whatever the circumstances or problem, gets us through for the long haul. Trusting God and doing God's will is the best guidance we can follow. Jesus can calm me as he calmed the sea. Remembering that Jesus is always in the boat with us provides the wisdom we need. In God's presence, discouragement is transformed into courage.

Lord, help us to trust in you.

#66

Walking with God is . . .   speaking an encouraging word.

"A word fitly spoken is like apples of gold." (Prov 25:11 RSV)

It was the first day of a new class. I needed encouragement to drive a long way and get the group started that I was teaching. My Quiet Time reading included this passage and reminded me that small things or routine teachings can bless and encourage. Tonight we were going to talk about leadership with people who were managing and leading programs for young children. This is work requiring much patience helped by knowledge, and encouragement is always needed.

These people are always working at the boundaries of several groups of which they are a part. Internally within their programs, they deal with a Board or owner with long-range concerns and goals. They also deal with the teachers' and the children's curriculum activities in a day-to-day time frame. Externally they deal with regulators, funding sources and their communities, in which there is an intermediate time frame. Furthermore, they are supposed to interpret each group to the other groups with integrity. Many workplaces have these three domains: policy and strategy, service delivery, and external connections—each with different goals and different time frames. Role conflict and role ambiguity are built right into the job. Support from any peer group, class, or professional association can help with these pressures in this "structured conflict." A word fitly spoken is like "apples of gold." Teaching and training can offer these words.

Lord, help us to be your hands and feet in encouraging those doing your work.

#67

Walking with God is . . .   listening in order to understand.

"Speak Lord, for your servant is listening." (1 Sam 3:9)

Learning and doing new things sometimes requires a zest for living that we may feel we don't have or that we thought only children had. Yet each of us is a child of God created with potential and possibility to do more and be more than we have in the past. This requires listening—for the Lord can speak in a profound way.

Sometimes, in a moment when we are not talking, the Lord speaks to us with the sounds around us. I had such a moment holding my first granddaughter after the family had all come home from her Christening at church. The sounds of family were all around, preparing the luncheon and talking to each other. Best of all, I got to hear my oldest son tell his next brother, the baby's father, just how to hold the baby to ease her stomach distress. This was promptly labeled the "Roger hold" (like a football). I felt like the Lord was showing me some of the joys of my labors in raising children that I had taken for granted, or thought I would never see. The baby, of course, slept peacefully in my arms. The noises around me were an answered prayer—prayer for their growing up years, prayer for grandchildren, and prayer for that day. What joys and possibilities exist in each moment of our lives, if we would only listen.

Lord, help us remember that "this is the day that the Lord has made.
Let us rejoice and be glad in it" (Ps 118:24).

#68

Walking with God is . . .   is knowing you are under the eye of the Lord.

"Go in peace. The mission you are on is under the eye of the Lord."
(Judges 18:16 NRSV)

Psalm 37 (v.5) tells us, "Commit your way to the Lord and he will give you the desires of your heart." This could be said to be the starter gate for a "Kingdom of God" vision for many things: better child care, the government moving into the information age, parent involvement with their children and in the schools, care of an elderly loved one, or work on a writing project, just to name a few. By visualizing solutions in some detail and then coming back from the future or "staying out there" in the future and "turning around" to "look back," one can see main stages or events that can lead to the problems being solved. What were major barriers that were overcome at each key stage in the solution? What measures of success could be used?

Now come back to the present and create a "first draft" or perhaps one could even write a newsletter that might come out in five years with articles on different aspects of the solution or program. This can include headlines, lead stories, items of interest such as promotions and retirements, or new groups set up. The power of the mind to visualize goals can never be underestimated. Knowing that your mission and vision are under the eye of the Lord is the encouragement needed, perhaps frequently, to keep going.

Many Old Testament heroes got very discouraged when the odds seemed to be against them. In Judges, they asked the priest to inquire of God if their mission would succeed. The response came, "The mission you are on is under the eye of the Lord."

We, like they, can know that God plus one is a majority, so that when things change and new opportunities present themselves, we are ready to move forward. We can go forward in peace. The mission we are on is under the eye of the Lord. The finish line is summed up in John 12:40: "Did I not tell you that if you believed you would see the glory of the Lord?" This may take five, ten, twenty, or even forty years and cannot always be seen, but often can be.

Lord, help us to persevere as we seek Your Kingdom.

#69

Walking with God is . . .   reacting to situations with understanding.

"God is our refuge and our strength, a very present help in trouble."
(Ps 46:1 NKJV)

My faith in God is partly based on a lifetime of receiving the love and blessings of my Creator. God knows me and prepares me for the right outcome in all situations. I try to let go of worry and let God into my life whether I am reacting to major catastrophes or minor irritations. Letting go of anger and trying to understand more about a situation has an impact for the good on my life, both physically and emotionally. Learning more about other countries and other religions may be a part of this understanding. Thinking of an annoying coworker as someone who has had a great tragedy in their life helps us to forgive minor slights. Often this is indeed the case, and the person just doesn't verbalize it. Stories that came out during the year after September 11, 2001, told of people fighting with coworkers, spouses, and having road rage, by their own admission, because they were so frustrated about people they couldn't save, or things that they couldn't do.

God can express love and acceptance through me as I listen to those I meet with thoughtfulness and concern. As I let go and let God into my life, God guides me through life.

Dear Lord, help me to turn this situation over to you,
and to allow your wonderful guidance into my life.

#70

Walking with God is . . .   seeing all people as God's children.

"There is neither Jew nor Greek, there is neither slave nor free, there is neither male nor female; for you are all one in Christ Jesus." (Mk 3:28 NRSV)

A friend of mine was serving as one of a group of new lay chaplains in a hospital near her work. When there was a death, her role on her duty day was to be with the family and pray with them. On a recent day, after a death, an older woman wearing a rhinestone Jesus pin appeared with the family. Thinking it was an Aunt or other family relative, my friend inquired and learned that she was the family's pastor. Backing off, she stood in the rear, when suddenly the woman was overcome and the hospital personnel brought a wheelchair. Apparently she had a heart condition that had flared up. When she felt better, my friend offered to wheel her back in to the family group, but her response was 'That's OK, baby, you go in. Jesus will hear your prayers as well as mine."

My friend felt like she was being empowered to do something she'd had doubt about, by this woman's honest and simple faith. She felt accepted to do something by a person from whom she didn't expect it, and this new empowerment greatly increased her capacity for ministry. Having seen the woman in a new light, she saw herself in a new light. All the things separating her and the group and perceptions of the world fell away. They were truly one in Christ and my friend felt carried by the faith of another.

Lord, help us to carry one another by heart and not by appearance.

#71

Walking with God is . . .   finding God in an age of technology and
being lifted up by your faith.

"The appearance . . . as it were, a wheel in the middle of a wheel."
(Ez 1:16 NKJV)

Human beings began communicating with each other many thousands of
years ago. In a presentation last year by a technology firm, it was announced that
700 million telephones were in use in the year 2000. With wireless telephones,
there are many more today. If we communicate with each other so much, ought
we to communicate with God more? I asked myself. Allowing time to read and
study is particularly important in some disciplines, but it is really important
to all men and women of faith, as it affirms that God will give the reader and
note-taker something that will be useful in the future in the service of others.
I know it is important to be lifted up by my faith to a level of self-confidence
and self-reliance at which I will be able to recognize, observe, and appreciate
the worlds around me. Ezekiel looked up and saw the wheels within wheels.
Reading the newspapers, using the Internet, or listening to a sermon, I became
aware of the many worlds around us and some of the wheels within them.

Communicating with God daily helps me to appreciate and apply some
of these new ideas or new learnings in new or unexpected ways. Making new
connections that will help a child, a teenager, a coworker, or a loved one can come
from daily communication with God, note-taking during sermons in church and
perceiving worlds within worlds or wheels within wheels. A database of helping
organizations can be an age of technology ministry of Christian charity. Finding
God in an age of technology can be just as direct as finding God in any age.

Lord, help us to open our hearts to you and
to appreciate the wheels and worlds around us.

#72

Walking with God is . . .   ordering your private world.

"God the Lord is my strength; he makes my feet like the feet of a deer, and makes me tread upon the heights." (Ps 18:33 NRSV)

Another translation of this verse uses the words "correlates me like hind's feet" (RSV). The word _correlate_ is like the word _coordinate_ and a hind is a deer—the analogy being the superb coordination a deer has to leap and run to high places. A creative environment helps us to do that along with our faith in God. Think about the place that inspires your creativity: the office? the kitchen? the home-office? the shower?

Then ask these questions, as I did when I was moving my University office to a home office and feeling overwhelmed until I realized I could prioritize by what was important to me, rather than by the size or amount of the materials to be thrown out or taken home. Questions regarding light included: do I need more or less light? Can I change the position of the lights? Allow more sunlight? Regarding sound—do I need more or less? Does a certain type of music inspire me? At certain times of the day? This is important if the hour affects your creative times. Regarding color and "environmental" art or objects: Can I add colors that either energize or soothe me? Pillows, posters, flowers, color on the walls were somewhat inexpensive, easily changeable, possible additions. Art and objects that are meaningful to me such as a seashell to remind me of the beach, pictures of family or a landscape that could enhance my creativity were also added. If money had been no object, it's fun to think of what I could do, and then to try to adapt some of these ideas to be affordable. Books tell me to also think about aromas and taste. What do I need more of? less of? Scents can even mask unpleasant building smells. In terms of diet, could I add or subtract some foods in order to enhance my energy? The fifth sense, touch, also needs thought: what do I need more of? less of? Are there some "toys" I could have there to focus my thoughts or to roll in my hands for a break? One February I took a large velvet pillow to the workplace office to make my computer chair more comfortable—and found that students, ages twenty-five to sixty-five, loved it. As you correlate and coordinate your creative energies and environment, the Lord will truly set you on your high places.

Lord, help me to organize and coordinate my energy.

#73

Walking with God is ...   seeing myself and you as expressions of God in my world.

"In Him we live and move and have our being." (Acts 17:28 NRSV)

Even before we were born, God was preparing us for life and preparing our way in life. The new research on babies' brain development shows more about how this happens. Infants in utero hear and remember their mother's voice, turning toward it on the first day of life. They also hear deep sounds better, and their father's voice is the second most familiar to them, plus the voices of any siblings that are at home. The human face is precious to them: whether it is smiling or sad, and they soon learn to imitate expressions. A researcher even found that if he stuck out his tongue at a newborn *forty-two minutes of age*, the newborn would imitate it! As a young mother I didn't know these wonderful things to try with my babies.

As spiritual beings, we are God's hands and feet in this world. Allowing our divine natures to show forth, using this miraculous "big brain," which is granted only to humans, and its development that we have been given, can lead to a new day full of ongoing wonderful blessings. The grace and caring of God *is* an ongoing blessing. "It is God who is at work in us both to will and to work for His good pleasure," (Phil 3:13 NRSV).

Lord, help us to remember that in You we live and move and have our being. We are not alone.

#74

Walking with God is . . .   praying for you and giving thanks for you.

"I do not cease to give thanks for you as I remember you in my prayers. I pray that the God of our Lord Jesus Christ, the Father of glory, may give you a spirit of wisdom and revelation, as you come to know him . . . . and what is the immeasurable greatness of his power." (Eph 1:16-19 NRSV)

This prayer is every mother's dream as she prays for her children and for other loved ones near and far. Additionally, letting children know that you are praying for them when they have a test (when added to the instruction) to (1) prepare well, (2) think what the teacher will ask, and (3) keep his or her mind sharp, can lift children up. A friend shared this prayer with me and her children have indeed done very well.

This wonderful intercessory prayer is great for all prayers for friends, as it prays for *HIS* will in many translations, and His will and wisdom and revelation are what you want for your loved ones (not necessarily your will or their will). So that they may "know the hope to which He has called you (or them)." It continues so that "you may know the riches of His glorious inheritance among the saints (believers), and what is the immeasurable greatness of is power for those who believe, according to the greatness of His power." Every parent knows he or she needs this much help, and this prayer assures him or her that it is present. He or she may need to ask, but God's help is always with him or her. These thoughts helped me raise four teenagers, and pray for them through college, and later job and marriage decisions.

Lord, share your greatness and wisdom with my children and my loved ones near and far.

#75

Walking with God is . . .   believing that all things are possible through God's power.

"Before they call I will answer, while they are yet speaking I will hear." (Is 65:24 NRSV)

Knowing that God is active in my life is knowing that even when I am confused God will show me the way. The security of this belief enables me to persist and persevere even when the results take twenty or thirty years, such as in raising children or writing materials and books that put forth new ideas, or even in making a quilt. By watching for God's hand and direction and being aware of His presence, I can fully appreciate the miracles He is working in the changes we see. With the Information Age, communications can come in *and be answered* in almost the same day from around the world. I know from my e-mail that if the date and time are from tomorrow to look to see if the message is from Australia or India or another faraway country across the International date line, that I have to figure out from the initials in the e-mail address. As people communicate and get to know each other *as people*, world peace becomes more of a real possibility. As we help our brothers and sisters both near and far (in my case with higher education information, and in English), we are working toward God's kingdom of love and peace. Just knowing that computers can translate languages, helps me to know that with God all things *are* possible.

> *Lord, remind me that before they call you will answer, while they are speaking you will hear.*

#76

Walking with God is . . .   knowing that God is watching over the ones I love.

"To this end we always pray for you, asking that our God will make you worthy of his call and will fulfill by his power every good resolve and work of faith." (2 Thes 1:11 NRSV)

As the mother of three teenage sons and a daughter, I often prayed for them, for their futures, and that my decisions and encouragement were right for them. Now that they are grown I can bless them across the miles in my prayers, in e-mails, and in telephone conversations. One son's wife brought in the tradition of saying "Bye, Bye, love you" at the end of phone conversations. It was a thrill to hear my two-year-old granddaughter shout out in Chicago's Midway airport—from her stroller, "Bye-bye, DeeDee (my grandmother nickname), love you." After September 11, 2001, we all are aware of how important last comments can be. One fireman was comforted to know that these were the last words his son and his wife had exchanged.

It has also been a great pleasure to be invited to attend church with each of my four children, although this didn't occur all at once. One son even gave the stewardship talk at his large metropolitan church that day.

As they reached their late teens, there were two sayings on the refrigerator: "A mighty oak is just a little nut that held its ground" and the other, a paraphrase of Psalm 12: "Blessed are the descendants of the (woman) who fears the Lord, for they shall be mighty in the land."

I saw the children taking peeks at these periodically when they came home from school and at other times. The message was: I believe in you—even if we're arguing about X, Y, and Z, today (fill in the blanks: clothes, rules, food, hours.) I pray for them, for all children and for each of my grandchildren, "Dear one—you are an expression of God's light in the world—a world that has been richly blessed by your presence."

Lord, protect this child and his/her joy and light in the world.

#77

Walking with God is . . .   looking back through three-year-old eyes.

"Choose this day whom you will serve" (Josh 24:15 NRSV)

As a child growing up during World War II, I was a three-year-old in 1941 when on December 6 Pearl Harbor was bombed. My family lived in Panama and within two to three weeks my mother and two brothers were on a ship to back to the United States, to New York and my grandmother's apartment there. We were there a few days until we moved to Winter Park, Florida to live with my great aunt Josie and be near the location from which my Father, an Army doctor, would be shipping off to war in the Pacific.

Leaving Panama we went through the locks of the Panama Canal. I remember seeing the great metal doors closed in front of the ship on a sunny day, and being disappointed that there wasn't more to see. Then my older brother, age five, came and said "come with me to see a German submarine behind the ship." I followed him and all I saw was a metal pipe sticking out of the water, the periscope I later learned. I was disappointed in my choice again that there wasn't more to see and I wanted to go back to my first location to see the locks. By then the boat had gone into the lock and there was only water all around—so not much to see!

I have not been back through the Panama Canal but this image has stayed with me as I looked at pictures, and remember events and feelings about them—even from this young age! Due to the importance in history this time and place gained more context. I later learned that the Japanese never planned to bomb the Panama Canal—they were only interested in protecting the Pacific rim for their own commerce. We were dependents and moved out quickly for fear of families being in imminent danger, which I didn't realize—it was just an interesting experience!

Lord, may all images that three-year-olds retain
be good and positive ones.

#78

Walking with God is . . .   feeling joy for many generations.

"For it is to such as these that the kingdom of heaven belongs."
(Matt 19:14b NRSV)

As the twig is bent, so grows the tree. Do we really want bent children? All the learning that children gain doesn't have to be immediate or useful—but it does need to be valued. Valuing learning and education is a marker of homes of children who are successful in school—regardless of socioeconomic status. All families are learning families, whether they plan to be or not. "Children learn what they live" is not just a familiar saying but has been validated over and over in research as the modeling of behavior is one of the most powerful teaching tools there is. This can be positive learning or negative learning, however. Children's minds are like high-powered computers. What we put in is the software and it develops and improves itself. Harsh physical discipline seems to work at first, but it messes up the software—just as some shortcuts on the computer do. Since children want to know how to be "grown-ups" almost every behavior of a parent is a model or an "imprint." To see a fifteen-month-old boy pick up his daddy's empty brief case or lunch box and carry it around—before he has the language to say what he's doing—bespeaks a powerful imprint.

But what a joy this awesome responsibility can be for parents—to form concept by concept and line by line, as if writing a story—a line that may go on through future generations for a long, long time or forever. What more valuable place to invest some time, energy, creativity, patience, shared wonder, and enjoyment than in doing something with a child, regularly, at least a few minutes a week if the child is young. For an older child, up to an hour of regular "pretend tea-time," as one family did, *on that child's level,* served at a time for which the child planned questions or topics to share. A three-year-old might want to help make cookies or instant pudding and talk about how it tastes, feels, smells, looks, and sounds (all five memory tracks are being laid down at this age). An older child might talk about school or special friends. Families that try this find that the children "save up" things they want to talk about. If the adult keeps any kind of journal or notes over time, they can see changes in the child's interests and concerns, just as in a family photo album. This time can even be on a regular long commute to some routine activity, such as childcare, work, or a sports activity.

Lord, help me to enjoy a child today.

#79

Walking with God is . . .   establishing a home with family values.

"For we are his workmanship created in Christ Jesus for good works which God prepared beforehand that we should walk in them." (Eph 2:10 RSV)

Children are growing and learning and laughing and responding, but they are on a train—the train of child development that replaces one stage with another in a predictable sequence. The laughing, helpful (but inept) three-year-old will be "too busy" to help much all too soon, and certainly by age eleven, twelve, or thirteen. The friendly, outgoing eight-year-old will be more inward and morose at nine. The teen with a crazy sense of humor, moods, and idealism, who leaves a trail, will be replaced with a busy, young adult in his or her twenties, sorting out how to get along in the world. As people live longer and longer in current times, it is important to know and understand something about the age(s) a child or children are in, and to enjoy *this* child at *this* age. As a child gets older, following the child's interests, drawing from the many ideas for parents in books and on the Internet, provides additional ideas for things to do or talk about.

A home where security, loyalty, kindness, courtesy, faith, truth, and love are the main characteristics can be developed by choice, regardless of the prosperity or income level of the family. These are the attributes that families hope to pass on to children, and to see in their lives and in their homes, later. But children must see these attributes modeled in their own home, whether with two parents or one, in order to live them out in their own lives. What's more, one won't hear about them on the radio or see them on television, so parents need to be sure *their* family values get equal time. Media literacy is another good topic for more education—including how music and lighting are used to affect the mood of the viewer. Children need to be told this. Even with both parents working, clear communication about their goals means that family members will keep re-inserting, and thus modeling, these behaviors in daily life—even though normal slipups occur. Ordinary folks, living daily, routine lives, can affirm these goals even if they feel stressed out periodically. Very few urgent interruptions are worth missing *this* time with *this* child, once a parent gets home from work. Some interruptions are inevitable, but working to reduce the number of interruptions yields benefits.

Lord, help me to find a special time with a child once a week.

#80

Walking with God is . . .   helping children have wonderful, positive
memories to return to.

"There shall be showers of blessings." (Ez 34:26 NRSV)

Children's lives are made up of memories, as they develop their memory "banks." The adult's job is to have more of these memories be good and full of love and laughter, rather than bad, if possible. Some even think memories are what hold a child steady as he or she grows older, and "anchor" a child by helping the child know what's good and what they want to repeat in their own children's lives. Saying something like "You are my beloved son with whom we are well pleased" to a twelve-year-old son would be a good idea for all parents of twelve-year-olds, as children need the reassurance that they are treasured as the blessing they are. One parent said this to her son and he responded "You are?" with amazement, reminding her that most eleven-, twelve-, thirteen-year-olds think that more is wrong with them than right.

When a child wanders, as does happen sometimes, there must be something for the child to *miss,* to remember with longing when they go through the low places in life, and hopefully, to come back to. Trying out new things and risk taking are important for young adults and even for organizations in today's world. Having a steady sense of the better way and core values to honor helps keep a balance when these new things go astray. Children need memories of a home they *want* to return to, and of a life they *want* to lead.

The greatest contribution families can make to a nation in these times is a stable home and a home where honesty, kindness, and integrity are taught. Some say this may have the greatest effect on an economy—new generations of intelligent, honest, creative, and optimistic young people with ideas in their heads and the kindness and integrity to carry them out and live lives of meaning in their own future homes.

Lord, help us to remember to love children with a love that makes them beautiful and special, and not just because they are *beautiful. Bless the children of today and help them grow and develop to be a loving, honest, creative generation.*

#81

Walking with God is . . .   continuous support of all parents.

"Do not grow weary in well-doing for in due time you shall reap, if you do not loose heart." (Gal 6:9 RSV)

Within actual families, styles of parenting and leadership are like a long garden hose. Any parent of adult children can tell you of family "traditions" their children described as adults that were originally put into place and done for some other reason. Examples include, "We always had to pick Daddy up"—we only had one car; "We watched that every Sunday night on TV"—because nothing else acceptable was on. When more positive images and activities, listening and encouragement, are put into the hose or pipeline intentionally, the children come out with more, and they come out with quite a lot even if a small amount or very little positive parent/family leadership is in evidence or consciously done. The love and care of parents, and their continuous support of children, do lay a foundation so that those they care for will have full and enriching lives. Therefore continuous support from the church or school in parent education program makes a lot of sense in helping children, parents, and families. This support becomes a "reinforcing system" and not just a minimal "balancing system." When the level of effort in parenting is present but low, the children's abilities may still tend to rise, but not as fast. A low flow of support effort from the church or school, adds somewhat to the level of positive parenting as a reinforcer for children, but a stronger effort from the church and school in parent education, encouraging parent involvement, will yield greater results.

Lord, help me to help parents know that their efforts are not in vain.

#82

Walking with God is ...   searching for God's wisdom in my own
family.

"Oh the depth of the riches and wisdom and knowledge of God!"
(Rom 11:33 NRSV)

Encouraging a family to develop a vision together of who they are and what they want to be helps children feel that their daily life is not just haphazard, and also creates a feeling of security. Discussion of goals and philosophy with the members of a family will help to define the values and the goals of the family more clearly. First explain that a goal or mission statement is like a map, showing where a family wants to be in the future. It should include, in some way, a pride in the uniqueness of our family, a future orientation, an imagery or pictures of the future that include a positive view of the future, such as the pursuit of excellence. Parents can ask family members to think about their values for themselves, or for the family ahead of time, and jot down some ideas or gather pictures from magazines. It may take several family (Sunday night?) suppers to form a consensus. Create, revise, and review the values and vision or mission statement or do a poster over as many gatherings as needed. Only then can goals (and even short term objectives) be developed that are in tune with the *values* of this family. In a family, if the home is clean, but there is no loving or caring or intellectual stimulation, maybe the *values* are not being highlighted. No one wants to raise nasty but tidy children, given a choice. Lack of cooperative talk and joint problem solving may not be modeling the very values a parent is hoping to impart.

A new theme or goal can be added every year as the vision gets clearer, adapts and develops. By brainstorming ideas and statements for the values, philosophy, or mission statement or poster, with the family, valuable new insights can be gained all around. Once the philosophy and new initiative goals are developed and clear, possible scenarios for improvement of one aspect or another can be generated. A scenario is a description of what a family might look like at sometime in the future. It is a description rather than a financial plan.

Lord, share your wisdom with us as we plan for our family.

#83

Walking with God is . . .   accessing the wisdom and knowledge of Christ.

"In whom are hid all the treasures of wisdom and knowledge."
(Col 2:3 RSV and KJV)

Family goals are needed, and the problem with family goals is that *if* they are **"go to work; come home; feed the kids; and go to bed,"** it is more than likely that those will be the goals of the children when they grow up. Having no plan or goal is like planning to go nowhere. If families put one-fourth or one-half of the thought and energy into thinking of family goals together, perhaps using the development of children as a framework, as they do for goal-setting in the workplace, more intentional and purposeful, positive results in families can be seen.

Informing family members' *perceptions,* about individual and joint activities and goals, would smooth many family discussions and is a benefit. Of course, this has to be done at an appropriate age level when working with children. One father made a "pie" chart of family finances, showing how big a wedge went for insurance and other things that children can't see. These concepts of developing a vision, goals, and learning for developing perceptions in a family, have been much more available to organizations than to families, until recently. They are essential for the fast-moving information age to build strong families, churches, and schools, to help them develop to their full potential. In identifying problems and solutions for a family, it is helpful to be clear on the values and goals.

Lord, help us to pray for your guidance in developing family goals and steps to them.

#84

Walking with God is . . .   developing and having a vision for our
family.

"I know the plans I have for you, says the Lord, plans for welfare not for evil,
to give you a future and a hope." (Jer 29:11 RSV)

What an intentional family becomes depends more on what it does than
on what is done to it. Families, through their decisions and actions, can help
shape their own destinies. They build on the idea of making the future happen
rather than letting events slide and then saying, "What happened?" The steps
in developing a scenario are brainstorming and then listing possible objectives
and steps for each part of a goal. But first it's a good idea to have the philosophy
and goals of the family be clear, so the following sample vision statement is
given. Families will have a different focus to their philosophy, but modeling that
there *are* values, goals, and planning is an asset for children, and is invaluable
for families.

A vision, philosophy, or mission statement might look like this for a
family:

- **We want the growth and development of each family member to
  their full potential.**
- **We plan to provide a safe, secure, loving environment in which
  that can happen.**
- **We hope to build excellence and achievement in education whenever
  and however possible: live near good schools, save toward college,
  and help with school homework in ways that are needed.**
- **We seek to serve the Lord God and belong to a good family place
  of worship nearby.**
- **We seek to leave the world a better place than we found it.**

The opportunity to vote on elements of the philosophy gives children a true
feeling of understanding and involvement and can be repeated yearly during
a family get-together for planning, perhaps around New Year's Day. In one
family in which a child became critically ill, remembering the family's brief goal
statement greatly helped the child feel that a family team loved and supported
him. The family even wore their family tee-shirts to the hospital room when
they visited him, and it gave him and all of them a feeling of family unity.

Family members also hear the many expectations other family members
have for the family and in voting for the elements favored by the majority, they

see that not all wishes can be met. If a family member feels strongly that his or her wishes should be followed, more discussion and underlying issues may need to be uncovered. This will save the parent a year or so of complaints and unhappiness, and thus can be a benefit. Or the family member may see that his or her wish cannot be worked into the budget, and try another solution such as some money-earning activities outside the home. For example, a teenager can see that asking for a car or a lot of new clothes might deprive his or her brothers and sisters of basic necessities, and look into getting a part-time job. A young child might learn why a pony is not feasible but a pet goldfish might be.

Lord, bless the vision for my family.

#85

Walking with God is . . .   being clear about our family vision.

"Write the vision; make it plain on tablets, so that a runner may read it. For there is still a vision for the appointed time . . . If it seems to tarry, wait for it; it will surely come, it will not delay." (Hab 2:2 NRSV)

All groups need to display their vision statements. One family with a sense of humor displayed this statement on their refrigerator door, "A mighty oak tree is just a little nut that held its ground." Another "refrigerator" vision statement of a single mother was a paraphrase from Psalm 112:1-2, "Blessed is the woman who is in awe of the Lord . . . . her descendants will be mighty in the land; the generation of the upright will be blessed." The teenagers in the home were feeling the usual self-doubt of teenagers but later did become business and family leaders. The importance of displaying a vision statement—even, and perhaps especially, a simple one—cannot be overestimated. The refrigerator door, of course, is seen often by all family members, and simple statements can remind children that parents think well of them for the long haul and that they can accomplish a lot with perseverance, despite daily ups and downs. One family measured how many decisions they made in one year at their family kitchen table meetings, by the number of times the refrigerator door opened and closed, and whether the adults gained weight!

Once the philosophy and goals are decided upon, the family leader can begin translating them into goals for the family, and then into a schedule or calendar for achievement of these goals. An adult's list of goals may look quite different from the family philosophy, while still remaining relevant. These goals might include

Remaining financially afloat by increasing income
Building quality into family life and learning, by focusing on specifics in the philosophy
Building morale, positive feelings, and family service to others

Lord, help us turn to You for divine ideas and guidance.

#86

Walking with God is . . .   enlarging your perspective.

"All things have been created through Him and for Him. He Himself is before all things, and in Him all things hold together" (Col 1:16-17 NRSV).

An old man said when asked about the peace and serenity in his life: "One thing to know is that there's only one center to the university and you're not it." Each of us sees the world from our own perspective. From that view each of us is the center of our own little world. A sense of entitlement, misunderstanding and conflict result because only God can be The Center of the universe, and of our little worlds, and of all other worlds. Our perception of ourselves, other people, our surroundings and our environment changes when we discover that God is at *The Center*.

Paul discovered Jesus Christ as the Center not only for his own life but for all life for all times and for all things. This view resolved conflicts as he and we become "ambassadors for change."

> *Lord, help us move forward exchanging your love*
> *for our service as your ambassadors.*

#87

Walking with God is . . .   showing respect and listening to all ages.

"Train up a child in the way he/she should go and when he/she is old, he/she will not depart from it" (Prov 22:6 RSV,/KJV paraphrase)

Show respect for a child by giving him or her a chance to tell you the story from a book or video he or she liked. Not only does the child learn respect by seeing it modeled and develop autonomy in thinking what to tell about, this is also great for language development. For example, one three-year-old wanted to watch the video *Lion King* (again) and the grandmother, who was babysitting, said she'd never seen it before. The child promised to explain it to her as the show went along, and did. When they got to "scary" parts, he even reassured her that this is a scary part but "it will be OK soon." Later, playing with blocks, the grandmother said, "Let's build a cage for the lions at the zoo." The child said, "Cage?" and hadn't known that lions are kept in cages. He spent the next six months building cages for animals in his pretend "zoo." Without the respect and listening that started with the video story, this fear of lions running loose and maybe down his street and the chance for learning might not have been uncovered.

Learning becomes much easier, and children "hear" what is being taught when they see good models or examples, feel loved, and have good experiences. Parents should give *themselves* a gold star (perhaps on the calendar?) when teaching has occurred beyond routine help and support. Parents' modeling attractive and warm, friendly behavior with respect also helps children be more accepted and popular with their own friends. Children raised with respect learn to show it to others.

Lord, help me to listen to children with respect.

#88

Walking with God is . . .   helping people feel good about themselves.

"You did not choose me but I chose you, and appointed you to go out and produce fruit and that your fruit should be permanent so that whatever you ask the Father in my name he may grant you." (Jn 15:16 RSV)

When I was a child in first grade, children in school were encouraged to buy ten cent "savings bond stamps" and paste them into a little booklet. When the booklet was full it was traded in for a ten dollar U.S. Savings Bond to "help the war effort" during World War II. My third grade brother and I took great pride in working towards this visible goal that was part of a bigger effort. Today children can learn from "visible projects" also.

Encourage projects that a child can plan and execute by him or herself: a picnic? a flower garden? Encourage family members to do simple "intact" projects that help, such as making gifts or decorations for the home, planning a schedule, or organizing a drawer or closet. Try to acknowledge and use each "project."

Encourage children to look at responsibilities in all their roles: family, household, _rewards_ for each: student and extracurricular activities such as sports or music. Agree together as what that might be such as making the team—after committing to go to practice; making a grade that is better; making little brother or sister's bedtime smoother by reading a story; being in charge of cleanup for their own room plus one other or more; doing their own laundry after age ten, or whatever similar task is needed. Teach children appropriate behavior and that discipline is learning responsibility and making some of these decisions on their own after considering the implications and consequences. Predicting and guessing or hypothesizing are valuable thinking skills.

> _Lord, help us to help children learn to think and be responsible_
> _as they grow toward your kingdom._

#89

Walking with God is . . .   recognizing effort in the family.

"And you will be children of the most high" (Lk 6:35 NRSV)

Ways to train children in responsibility might include giving or delegating a small section of a task at first, on a regular basis, and with something specific to do. This builds a *sense of achievement* into a child's task and also some responsibility. Or delegate another child to train the first child as in "Please show Susie how to vacuum the floor."

Emphasizing the *value of the work* itself is one of the easiest things to reinforce, but it is often not done. Remind people of the family's philosophy or vision/mission statement regularly: in notes, in e-mail or letters if they're away, or on a bulletin board or the refrigerator at home. Say, "We believe in having an excellent family," reminding children that they can use the power of their minds to make their lives better or whatever simply stated goals the family may have. The goals can be new and fresh every year, to keep them fresh and interest in them high.

Some simple ways to give recognition and awards for achievement in families include featuring a "Family Member of the Month" on a bulletin Board or on the refrigerator. Tell about hobbies, interests, favorite jokes, and school or work achievements. List compliments given that person, child or adult, or have family members do this. Give a certificate with a gold seal on it at a family supper for a child's *first* contribution to a family project. Mention names of those who have helped in a letter to grandparents or other relatives. Give "thank you" notes at the end of a project to those who have helped in extra ways. This promotes *their* writing of thank-you notes. Acknowledge and implement family member's ideas whenever possible. Affirm and validate their input at family gatherings for solutions that are useful. Praise the family member for a specific contribution in front of the rest of the family. Reinforce and complement children's positive interactions with each other. Involve children in writing or dictating paragraphs for the holiday newsletter or for thank-you notes.

"Children are a blessing from the Lord." Lord,
help us help our children to be *a blessing.*

#90

Walking with God is . . .   praying for God's help in solving our problems in the days ahead.

"I pray that from his infinite resources He will give you mighty inner strength through his Holy Spirit." (Eph 4:16 NKJV)

Praying for God's infinite resources immediately reminds us that God has all the money in the world, all the knowledge and power in the world, and all the connections in the world. Our lack is usually a lack of imagination for how to access one or more of these resources. Have we connected to the educational experiences we need? Have we connected to people who might have answers to our questions or at least who could help us form clearer and better questions? Have we identified or do we *know what we don't know?* This last is always a good for insight and perspective!

Often, *knowing what we don't know* is a first step in problem solving and helps us to break down a problem into parts and then into manageable steps. The listing of actions or activities on a calendar keeps a measurable time line in front of us as an individual, a group, or *even a nation*. In Jonah 4:11, the Lord says to Jonah, "I am concerned about (Nineveh) which doesn't know its right hand from its left."

Lord, we pray that you will be our companion, and help us keep the hope that you have revealed to us in your scriptures. Help us to know our right hand from our left especially after the 9/11 experience, and know the path on which to proceed.

Dad + Brennan

#91

Walking with God is . . . helping each other.

"For where two or three are gathered together in my name—I am there in the midst of them" (Matt 18:20 NKJV)

In an analogy for families and organizations, one man found group lessons from the South American rain forest. It is very large, very balanced, very diversified, and it supports itself on very scarce resources. To him, having a vision means seeing the forest not the trees. It means turning obstacles into opportunities. Since a rain forest has almost no resources, it must learn to adapt for what it doesn't have. The soil is thin, and there are few nutrients. Some families feel that this is their situation also. However, there are many examples of strong families with few resources that valued education and their spiritual roots, and effectively reared their children to be well-rounded, productive adult citizens. These families were able to help their children develop to their fullest potential even though economic resources may have been scarce.

Rain forests are the home of millions of plants and animals, perhaps two-thirds of the biological diversity of the globe, yet they are so balanced that the system is more efficient—even in using wastes for food, more creative, and more agile than any "organization" in the world. Organizing a family like a living system might carry lessons for the successful family (or organization) in the twenty-first century. A vision that sees benefits and increases them and sees needs and fills them works to this end.

Families that plan, take steps, and have a vision for their family are part of the parenting that is needed in a global information age. A family, like an organization, must have a reason for being, a purpose including love. This purpose and its design is its most important asset, and inspires learning, adapting, and productivity from members of the family that are creative, educated, intelligent, and moral.

Lord, help us to support each other so we can stand up and be tall like trees.

#92

Walking with God is . . .   helping us each to know and see the picture of what we can be.

"We must always give thanks to God for you, brothers and sisters, as is right, because your faith is growing abundantly, and the love of everyone of you for one another is increasing." (2 Thes 1:3 NRSV)

Many families feel more like a large jigsaw puzzle than a family. There is an assortment of abilities, interests, and personality traits and then these are impacted by family economic circumstances, stages of child development, educational opportunities, tragedies, triumphs, and all that life brings their way. Having a picture of the completed puzzle on the top of a puzzle box to guide whole sections taking shape is enormously helpful, if not an absolute requirement for puzzles. A family vision is about designing a plan or picture for the "top of the box." It is also called a vision, to help families grow and learn, to have the sections taking shape in a direction in which they want to go. The rain forest can continue to give us examples as a "living jigsaw puzzle."

Lord, help us be together as we pray in Christ's name.

Brennan Blake
Valerie

#93

Walking with God is . . .   adapting and changing.

"He will not let your foot be moved; he who keeps you will not slumber." (Ps 121:13 NRSV)

The design principles of the rainforest include getting feedback, adapting and changing, differentiating—being unique—being yourself, cooperating, and fitting in well (being a "good fit" perhaps in a unique niche). Some see *feedback* in two categories: *advanced feedback* when one sees a curve in the road coming, and *immediate feedback* when one doesn't see a cliff coming, drives off it and gets hurt. *Advanced feedback* is better of course, and making predictions can be fun and interesting. The human senses are one of the best feedback systems in nature: seeing, hearing, touching, tasting, and feeling. But collective feedback systems at the level of the parent's friends' group and community have hardly been developed.

In a family allowing and encouraging feedback, also called two-way communication, and building on the feedback as a source of creativity, is a strategic support. Knowing the costs and benefits of everything a family does in advance is a good kind of advance feedback. What is the benefit of a well-raised child? the cost? the cost of a poorly raised child? (This cost can be very high.) To know these benefits and costs, input from every individual involved *early* is needed. An "early warning" system is invaluable, such as planning on things to notice.

The next lesson, *to adapt and change*, is much easier when people, including families, are creative and innovative. Problem solving encourages creativity and innovation and applies new and not-so-new applications to some familiar problems, such as "Should the family move? If so, where to?" or whatever.

A third, very welcome lesson from the rain forest in the twenty-first century is to *differentiate, be yourself, be unique.* In the rain forest, if two organisms reside in the same niche, one becomes extinct. In business, if two businesses have the exact same niche, with the advent of Internet advertising and electronic commerce, one business will thrive and the others will adapt, if ever so slightly, or become extinct. Families building on their uniqueness may be a key for a family for survival with serenity. One research group predicted that in an age tied together economically by electronics, many different cultures, religions, and nations would increasingly become the norm.

Lord, help us to adapt or change what we can, be at peace about what we can't change, and to know the difference.

#94

Walking with God is . . .   developing deep roots.

"I am in the father, and you in me and I in you." (John 14:20 NRSV)

Cooperating while retaining the specialness and core competency of family members is another design lesson that can be seen in the rain forest and also in a stand of bamboo. The many tall bamboo shoots hold each other up and grow taller *together*. Sending out more shallow roots every spring enables them to grow in a broader swath.

Both organizations and families can be very productive with scarce resources if they hold each other up. A family that is small might need a deeper root system, in the same analogy and look even more to the Lord. These roots can be spiritual and family connections. If it is a small family, these might be interpersonal connections and supports for the family from the community.

Families that encourage children to look for their own unique and special talents and abilities, and apply them where they best fit, will have children that excel and prosper. Families (and organizations) that only create problems will not.

Lord, help us to fit in with your plans for us.

#95

Walking with God is . . .   finding God's purpose and vision.

"Fear not for I am with you, be not dismayed for I am your God, I will strengthen you and I will help you. I will uphold you with my victorious right hand." (Is 41:10 RSV)

Families *and* organizations do better when they live for a purpose. Finding this purpose and vision, writing it down or capturing it, and taking steps toward filling it develops and sustains those involved and promotes growth and excellence in new ways. Above all, it is important not to evaluate efforts too harshly and too soon—certainly not in less than two years, and hopefully, not before six years have gone by. Depending on size and scope of the group involved, it takes six months to two years of input, six months to two years of attitude change, and six months to two years to get results or "outputs" in any new effort, according to management theorists.

A pilot doesn't get on a plane and hope it goes to the right place. He or she has some sense of where it is going and a mapped plan. Individuals are the pilots of their lives, and having a vision helps individuals, parents, and families, churches and schools create the change they want to see. Having a sense of purpose also contributes to a longer life according to numerous centenarians studied.

Children take about twenty to thirty years to mature. Many young people seem very unformed in their middle twenties and at twenty-nine and a half, things seem to fall into place—job, marriage, education completed, etc. Therefore, "don't judge them until they're thirty" has become a saying. It is important to adapt, but if mind and spirit are in harmony, the vision and purpose of the family—to preserve its love, honor, excellence, and productivity—will turn out to be a true and productive vision for families in the twenty-first century.

Lord, help us to pilot our lives in the way you would have us, with your guidance.

#96

Walking with God is . . .   understanding the forces and
impacts of change.

"I the Lord do not change." (Mal 3:6 NRSV)

The driving forces and impacts of social, intellectual, economic, political, and technological change as seen on many horizons: global, national, regional, and local can influence many changes. Reviewing them gives one insight into other changes and challenges. Individuals can construct a chart showing impacts at the global, national, regional, local, family, and individual levels of changes that can be identified. The forces causing change can be divided into categories, such as political, social, economic, physical, and technological. You might want to add even more categories.

In the political forces category, the global peace that existed for many years at the end of the twentieth century made global economics possible. In addition to the U.S. and U.N. forces' wars on terrorism, "hot spots," localized wars or fighting, erupt, but these can be local or regional in nature. These usually erupt over cultural, religious, and historic animosities. Understanding these animosities better through more knowledge of world history and world geography can be a springboard for family and school learning, and can sharpen one's predictions about what might happen next. For instance, encourage children to read library books on different countries to inspire new thinking and insights. Invite interesting guests or students from other countries for a meal.

A national impact of these political forces includes immigration changes. Regional and state impacts can be seen in politics as regions and states are beginning to deal with global corporations and to send invitations and tax benefit packages to international businesses. Diversity in community politics causes elected officials to be more representative of the diverse populations they serve. Families feel less constriction and segregation as more kinds of jobs and people are welcomed in the workplace as well as into new housing. Individuals can taste national and international travel in person and on the Internet. E-mail coming in on one day can be from Belgium, Sweden, New Zealand, Australia, and South Africa—limited only by the language of the sender or the receiver. Political changes are having an impact on every level and are often felt by individuals.

Lord, help us understand the history and culture of other nations.

#97

Walking with God is . . .   helping build a bridge between the "haves" and the "have-nots."

"Just as you did it to one of the least of these . . . you did it to me."
(Matt 25:40 NRSV)

Economic changes are having a global impact. Anyone can tell this, who has used an ATM bank machine in a foreign country and determined the foreign currency they would receive from their home bank account by pushing a button to make the selection. Tariffs being reduced between countries have encouraged international trade and have increased imports and exports from some countries. Economic growth resulted, which was predicted since1990, but at the time was considered to be too optimistic. Economic recession also proved to be global. The information age has prompted and facilitated these opportunities and challenges to developing trade and prosperity.

Impacts on the workplace can be seen as more and more businesses include e-mail, telephone, and Internet/electronic ordering, and the staff and technology to support them. Schools for grades kindergarten through twelfth grade are using e-mail for parent conferences, announcements, Web sites, and small group meetings. Families, individuals, and organizations are benefitting by the convenience and lower cost of goods and services acquired in these ways. Some said electronic commerce would completely change everything we do and how it is done. Electronic ordering and online federal grant applications (www.grants. gov) and services are mostly here or are just around the corner.

Parents helping their children be creative and innovative will be important, as a key driver of the coming economic era is innovation. This includes commitment to continual renewal of systems, processes, and information delivery methodologies, such as e-mail, document storage, Internet sites, PDAs, and other kinds of electronic interactivity. We are continually challenged to update the content, the tools, and our approaches. Learning to learn continuously has become a key and critical life skill. Helping those less fortunate than we are will be enabled by data clearinghouses of resources, e-mail to other countries—plus knowing what people need.

Lord, help us to follow your lead in using our resources to help and interact with others in your world.

#98

Walking with God is . . .   listening and respecting where others are
"coming from."

"For my thoughts are not your thoughts, nor are your ways my ways, says the Lord." (Is 55:8 NRSV)

Sociocultural changes are having new impacts at every level. As people travel and learn more about many societies and cultures whether in person or via the Internet or both, service and human relationships improve. "Meet them where they are" is not only a good teaching-learning practice, it provides opportunities for prosperity, service, and good relationships. Families that expect courtesy and respect, give it. However, this also requires learning where people "are coming from." Think of the old mountaineer's comments, when asked "How do you get to North Mountain?" He answered, "Well, to begin with, I wouldn't start from here." Look carefully at the starting points of getting to know people. Population growth increases individual and family opportunities to learn about other cultures and individual people in them, partly because there are just *more* people.

Electronic communication speeds all communication. Leaders are challenged to become facilitators and teachers about resources that can be accessed as direct delivery to individuals. Direct delivery of information to parents might include lists of Web sites, learning activities for children by age group, and other "knowledge management" for parents. New tools bring access and resources of multimedia information for parents and for teachers. As church members and parents become involved in *producing* information for each other, and for others on a blog or Web site, their knowledge and ideas will be part of the coming together with communication and computers to enhance a new era. These sites can be shared with the world, as a "visit counter" installed on a web page will tell the viewer. One home learning activity Web site (www.homelearning.org) was accessed by people in France, Israel, Holland, New Zealand, and South Africa—reminding the sponsors that child development stages and activities are universal and without geographic boundaries. People can access a collective information resource from any time zone or location.

*Lord, help us to use the technology you have
given us to help other people.*

#99

Walking with God is . . .   knowing that the Lord is with me regardless
of my location.

"Lord, I love the house in which you dwell, and the place where your glory
abides." (Ps 26:8 NRSV)

Physical changes and location or "place" are less important today, as in the
work world "place" has become less important in an era of international business
and telecommuting from home, a telecommuting center, or from a vacation are
not unusual. The networking of regions, countries, and far-flung employees has
become easier and more commonplace with more implications and opportunities
for developing new services and improving workflow. Nationally, families move,
or don't have to move, as information age jobs replace industrial age jobs. One
result is that regions seem smaller and more manageable, especially as "distance
learning" becomes more commonplace for courses in education and training.
"Desktop video," a webcam or a small camera on top of or in the computer, and
conference calls are used for everything from small meetings to job interviews.
A constant challenge is to keep the content and meaning of a new initiative in
place while utilizing technology to improve the communications needed.

Much comment has been made about distances across a city or a nation
becoming less important as "physical place" becomes less important with the
use of e-mail, fax, wireless telephones, PDAs (personal digital assistants), and
portable laptop computers or netbooks. "Snail mail" has become the nickname
for a letter sent by the regular postal service. Families can utilize technology to
stay close and benefit from the increased knowledge base readily available in the
home with a personal computer and the Internet. For families, parent involvement
in schools can be facilitated with e-mail and wireless phones to and from the
teachers for "one-sentence conferences" and also for online group conferences.
Quality time and bonding across generations can be pushed to a higher priority
and be enhanced by e-mail or even texting with grown children.

Since immediacy becomes more important as "place" becomes less
important, individuals are challenged as time and space become redefined for
individuals and organizations. Taking a laptop computer to a meeting to access
a database of resources available makes a lot of sense and "saves time."

*Lord, help us feel close to you as well as to our loved ones. Help us to
communicate with You as often as we do with them. Help us to remember that
"surely the Lord is in this place."*

#100

Walking with God is . . .   feeling God's healing strength and energy.

"Do you not know that your body is a temple of the Holy Spirit within you, which you have from God, and that you are not your own? For you were bought with a price; therefore glorify God in your body." (1 Cor 6:19-20 NRSV)

Bodily physical fitness interests have swept the country for individuals, especially for those who are then avoiding retirement and nursing homes until a much later age. This is thus pressuring the health care industry and in turn building the tourism and recreation industries. Many new earning opportunities should be present in these areas. Schools are benefitting from active volunteer "adoptive grandparents," and helping professionals can benefit from "mentor grandparents" for parenting groups.

Maintaining the "temple of our body" is a God-given responsibility, now that one hundred years of life are more possible. When you or I are out walking or jogging, go a quarter or a half a mile farther! Then, when we have to return, we've gone half or one mile farther than before. Now you're even fit enough to put up the Christmas tree. "A desire accomplished is sweet to the soul" (Prov 13:19). Eating the right foods, getting enough exercise and enough rest are all part of a "fitness plan" for God that we can adopt for ourselves.

Lord, help me to stay healthy and fit for you.

101

Walking with God is . . .   using technology to learn something new
every day.

"Call to me and I will answer you, and will tell you great and hidden things that you have not known." (Jer 33:3 NRSV)

Technological sources and impacts of change are with us every day. The knowledge is exciting that information, and access to it, doubles every eighteen months or less and that this has been happening for some thirty years; the Internet has increased access to information and has increased the exchanges between people in general, without regard to race, creed, country, color, status, or gender. The Internet "year" has become forty-seven days for improvement and increased access. Information one couldn't get two years ago, one complains about getting *too slowly* today. Technology has increased and impacted or influenced all of the sources of change mentioned so far in these devotionals, and at almost all levels. The national and global information infrastructures can, and do, enhance all disciplines: government, education, health, the arts, business and commerce, and more. Many of these sectors have reengineered their "enterprises" to improve the results of their original mission, building on the facilitation and benefits of technology. The U.S. Government "Service to the Citizen" initiatives with larger government information databases available to individual citizens on request, via the Internet and CD-ROMS, is but one example of this, but a very helpful one to school children doing homework research. For example, see *www.nasa.gov/* for air and space and solar system information.

In the community, more technology is readily available for purchase through stores, discount stores, mail order, and is free at public libraries. Classes and tutorials of all kinds are available in all settings, and to individuals at home through almost every software application's "Help." Distance learning from institutions of higher education is reaching out with nonplace-centered credit courses, and degrees, and noncredit courses and certificates, and so is the training industry. Families and individuals are challenged to grow and learn at home and at work, as they surf the Internet and have access to museums such as the Louvre at www.louvre.fr/ and libraries such as the Library of Congress at www.loc.gov. Professionals in all fields are using communication technology in their work and for personal use, especially the wireless phone, and notebook, netbook, laptop or handheld computers.

Lord, help us to learn from each other in new and meaningful ways.

#102

Walking with God is . . .   thinking of others.

"And God is able to provide you with every blessing in abundance, so that by always having enough of everything, you may share abundantly in every good work." (2 Cor 9:8 NRSV)

When my four children were small, the time before Christmas became a time of bickering and "antsy" anticipation. Remembering a tradition from my college dormitory years, we instituted "Secret Santa" during the Advent season. Everyone, including Mom and Dad, drew a name out of a hat and did one or more good deeds a day for that person. Then they would leave a note saying "from Secret Santa." Much attention was put into disguising handwriting, I might add. A pencil, a stick of gum, a candy bar, a bed made or turned down—all became prized surprises and certainly changed the atmosphere of the home. Instead of arguing and fighting, thinking of another became the daily focus. On Christmas Eve, the "Secret Santas" were revealed along with the children's gifts to each other and Mom and Dad. This way the pencils and macaroni plates lovingly constructed or saved up for and bought were not eclipsed by larger gifts Christmas morning, and the gifts were greatly savored: The happy cry "Oh, just what I always needed!" for an eraser, for example.

Even to this day, my children's children exchange the gifts from each other and to their parents on Christmas Eve, be they far or near from me. The gifts have matured, as have the givers, but learning to think of others and anticipate the needs of others stayed with them.

Lord, help us to think of others and to teach this to children.

103

Walking with God is . . .   thinking of others in the wider community.

"And God is able to provide you with every blessing in abundance, so that by always having enough of everything, you may share abundantly in every good work." (2 Cor 9:8 NRSV)

My daughter's children spend a day or two before Christmas culling through their toys to give at least ten to "the poor children," at whatever agency my daughter and her husband have selected that year. One year it was the unwed mothers' group, and that generated somewhat unwelcome questions about what happened to the Daddy? The children then have room for new, more interesting toys, and watching them choose what to pass on is instructive, to say the least. Their decision making and reasons spoken aloud can be very interesting! One was "I don't like purple anymore." Or, "This book is too baby-ish for me."

Again, the donations will mature, as will the givers, but learning to think of others in the wider community and thinking about the needs of these others hopefully will stay with them.

Lord, help us to think of others in our communities and to teach this to children.

1/16/2009

#104

Walking with God is . . .   being aware of a new season for
experiencing the wonder of God.

"Let me abide in your tent forever." (Ps 61:4 NRSV)

Christmas season is always a busy time. Delivering a loaf of freshly baked bread to a neighbor, I was treated to a wonderful sunset, with pinks, purples, and "glory shining." I was reminded that God is always with us and there is always a new season for experiencing His wonders. The next day, during the regular church service, the Sunday School Christmas pageant reminded me of the time when my three boys, ages six, four, and two were the three kings, and my daughter, seven months, was the Baby Jesus. I always had thought only a third or fourth child in a family would be allowed to be handled by a nine—or ten-year-old Mary—although the role required only lying in the manger. During the second service Mary even gave her a bottle! Later it also reminded me of the pageant my grandchildren were in when the child dressed as the star got tired and sat down on the altar steps. The pageant looked different without the star! God's wonders always bring an overwhelming sense of peace and joy, and an awareness of God. This consciousness of the presence of God stayed with me each time as I went about my routine chores.

Whether with natural wonders or the gift of children learning about the holy birth of Jesus, the Christmas season lends itself to experiencing God's presence anew, but any season will do. Spring is beautiful, summer is lush and full of outdoor experiences, fall brings cool, crisp air, and winter brings Christmas.

Lord, we pray that you may evermore dwell in us and we in you.

#105

Walking with God is . . . touching Jesus to be healed.

"Jesus turned, and seeing her said, "take heart, daughter; your faith has made you well." And instantly the woman was made well." (Matt 9:22 NRSV)

Just as the woman with the flow reached out to touch Jesus's robe to be healed, many Christians today, who feel their life is "draining away" can reach out to "touch Jesus and be healed." This analogy for modern times was developed by a member of my Bible Study group. When people reach out to touch Jesus, they may pray, go to church, read, or meditate on the scripture, and talk to other Christians. Over time, as their insights come together, they can be healed. As they feel the grace of God and Jesus's love, joy, and peace in their lives, this healing continues.

Nathan spoke to David in 2 Samuel 12:1-9, and in community we can be "Nathans" to each other—helping one another to listen to and understand the Lord and His guidance. The need for healing is as great as it was two thousand years ago, and touching the hem of Jesus's robe is still possible, figuratively speaking. As we walk with God, the abundant *more* He has for us in prayer and in living becomes a healing force in our lives and the lives of others.

Lord, be a healing force in my life and in the lives I touch.

#106

Walking with God is . . .   enjoying your grandchildren.

"I will make of you an eternal excellence, a joy of many generations."
(Is 60:15 NKJV)

Enjoying grandchildren is one of the greatest pleasures of life. Looking at this little one—who may have the "aspect" of an older family member as a child or an infant—a grandparent can "see" how the child of two, might look in five, ten, even fifteen or twenty years later. Then watching this child develop, with his or her own unique personality, overlaid with modern phrases such as "I hate it when that happens"—when the two-wheel bike won't respond as expected for the six-year-old, or "that's cool," is a lot of fun.

Our spiritual walk, what we say and do, likewise will imprint on these little ones also. We can try to model our lives after Jesus so others, especially children and grandchildren, can see and know the love of Jesus in us. For instance, we can minister to them and others as He would have done. Sharing our joy in the Lord with them helps them to develop their own joy to pass on to their future generations.

You will indeed become "an eternal excellence."

Lord, help us to share your joy, strength, and peace.

#107

Walking with God is . . .   counting the apples in a seed.

"Did I not tell you that if you believed you would see the glory of God?"
(John 11:40 NRSV)

When my daughter was in seminary, studying to be a minister, I came across the phrase "how many apples in a seed." It seemed backward. As a nursery school teacher in my earlier years, I had often cut an apple in half, sideways, to show the children the "star" that the seeds make in the center. But this phrase "counting the apples in a seed" means that you plant the seed, grow the apple tree, and count the apples produced. The whole process takes years, yet one seed actually can produce many apples that then have many seeds. How like preparing a young person for the ministry.

Later as an Associate Pastor for Youth in first one and then another large church, my daughter averaged one hundred young people in her teen groups, increasing and doubling previous numbers of attendees. Also she was modeling a new professional role for some of the young women. Indeed there were many apples here, and only ten years had gone by. The young people she has helped, especially through life crises, stay in touch with her and visit her and her husband and three children. She has even performed some weddings for them.

Every day the wonder of God's grace fills us with awe: the beauty around us, the love of God, and the wisdom and insights we receive—all given freely and unconditionally. Surely it is "the glory of God."

Lord, help us to see your glory in our family and surroundings.

#108

Walking with God is . . .   learning about other countries.

"Enlarge the place of your tent, stretch your tent curtains wide, do not hold back; lengthen your cords and strengthen your stakes. For you will spread out to the right and to the left." (Is 54:2-3 NIV)

A recent observer commented that the U.S. views China today in the same way that nineteenth-century Europeans viewed the U.S.: having lots of natural resources and cheap labor from exploitation of immigrant and even slave labor 150 years ago, and as having a casual attitude toward copyright and patent laws protecting mainly British books and inventions. The U.S. benefits today from many inexpensive products, but as China grows and develops our U.S. tent will include more from this huge nation.

All the factors mentioned played a part but were not the full story of America's rise, nor do the similar aspects of modern China's behavior fully explain what China has achieved. China's large-scale economic shifts are effecting more than purely the economic level, as is always the case. There are environmental, political, and social changes and goals as well as economic goals. America debates the China "opportunity" and the China "threat," but these seem distant and theoretical from the perspective of the Chinese cities.

Chinese cities that are fast growing seem like fast-growing cities in the old American West: brash, transient, unmannered, full of opportunity, and rough. Factory workers in the Chinese city of Shenzhen earn $100 a month, but get free food, free uniforms such as red company jackets and blue jeans, and free dormitories. Thus they are able to save far more than U.S. workers. Many, of course, send money home to their families. They are earning about $.50 an hour compared to the $7.00 an hour minimum wage range in the U.S. United States workers do not save even 10 percent of their wages after paying for food, house, medical care, and insurance, it has been found.

It is interesting to note that the two leading U.S. exports to China by volume are scrap paper and scrap metal, from recycling. As America is enlarging its tent and helping developing nations, it is important to respect the human-ness of each person in each of these countries—their brains, abilities, and innate cultures.

Lord and Creator of all, may we see potential in all people,
regardless of their circumstances.

#109

Walking with God is . . .   visiting schools in other countries.

"Even there thy hand shall lead me, and thy right hand shall hold me."
(Ps 139:10 RSV)

On a trip to China with a group of educators we visited a school in a Han village built in AD 1400 in the Ming Dynasty era, for the soldiers sent to protect those building the Great Wall of China in its last phase. The soldiers intermarried with local people and stayed. The village was very old, dirty, and primitive, but it did have electricity. The school, originally donated and updated by a group of Americans, needed books and a computer for its library. Our education conference made donations toward this and enjoyed a dance in costumes performed for us.

The children were darling as usual. The educators were asked to perform a dance in return and performed an unplanned dance of the "Hokey Pokey"—and no surprise—everyone in the education conference group knew it! The Chinese watchers loved it and tried to imitate the steps. Even the elderly Chinese women were doing it. International relations can be helped more easily than one would think! Our performance was enjoyed by all.

Lord, help us to remember that children are children the world over.

#110

Walking with God is . . .   seeing children in other countries.

"Let the little children come to me and do not hinder them, for the kingdom of God belongs to such as these." (Luke 18:16, Mk 10:14 ESV)

On the same trip to China, we visited what was called "public kindergarten" in Guyang, in Guizhou province. Guyang is a "small" city of only 3.6 million, which is the same size as Washington, D.C. By comparison, Beijing has 18 million in population. At the preschool the three-, four-, and five-year-olds came to meet us calling out "Pleased to meet you" in English, the only words they knew. But we knew less Chinese than that! They danced outside with us and for us, to loud and peppy music. The play yard had plastic wheel toys—the same type one finds in U.S. pre-schools. After visiting classrooms and holding a meeting with the teachers, we went on to visit an elementary school. There we watched first graders learning calligraphy. The children start with pencils and move up to indelible black paint and brushes. Of course some paint wound up on the floor. None of the schools, nor the University we visited, were heated, so the children all wore jackets, and the adults wore coats, as it was December. The first graders then gave their calligraphy efforts to us as gifts! I passed mine on to grandchildren ages five, seven, and nine.

Lord, help us to enjoy the joy and smiles of all children.

#111

Walking with God is . . .   contemplating the beauty of the human mind.

"We have the mind of Christ." (1 Cor 2:16 ESV)

It is awesome to contemplate the full complexity of the brain, tens of billions of neurons connected through trillions of branches acting through complex patterns of neurotransmitters. One can add what is known about baby and early childhood brain development: A three-year-old has 3 trillion connections that are carved away by non-use to the 1 1/2 trillion connections that most adults have. Neglected children often carve away more, unfortunately. A powerful picture emerges of the brain we all carry.

Today we have the power to enhance our minds by three very different approaches: by education, by computers, and by techniques of neurobiology. Education, of course, dates back to prehistoric times, computers are a modern invention, and neurobiology is only beginning to realize its potential for expanding normal minds and restoring brains damaged through accident, disease, or heredity.

Scientists now see that proposals to simulate the entire brain in molecular detail on a computer, as in artificial intelligence, seems presumptuous. But we are beginning to know what we don't know. We can be grateful for the wonderful brain every human being has been gifted with and respect our own and other's talents and abilities, both known and unknown to the individual.

Creator God, thank you for the wonderful gift of our mind. Help it to expand and help us to help children learn and gain thinking skills. In Jesus name, Amen.

Maddy

#112

Walking with God is . . .   not letting your heart be troubled.

"Let not your heart be troubled, believe in God, believe also in me."
(John 14:1 NRSV)

During a messy divorce and reentry into the work world with four children in college, these words sustained me on many a night when I couldn't sleep. I would get up, get pen and paper, and write these words from John 14 across the top of the page. Then I would list and number my concerns down the left-hand column. This helped my thoughts slow down. Then across from each one I would list a Bible verse from a large page of positive verses a friend had given me from her Bible study group. In doing this God would help me to see a situation more clearly. Then, as I am writing, I am turning the situation over to God. Without fail I would receive an answer in the Bible verse (or two) for each problem that suddenly seemed appropriate. A frequent choice from Isaiah 41:10 was "Be not dismayed, I will strengthen you, I will help you; I will uphold you with my victorious right hand."

Another favorite was "my presence will go with you, and I will give you rest" (Ex 33:14 NRSV). I would feel the love of God and that God would see me through. Anguish was replaced with peace, calm dispelled fear, and I would go back to sleep in about thirty minutes total.

One list I found later included "show house contract to two lawyers." The next year a list had "choose new slipcover for blue chair." Things had gotten better. The importance of my worries had shrunk. When we focus our thoughts on God, we can be sure God will be with us, to comfort us, guide us, and help us. However we express our prayers, God welcomes them and responds. This written approach to prayer for worry and anxiety is always available.

Father, Creator of all, may we see that God restores and
cares for us at all times and in all situations.

#113

Walking with God is . . .   imagining a universe that is larger than you thought.

"The heavens tell the glory of God, and the skies announce what his hands have made . . . But their message goes out through all the world; their words go everywhere on earth." (Ps 19:1-4 NIV)

David wrote this psalm and he knew that God created the stars and that it was God, not chance, that set the stars in their specific places, as we know from Psalm 8. David also knew, like most of his contemporaries, the meanings of the names of the stars. And he knew that the expanse of the stars had a divine purpose. In Genesis it says, "God said let there be lights in the expanse of the heavens to separate the day from the night and let them be for signs and for seasons and for days and for years." The stars had a double purpose marking time signs, as well as for showing prophecies.

The stars are God's ancient sign language to communicate with their regular appearance and reappearance in regular order during the course of a year in order to tell the story of God. The stars are God's ancient sign language to communicate the Gospel before the dispersion of the peoples of the earth and before writing was a tool of civilization . . . before writing became widely used for the preservation of truth. Parents communicate with babies with sign language before they can speak. God communicated the gospel Word to us through the stars, before the Written Word came to be and before the Incarnate Word came to be.

My grandmother's grandfather was Simon Newcomb, who was the preeminent astronomer of his time in the late 1800s and early 1900s. Newcomb stated in a famous paper entitled "Extent of the Universe" two astounding facts: "The universe, vast though it is, shows certain characteristics of a unified and bounded whole. It is not chaos, it is not even a collection of things, each of which came into existence its own separate way . . . . the Milky Way itself is a single structure." Newcomb and many other scientists both historical and modern, have pointed us to the truth of God in our Universe. (See *The Language of God* by Francis Collins. See also *God's Voice in the Stars* by Kenneth Fleming). In the Christmas story of the gospels, the wise men followed the star to Jesus. These men were also men of science and learning. We too can too can hear and see the communication of God through the night sky, through the earth, through the person of Jesus, through the wisest of men, and through the Holy Spirit's direction. God is showing you himself in many more ways than you know. You will find that you are really loved.

Lord, help us to know that we have to stand back to see the big picture.
Rev. Allison Jones Lundeen

#114

Walking with God is . . .   standing back to see the whole picture.

"Commit your way to the Lord, and your plans will be established."
(Prov 16:3 NRSV)

Whether looking at stars or growing a family or looking at a quilt, you have to stand back to see the whole picture. Quilt makers will tell you that they don't start with all those little squares that need sewing together, they start with the whole picture or design.

The Aids quilt, which fills the whole Washington, D. C., Mall, may have to be seen from a helicopter to take it in, but the big picture tells the story of many people dying of this disease. Each square is as big as a rug and represents a deceased person, remembered by loved ones. More money has been put into Aids research, and now the disease has slowed its death toll, at least in the U.S.

Families also have to be seen from the long view or "standing back." Children are a twenty-one-year or longer project but as young adults, they can make their parents very proud. I love the weddings of my friends' children for I knew these children when they couldn't walk or talk, or even feed themselves.

Lord, help us to stand back when we see chaos
and look from a higher, longer view.

#115

Walking with God is . . .   relaxing and letting God pull you up.

"I am the vine, you are the branches: the one who abides in me, and I in him, that one bears much fruit." "I am the bread of life." (John 15:5, John 16:35a NRSV)

At a church service recently, the minister brought in a loaf of bread, bunches of grapes, and a full—size water ski. Her message, especially to the large confirmation class, was that with Jesus as your root you can do much more than otherwise.

When she got to the water ski, she asked how many in the congregation had water-skied. A majority raised their hands. Then she asked, "How many had *tried* to water-ski?" More raised their hands. I knew she was a good water-skier and she went on to say that in water-skiing you have to hold on to the rope, but there comes a time when you have to relax and let the boat pull you up. Then you hold on tight! You will be riding over and around bumps, waves, and "chop" in the water. Her analogy, for teenagers and adults, was to let the pull of God as well as your holding on tight, be part of the effort as you ride out the bumps and waves of life.

Lord, teach us to relax and seek and accept your help with challenges.

#116

Walking with God is . . .   accepting the power and support of God.

"If the spirit of him who raised Christ from the dead, lives in you, he who raised Christ from the dead will give life to your mortal bodies also through his spirit that dwells in you." (Rom 8:11 NRSV)

Anyone who believes in Jesus will find astounding power and support in this verse. As families raise children and seek to "stay afloat," there will be times when you feel that "the power that raised Christ from the dead" is needed. Christ came to lift up and not to condemn. The efforts we make may seem to bring slow results, but over the long run, results will be showing. Curbing negative self-talk, that is, not condemning plus prayer and daily time with the Bible, bring the serenity and inner peace so needed in family living. Maintaining a positive attitude with encouraging words for children just mastering self-mastery, self-control, and self-discipline is building in the right direction. "Living water" will be flowing from your heart for walking with God, sharing love and family living.

Lord, help us to stay afloat as we seek your peace.

Kerry

#117

Walking with God and family living means . . .   looking ahead and knowing something about child development.

"Your abundance at the present time should supply all your want."
(2 Cor 8:14 RSV)

When you're a first-time parent, you "need to know it will be OK in six months" as one mother said. Child development moves so quickly that whenever a stage seems unpleasant (such as colic, or the "terrible twos") the child will move on to a new stage, perhaps even before the parent can figure out what to do. Without knowledge of child development, parenting is like going somewhere in a car without a map. The chances of getting where you want to go are greatly lessened. The car (or child) will keep on going but probably won't wind up where a parent wants him or her to be. Just as in looking down a road, one can see cars and the road ahead. One can see that at a distant point on the highway there is construction. This is in essence looking into a future time frame—if only for a few minutes.

When people look ahead on the road and see construction, they change lanes, noting that in one lane far ahead, cars are moving more effectively and faster. They *anticipate* that it will be more advantageous to them to move into the better lane. In this way they also might stop, or move over, when they see or hear on the radio that there is more road work or an accident up ahead.

Many drivers will not look, some will not see, and a few, not knowing how to use the information they see that is laid out before them, will change into a faster lane beside them at present, and wind up in a slower lane up ahead, or even in an accident. This perceiving of a future order and acting now to move toward it or away from it is what knowing about child development and how to update it as children grow is all about.

Lord, help us to learn what we need to know.

#118

***Walking with God and
family living means . . .***   valuing the mind of a child.

"We have the mind of Christ." (1 Cor 2:16 ESV)

Every child is born with 3 trillion brain cells, but all the connections between them are not in place yet. What is reinforced will be used and connected, and what is not used will carve away. This is how all human beings become unique. Children's brains ARE different and are much more fully connected at age five than at age two. Abstract thought doesn't really pick up until ages eleven, twelve, or thirteen according to the famous researcher Piaget, who calls this "formal operations." This means that talking about something that a young child can't see (is "abstract") is much less effective than showing the child an object and explaining what it can do. At ages seven to eleven, Piaget calls this "concrete" operations (you can see it, like concrete), and for ages four to seven, it's called "pre-operational," just previous to concrete operations.

The great gift of 3 trillion brain cells is more likely to be 1 and ½ trillion as the child reaches ages five or six, but there is still time for children to learn and absorb more. A child's IQ is 50 percent in place by age three and 75 percent in place by age seven, so these early years are very valuable.

Understanding the differences in brain structure that evolve and how children develop at different ages will help parents to better understand what approaches, methods, or words might work better on different issues at different ages with their children. Arnold Gesell and the Gesell Institute offer helpful materials on what children do (not on what a parent *should* do).

*Lord, help us to understand the different ages and
stages of our children.*

#119

**Walking with God and
family living means . . .**   knowing what parents need to know about
child development.

"I have learned in whatever situation to be content." (Phil 4:11 ESV)

It is well to keep in mind the alternating "equilibrium" (smooth) and "disequilibrium" (breaking-up and inward behaviors) described by Gesell and others. The pattern or "cycle" of development can be seen clearly and has been validated and revalidated by a variety of researchers.

The *smooth* years are relatively calm, and the child has consolidated forces and meshes well with his or her environment. Generally this child (plus or minus six months for a particular child) is able to do most of what the child aspires to do. Ages three and five and ten are often good examples of this "balanced" period that is in equilibrium. The child also meets demands of others as well as from himself or herself with satisfaction.

A *"breaking-up"* stage generally follows when the child outgrows the "old" self and becomes contrary and at odds both with himself or herself and the environment. It's as if the old self (like an eggshell) has to break up to allow room for growth and expansion of the new self. Some need for order causes these children to be ritualistic, for example, try putting a two-and-a-half-year-old in the wrong chair for a meal to observe this importance of ritual, resulting in a big complaint or fuss. These children can be described as "boiling and bubbling," and they can't explain it to others because they don't understand it themselves.

Then comes a *"sorting out"* stage with a temporary quieting. They have figured out that different tasks, places, and situations have different behaviors related to them. They also associate a result with a specific problem or cause—sometimes wrongly. (For example—one of the worst is—Mommy and Daddy divorced because I was naughty).

Lord, help us to understand how our children are sorting things out and to be content as this progresses.

#120

***Walking with God and
family living means . . .***   understanding equilibrium and cycles in
children and families.

"He began to be in need." (Luke 15:14 ESV)

"Inwardizing" comes after an outward or "sorting out" stage. This comes when a child wants order with little change, and is fearful of the unexpected. The child likes to depend on what he or she can control in this effort to fit the world within himself or herself. At last they've nearly figured themselves out—"Don't bother me with new stuff" characterizes this period. Seven—and eleven-year-olds are often inwardizing.

Expansion follows with the exuberant eighteen-month-old, four-, eight-, and twelve-year-old. "Run, don't walk, yell, don't talk" characterizes the four-year-old in this period. Constant motion, noise, and vigorous movement and change are the key to these ages.

"'Neurotic' and fitting together" comes next as the child is again inward, intricately meshing forces and separating fact from fantasy. These ages can be called "bothered" because the child has a glimpse of what's possible but can't do it yet. Theses children aspire to do more than they can manage or handle. Nine-year-olds particularly can be very quiet. Fifteen-year-olds want to drive—in fact, it is often their most difficult teen year. Parents need to know this, and that it is a natural sequence of an order, building toward a new person.

Next follows another smooth period, hopefully at sixteen, when the child is again in equilibrium, and the cycle starts over.

Lord, give us patience as this rosebud of a child unfolds and unfurls.

#121

Walking with God and
family living means . . .   encouraging children to success in life.

"Your Father knows what you need before you ask him." (Matt 6:8 ESV)

Self-esteem or self-confidence affects how a person manages his or her needs, deals with others, produces in life, solves conflicts, and searches for meaning in life; these qualities also affect whether or not a person is able to develop close relationships and take responsibility for meeting others' needs. Self-esteem and a positive self-image go hand in hand.

The feelings of belonging and significance that a child gains in the family can help him or her to be successful in every area of life. Self-confidence and a sense of achievement can be built up in children the same way it can be in adults, but must be done in smaller steps. Children need encouragement and opportunities to try new things. Children need to feel worthwhile and need to have a sense of self-respect just as adults do. Often, aggression in children is a symptom of a poor self-image.

Lord, help us to provide a home with learning opportunities for children.

Brad + Blake

#122

Walking with God and
family living means . . .   sharing decision making and respect.

"You have need of endurance, so that when you have done the will of God you may receive what is promised." (Heb 10:36 ESV)

Steps that build self-esteem include opportunities for decision making. Children need a chance to make decisions. When providing such opportunities, parents should limit choices to two or three, since too many choices are frustrating and confusing to young children. Some appropriate decision-making opportunities for a young child include such things as choosing which vegetable or fruit or dessert the family will eat for supper. Parents can talk about color, smell, size, and taste. Selecting the clothes he or she will wear is also good decision making practice, again, allowing a child to make selections from a limited number of options.

Sharing a grocery shopping trip with a parent is another easy-to-do activity. This can include making a "shopping list" for the child by pasting various labels on to a piece of cardboard from empty cans or boxes of food that the parent plans on purchasing during the shopping trip. A parent can ask the child to match and find these items and put them in the cart. The child will feel good because he or she is big enough to help, which boosts his or her self-image. The parent benefits, too, because the responsibility of helping keeps the child busy in a productive way. Another example is offering the child the opportunity to choose between two items to buy in the hardware or clothing store, when the parent has no preference for one or the other. How nice it is to have one's opinion valued and respected.

Lord, help us to teach children respect by showing respect for them.

Deciding
to add
another
brick.

Mogan

#123

***Walking with God and
family living means . . .*** offering choices.

"The Lord loves the righteous." (Ps 146:8 NASB)

Making choices can be a useful ploy for parents to enhance discipline and learning situations. Offering a choice of alternatives to the child when he or she is absorbed in a behavior of which the parent disapproves gives a chance to build something positive while correcting behavior. This opportunity can turn an unhappy situation into a learning experience. It also will help avoid a power struggle and will give the child the responsibility of making an appropriate decision. For example, the parent can explain to the child, "Crayons are for paper or coloring books, not for magazines (or walls). Which would you like to have, a coloring book or some paper?" A calm approach teaches the child something important: Some things are for coloring on, others are not. It may take several reminders before the child remembers and obeys the rule, but he or she has not been "put down" by a frustrated, angry adult. The child has learned something, and he or she knows what materials to ask for next time. After two weeks, can parents see a child's progress? Is he or she handling some object more carefully?

Lord, help us to use a calm approach when offering children choices.

#124

Walking with God and family living means . . .

modeling enthusiasm for interesting new challenges.

"All the nations of the world seek these things, and your Father knows you need them." (Luke 12:30 ESV)

"Nothing succeeds like success." Children who learn this concept early—that they CAN succeed in small efforts—will have confidence in their own abilities to tackle greater tasks later. What children think about themselves and their abilities will greatly influence their potential for success as they grow older. It will also affect their enthusiasm for meeting new challenges and will shape their outlook on life. Parents who know what can be reasonably expected at different ages give their children a real edge in building their confidence and abilities, by not expecting too much or too little at particular ages.

Adults can help children build a positive self-image by providing opportunities for them to prove to themselves that they are capable, worthwhile people who are worthy of respect. Children can invite parents to try some of the activities that they enjoy or ask parents to be "an audience."

Lord, help children develop for tomorrow's world.

#125

**Walking with God and
family living means . . .**   seeking stability and harmony in families.

"Trust in the Lord always, for in the Lord Jehovah is your everlasting strength."
(Is 26:4 LB)

Like ships' pilots who steer ships through rocks, shoals, and fog to the harbor, all parents have days when they would say about family leadership, "Where is the harbor?" "The fog is too thick!" "Why are there so many rocks?" Leaders of all kinds need to have wisdom, for if the leadership of a family is not well done, the family won't function well or meet its goals. The fog rarely lifts. A well-known management professor called this "paddling in permanent white water" as a description of families and society in the twenty-first century trying to maintain or reach stability and harmony in a fast-paced information age. Parents also need to generate encouragement, confidence, and commitment in order to have a family with a sense of teamwork. It is rewarding to be a part of a family about which family members are proud and enthusiastic.

Lord, help us to build encouragement, confidence, and wisdom in our families

Valerie

#126

***Walking with God and
family living means . . .*** practicing decision making.

"Before they call, I will answer, while they are still speaking, I will hear." (Is 65:24 NRSV)

I overheard this on a telephone call to my daughter when she said to her own daughter: "Are you going to eat your ham or do you want to keep on whining?" Long pause. I hear a little voice say "I whining." Probably only a first-time mother would pose such a question to a twenty-three-month-old, but the child was exercising the decision-making opportunity offered her, which was better than her language skills. She knew she didn't want the ham—the other choice given. Early practice in decision making is valuable for children, and this is a good example of an unimportant (to the mother—sort of) choice that a child made. Families and individuals that practice decision making become better at it, and become stronger and more effective as they gather information to make and act upon informed choices.

Lord, help us to become stronger and better at decision making.

#127

Walking with God and
family living means . . .   leading effectively.

"Let the little children come to me, and do not stop them; for it is to such as these that the kingdom of God belongs." (Luke 18:16 NRSV)

Having an outstanding family requires leadership and decision making. Family leadership or coleadership involves decision making. To lead effectively one needs to plan for change that improves the family situation. This change may involve achieving new goals using old practices, continuing to work toward old ongoing goals using new practices, or aiming for new goals using new practices. Research has shown that at any time the leader involves family members (or members of any organization) in the planning and decision making, the leader builds commitment. But how is one to do this? And when? Furthermore, planning should be a continuous process as new resources, new goals, or new needs arise. A plan can be considered an interim step, so it is essential that the planners get together at regular intervals to adapt and improve plans that have been made, and to generate new plans. Families can do this at any family dinner together, or another gathering time.

Lord, we pray for the children of the world and envision them attaining their full potential as beloved children of God.

#128

**Walking with God and
family living means . . .** increasing group decision making.

"You shall receive power when the Holy Spirit has come upon you; you shall be my witnesses . . . to the ends of the earth." (Acts 1:8 NRSV)

Many in-depth family processes or family management materials are available on leadership and motivation and in the literature. However, a basic premise behind leadership is that the more power a leader gives away, by involving others in decision making, coordination, or planning, the more total power a leader or family coleader has. Not all decisions are appropriate for family group involvement, however, so further analysis of the *decisions* that need to be made, and *how* the decision can be made, are needed.

Lord, help us to analyze our decisions and not just blindly rush in.

Shall I touch it?

Maddy

#129

***Walking with God and
family living means . . .***   learning from other cultures.

"Do not fear, for I am with you; do not be afraid, for I am your God. I will help you, I will strengthen you, I will uphold you with my victorious right hand." (Is 41:10 NRSV)

Some young families and some cultures rely on the extended family as part of their "organization" more than others. This is partly due to geographical location of the extended family members in all cultures. The African-American extended family traditions can be traced back to African societies in which newly married couples are not expected to start their own households but become a part of a large extended family that helps with all aspects of life. Today, more of these families than other cultures' families have relatives, in addition to their own children, living in the same household. These parents see more of their kin during the week and perceive them as significant figures in their lives. By providing emotional support and sharing resources, the extended family helps to reduce stress including that of poverty and single parenthood. They help with raising children and provide basic information about child development to young mothers. More positive interactions of preschoolers with the adults around them can be seen in extended family living, but moving out to an independent household with the help of nearby relatives is related to improved child raising, as mothers mature. These benefits of kinship continue into adolescence and greater self-reliance, emotional well-being, and reduced delinquency are seen in the children of mothers who have been helped by extended family to develop and implement effective parenting skills.

Lord, help us to remember that even with a parent or family member on which to rely, let us be reminded that You are there for us.

#130

**Walking with God and
family living means . . .**   enjoying brothers and sisters.

"For we are his workmanship, created in Christ Jesus for good works, which God prepared beforehand that we should walk in them." (Eph 2:10 NASB)

Brothers and sisters in families of all cultures contribute comfort, sharing and teaching models to the family group, as well as interactions that differ greatly from parent-child interactions. Since siblings relate to each other on a more equal footing when they are close in age, the children learn to take another's perspective and develop competence in relating to other children outside the home thus predicting favorable adjustments at school and in life. During the school years, siblings continue to rely on each other for companionship, emotional support, and assistance with tasks, even while occasionally fighting. As an effective ladder for children's learning, an older sibling teaching a younger child a task or how to do a finger-toy construction project produces considerably better performance due to the younger child observing, imitating, and asking for input and explanations. This peer learning can be damaged, however, by parents comparing siblings negatively to one another. Even in adolescence, a large survey shows this attachment to a brother or sister remains strong, although dropping somewhat as a child seeks to be an independent young adult.

*Lord, help us to build our children up and not compare
them to each other in negative ways.*

#131

***Walking with God and
family living means . . .***   reaching out to the family we have.

"I will lift up my eyes to the hills; from whence shall my help come? My help comes from the Lord, who made heaven and earth." (Ps 121:1-2 NASB)

Fairness and modeling positive communication within the family, including interactions and opportunities involving planning and decision-making, gives children social skills that will carry them into adult life. Despite today's average nuclear family size that is smaller than that in past generations, 80 percent of American children grow up with at least one sibling. Extended family support relationships in all cultures become even more important as nuclear families get smaller. When actual gatherings of extended family are made less possible by distance, there are still many one-to-one telephone conversations and e-mail exchanges for gathering information and support that help young families make decisions.

Lord, help us to hear from several generations when making decisions.

Brad & Belle!

#132

Walking with God and
family living means . . .   supporting newly combined families.

"You will know the truth and the truth will set you free." (John 8:32 LB)

Divorce and remarriage test the decision-making abilities of families of young children, as transitions occur in housing, income, family roles, and family responsibilities. Marital breakup is quite stressful for children but there is great variation in how children respond. The parent's psychological well-being, the particular child, and the social support within the extended family and the community, are factors that make a difference. Decision-making skills that have been practiced early and on less stressful issues are helpful. They are also helpful in remarried or "blended" families as new issues and difficult adjustments arise as new child-rearing practices, new rules, and new expectations emerge that can be a stressful switch from familiar practices. The child's adaptation relates to the quality of the total family functioning; it has been found by researchers who interviewed many children of divorce. Parenting information and classes can be very helpful when a newly remarried couple with a blended family needs to consider many child-rearing practices, not just those inherited from their own homes of origin, to consider and implement, for their new life together.

Lord, help us to learn and grow together.

#133

Walking with God and
family living means . . .   knowing there is a plan.

"For surely I know the plans I have for you . . . plans for welfare and not for harm to give you a future and a hope." (Jer 29:11 NRSV)

    Families, of any type, can practice their group decision-making skills on first smaller and then larger issues. One family said you could always tell when they were making a lot of decisions—you could hear the refrigerator door swinging open and shut. They would sit at the kitchen table on a Saturday or a Sunday afternoon—near the refrigerator, and "eat a lot." The mother added "last year we all gained weight as we had a lot of decisions to make." Even the youngest children would participate, but they would be allowed to leave the table. The mother concluded, "It helps the kids to know there is a plan."

Lord, teach us to include all those affected in some part of the decision making.

#134

Walking with God and
family living means . . .   helping decision makers look at a problem.

"If you give a little, you will get a little. A farmer who plants just a few seeds will get only a small crop, but if he plants much, he will reap much." (2 Cor 9:6 LB)

Extended family organizations may be the usual help or an occasional asset in decision making, for example, in deciding about buying a car. Experts suggest that decisions that are made that impact others are the ones on which to try using decision tools, such as a decision tree or even a straw vote. A decision tree might start with two branches for buying a new car, for yes and no. Then other branches such as buying a used car or repairing the old car can be added to show more choices and their costs and benefits.

In a decision with only two possible outcomes, and in which the leader has no preference (as in the earlier "ham versus whining" example), Dad or Mom can flip a coin or just leave a choice open to a child. Listing the pros and cons of a decision in separate columns on a paper is a useful strategy for slightly more complicated decisions. The benefit of decision-making strategies is that they help the decision makers look at a problem in a more systematic way, and consider relevant questions that may not at first have been apparent. This helps children break down problems also. An adult in the family can delegate most "simple" decisions to an appropriate family member, after parameters have been set. For example, "The yard needs mowing and to be cleaned up and kept green, by being watered and fertilized. This means trash picked up and mowed every two weeks. Dad/Mom (the adult) can do the fertilizer. We can alternate who does the rest or if Joe (age twelve) will do it, some other jobs can go to someone else." Communication patterns in healthy families show that discussions are often task-oriented (not person-oriented and family members are intent on problems to be solved, with as much clearness about standards as possible.

Lord, help us to be clear and to learn to make sound decisions.

#135

***Walking with God and
family living means . . .***   building decision-making skills.

"A generous person will be enriched, and one who gives water will get water."
(Prov 11:25 NRSV)

Much has been written about the benefits of delegating decisions to the
lowest level, to build commitment all through a family or an organization. An
example in a family might be: "This year the children will decide on where
to have the Fourth of July picnic." Or just watch a preschooler in a grocery
store enjoy picking out which choices of crackers or cereal for the family.
Poor decisions have resulted in almost one-half of the youth in the U.S. by
1990 engaging in one or more problem behaviors: substance abuse, school
failure, delinquency, or premarital, unprotected intercourse. Choices made in
adolescence may have lifelong consequences for health, career, psychological
well-being, and social acceptance for these teens when they are grown up.
Children begin making decisions that have consequences when they are very
young. As they mature, the number of decisions will increase.

At about age ten, the beginning of early adolescence, the child's control of
choices will or should about equal the adult's control of the child's choices (that
is be 50-50 or half time). Decision making needs to gradually shift from almost
complete control by parents to almost complete control by the young adult, with
continued monitoring, input, and support from the parent. By age twelve some
children are capable of a planned approach to making choices. This is important
because this is the time in which many decision-making skills are developed.
By ages thirteen and fourteen, young people can think more abstractly, so young
teens are finding their own solutions to many problems and testing their own
ideas. By ages fifteen to seventeen, adolescents are beginning to make important
long-range decisions about education and career. Teaching a child to make
decisions is more helpful than making decisions for him or her, just as giving a
person a fish is less helpful than teaching him or her how to fish.

Lord, help us to teach children wisely, at each age, as they are growing up.

#136

Walking with God and
family living means . . .
reducing grumbling with good decision-making processes.

"Be strong and do not lose courage, for there is reward for your work."
(2 Chron 15:7 NASB)

A decision tree is useful for decisions that are more complex. A decision tree can be generated with family members participating in a family meeting setting. This can be a helpful tool to encourage discussion and inform all involved, before taking a vote. Or a simple tree can be used at home, alone or with the family, to solve personal problems such as whether to buy a new car, repair the old one, or buy a used car. The issues for a car problem might start out with the need for reliable transportation and four choices: (1) Buy a new car, (2) Buy a used car, (3) Repair the old car, and (4) Take public transportation or car pool. The choices could have additional lines attached to boxes to the right as details are considered such as makes of car, uses for trips, or size and car pool arrangements. In dealing with this in a chart the family group or decision makers first decide the smaller details in the boxes farthest to the right of the list and ranks them from +1 to +10 or -1 to -10 on preferences and "gut" feel. In families this builds commitment and interest, and some learning about cars occurs. Without group input, complaining and grumbling can result when the old car is in the repair shop or breaks down again—if that is the choice that has been made.

For example, repairing the old car at Dealership A might be the favorite if people don't mind waiting a week. If they don't want to wait and they need a low-cost repair, Dealership B might seem better. Checking availability of used cars and new cars seems to be the best idea if financing is feasible and available. Asking a teen to check auto newspaper ads can get useful information. A family group can choose their own topic and practice predicting results and outcomes as they build their chart and boxes of additional details. Practice in predicting consequences and considering alternatives is useful to all ages. Teenagers usually enjoy researching the car issue in newspaper classified ads, car advertisements, and Web sites.

Lord, help us to build children's decision-making skills with practice.

#137

Walking with God and family living means . . .   planning for abundance.

"God is able to make all grace abound to you, that by always having enough of everything, you may share abundantly in every good work." (2 Cor 9:8 NRSV)

A simple decision chart for an annual holiday picnic, or an extended family gathering might center on whether the meal was lunch or dinner, and whether it would be barbecued or brought cold. Children of all ages can understand this simple issue. A chart might start out with choices for a summer picnic: (1) Cook, (2) Not Cook. Then discussion (or information gathering) focuses on whether Parks A and B allow cooking, at what hours, and with how much advance notice they require. The chart begins to look at details about Parks A, B, C, and D: Park A—weekends only, four miles away, is free, and has swing sets; Park B—requires one week's reservation, is six miles away, and is free; Park C—is a theme park, is twenty-five miles away, and has expensive rides, but people can go any day; Park D—requires no advance notice, is next door—is a local park, and is not exciting, but is free.

There could be additional boxes of details placed to the right of the choices, as one considers more details, possible swimming, amusements, or driving arrangements. In dealing with this chart, the family group first decides on the boxes the farthest to the right. To start deciding first rank all the considerations on a preference scale of + 1 to + 10 or -1 to -10. The chart shows that Park D becomes the favorite if people don't mind not being able to cook. If they still want to cook, Park A seems better. This question could now even be presented to a family meeting with a choice between Park A and cooking, or Park D and no cooking. The factor of whether the family consider Park D exciting or not, or whether that is even important to the family members would surface. Park C might get vetoed by the adults as much more expensive and crowded on holidays. Next, decide on lunch or supper, and what food to have. This example may seem very simplified, but in today's busy life with the busy family members who are various ages and in various stages of life, it is a "safe" and useful practice exercise in group decision making for the family.

Lord, help us have an abundance of everything for every good deed and family plan.

#138

Walking with God and
family living means . . .   giving all the family a chance to weigh in
with decision-making ideas.

"If you give, you will get! Your gift will return to you in full and overflowing measure, pressed down, shaken together to make room for more, and running over. Whatever measure you use to give—large or small—will be used to measure what is given back to you." (Luke 6:38 LB)

Using a simple chart or writing down ideas is helpful in making group decisions with a family. For instance, with the picnic example, a discussion also gets family members interested, and they will go out and research other parks and bring in new information for another time or coupons for discounts on a theme park with expensive rides. This is building commitment and interest and also planning to have fun. When this decision is looked at as a family decision of low importance, but needing commitment, and with uncertain group interest or group commitment plus few pressing time pressures; but also as having learning aspects, the analysis for decision making recommended might be: consulting those making the event happen, and delegating the decision and its implementation. An autocratic or "bossy" decision might seem speedier, but can lose the support of the family and result in complaining and grumbling and a "why bother?" outing. The remaining question for a family leader, or any leader, however, is how many people should be involved in a given decision? And HOW does the parent involve them?

Lord, help us to give generously with decision-making
opportunities so that we may reap the full measure of synergy,
good ideas, and future decision making skills.

#139

Walking with God and family living means . . .   getting help with gathering information.

"Jesus answered them: Have faith in God." (Mk 11:22 NRSV)

Often the adult does not have sufficient information to decide alone, but knowing that much, at least "knowing what you don't know," is a start. In seeking more information people can then start reading materials about others' experiences and asking people for more information. Talking to car owners or car experts or other dealership customers is an additional approach for car issues. The leader might also ask the family members to start researching this problem as "the family is looking into it," without necessarily stating the plans under consideration. Teenagers greatly enjoy gathering car information. Alternatively, the adults involved might talk informally with friends who have accomplished a goal such as other families that have bought a car or that have moved—another big project requiring a lot of decisions. For a family outing to a theme park, family members could research what friends have been there, how long it took to get there, and what the actual cost was.

If one doesn't know where to get the information, or the money or the supplies or even the possible people to be involved, then it is likely that a wider family group will need to be involved. However, "knowing what you <u>don't</u> know" is a great strength because at least you can start to find out the answers or ask the right questions that need to be asked. This is an important part of thinking and developing positive approaches for decision making for individuals, parents, families—especially teenagers, and even for organizations. By opening the problem to a wider group, more friends, more relatives, more resources, and more ideas will be brought into the whole project. Looking together for information and then for solutions, builds commitment and interest in any project.

Lord, help us to know what we don't know so we can ask good questions.

#140

Walking with God and
family living means . . .   sharing information.

"A generous person will be enriched, and one who gives water will get water . . . . a blessing is on the head of those . . . who seek good." (Prov 11:25-27 NRSV)

If family members will be the ones carrying out a decision (such as taking the car in for repairs or warranty work), then giving the family members enough information and a range of choices to gain their acceptance will be the key to a positive success or a complained-about failure. Pointing out that trips to work, to school, or to have fun are all delayed until the car is repaired keeps the big goal in sight.

Does the family share the goals to be attained in solving this problem? When family members share the goals, the family group can look together for solutions that are in the best interests of the family. Starting with planning to have fun together is an easy first step if work and school are not involved. In a family, people tend to share goals that they help to select. Some allowance for maturity level in a family will have to be made, obviously, as a four-year-old goal might be the goal of having waffles for breakfast, lunch and dinner—but the goal of "help all the children grow up to be happy and healthy" is one any age can share.

Lord, help us to share our goals and thus our planning.

#141

**Walking with God and
family living means . . .**   learning that involving others can be the
fastest way to a solution.

"The upright will dwell in thy presence." (Ps 140:13 NASB)

Sometimes involving the family group is the *fastest* method for solving a particular problem. For instance, if a family needs to move to a new location for a job or other reason, if this is just announced as a flat statement (the bossy, autocratic method), family members may complain for two to five years after the move and other problems can arise. If three to six months of discussion occurs, complemented by subscribing to the newspaper in the new location and researching the schools (gaining more information), the fastest solution of three to six months to involve all those (who can talk) may be the best and the smoothest. Even very young children can learn about moving vans and travel, and learn to view change as a planned adventure.

*Lord, help us to remember that involving everyone
early can save a months of grumbling.*

#142

Walking with God and
family living means . . .   knowing when to involve others.

"The Lord is with you when you are with him. And if you seek him, he will let you find him." (2 Chr 15:2 NASB)

How much to involve the family is always a question. The family group becomes involved in more and more ways as the solutions progress from individual or autonomous to family group decisions. Young people learn to make decisions by observing their parents. They need opportunities to practice and discuss realistic decision making, and practice in predicting a variety of consequences. One research study found that adolescents are more likely to participate in family decision making when they see themselves as in control of what happens to them and if they feel that their input will have some bearing on the outcomes of the decision-making process. Adolescents may place a different value on some of the consequences—and often let peers influence their decisions, especially about risky behavior. Therefore this makes it even more important that parents take into account consequences from the adult point of view—but also to consider the influences and values of their teenager.

In individual or autonomous decisions the adult makes the decision herself or himself using the information available, at the time. Or if the adult needs more information, he or she can obtain the necessary information from others and then decide alone. A parent can ask family members, "Where would be a good location to live in this town?" and other questions. The family leader can tell the family his or her plans or not, as he or she thinks best, but the family is not part of the decision, only information providers. In a cooperative solution, the leader can talk one-to-one with family members without meeting with them as a family group. This can be done informally over time, at the dinner table or anytime, even in the car, or in a number of ways. Finally the family leader makes the decision that may or may not take their views into account.

Lord, help us to build on each other's ideas.

#143

***Walking with God and
family living means . . .***   learning how to decide.

"The Lord is the one who goes ahead of you; he will be with you. He will not
fail you or forsake you. Do not fear or be dismayed." (Deut 31:8 NASB)

    In another cooperative solution, the adult may finally decide alone, perhaps
not even using the family members' advice, but this time they come together in
a family group to give their suggestions. This allows everyone to be familiar
with the question and also provides a situation in which they can build on each
other's ideas. If the parent should decide later that he or she does need their
help and input, at least they would know what he or she is talking about. Of
course, if the family leader does follow their advice, he or she lets them know
and praises them for their help. If the family leader doesn't use their advice, he
or she can explain that circumstances were such that another solution seemed
better at this time, if an explanation is appropriate or needed.

Lord, help us to praise each other's ideas.

I've decided to play on the climber.

#144

**Walking with God and
family living means . . .**   opening a challenge to many inputs
and ideas.

"I am the vine, you are the branches. Those who abide in me and I in them bear much fruit, because apart from me you can do nothing." (John 15:5 NRSV)

In *group decision making* a family group decision maker shares the problem with the family group and then acts as a discussion leader while everyone generates as many ideas as possible. This is wonderful practice for children, and they are usually impressed by the parent's neutrality in the facilitator role. The vote on the best solution is one the family leader is willing to adopt and implement, and of course, it has the support of the entire family group. This might be very helpful if the family leader knows he or she wants to have a picnic or even to move the family for a new job, but is not sure exactly where to locate. The family leader would probably want to have a new home convenient for the family, however, and needs help in defining that. This larger family group solution concept is especially useful when one knows that one wants to do something big, but one doesn't know how to go about doing it or even where to learn how. By opening the problem to the family group, more resources and more ideas can flow in from the whole family group. They may decide they want to know more and guests can be invited over and information gathered, as everyone learns more and has time to get more information from friends and acquaintances. A teenager may know someone in the high school who has just moved from that location. Interesting problems attract interested people, and the family leader will find all sorts of resources becoming available. Also allowing some time gives "the grapevine" time to work, and a family member might ask a neighbor or some other person, key "how to do it" questions, which would be inappropriate or too time consuming for the family leader to ask.

Lord, help us to seek the best solutions with your help.

#145

**Walking with God and
family living means . . .**   asking with faith.

"Ask and it shall be given to you; seek, and you shall find; knock and it will be opened to you." (Matt 7:7 NASB)

Decision making is indeed key in leadership processes, whether in a family or in an organization. However, the ability to structure decisions and then break them down into manageable parts is necessary in decision making, and these skills can be learned by adults and children. Sometimes making a decision one's self can be the *slowest* way to a resolution when family group support is needed and family group involvement would be better (and faster). Taking three to six months to involve the family (or a staff), is often the fastest decision approach possible when a large decision is involved and when an individual decision might result in years of grumbling or controversy. The key decision-maker family members need to be well-informed and well-versed enough in the particulars, especially the main issues, to agree with any of the decisions that are very important and thus to deal with the later consequences, such as the repaired old car breaking down again. If each is convinced it is a good decision, it will be one which he or she can support wholeheartedly. This means they must possess knowledge and comprehension of the significance, the nature, and the implications of a situation or a plan.

Teaching children to explore the implications of various alternatives in decision making and the responsibilities that will be involved is a valuable "thinking skill" teaching that goes on in families. The classic example is that if a child wants a pet, discussing the responsibilities involved in caring for various kinds of pets: puppy, kitty, bird, goldfish, turtle, or horse.

Lord, help us to teach children and to keep the family informed.

#146

Walking with God and
family living means . . .   valuing thinking skills as children grow and
develop.

"And be sure of this—that I am with you always, even to the end of the world."
(Matt 28:20 NASB)

    Developing thinking skills at home is a continuing and rewarding surprise
for parents. This development also builds language skills and ability as educators
know. Decision making involves making choices and selecting among alternates
on the basis of laws, principles, generalizations, and rules. Families can ask,
"What *should* be done? Where will it lead? Is it good or bad?" Children need
opportunities to make real choices that involve comparing, observing, imagining,
and other attributes of thinking. The parents can help children clarify values
that they think about, repeat often, affirm, and prize. A parent can thus hold
up a "verbal mirror" to the child and ask, "Is this what you mean? Is this what
is important to you? Is this the way you see it?" or "Would you do this often?
Have you thought a lot about this?" Children need opportunities like this to
discuss their decisions.

Lord, help us to help children to clarify their values
and learn to think clearly.

#147

***Walking with God and
family living means . . .*** recognizing a possible problem and
alternative solutions.

"I am the Lord your God and no one else; and my people shall never be ashamed." (Joel 2:27 KJV)

When children recognize a problem, it becomes easier to realize when a decision may be needed. Describing alternative solutions and predicting alternative results are good practice for human beings, ages three to one hundred. Even two-year-olds can handle two choices occasionally, but are not famous for being good at it. Choosing an alternative solution and being able to live with the choice is a good life skill for all ages. Should a child put all his or her favorite books on the top shelf or the bottom shelf? This is an example of a decision that would be meaningful in his or her life and that the child could practice living with. Most parents would be comfortable with any choice the child makes.

Lord, help us to live with our choices or change them.

#148

***Walking with God and
family living means . . .***   helping children see that their input is
important.

"Look I have been standing at the door and I am knocking. If anyone hears
me . . . I will come in." (Rev 3:20 LB)

Parents can help young children to have confidence that the decisions they
have a part in are important. They can practice respecting children's opinions
and decisions and ask them to respect theirs. Making sure this is two-way respect
enhances the relationship with a child. Families can share some adult concerns
for adult decisions so that children can begin to understand the process adults
go through when making up their minds, such as researching which car or TV
to buy, considering what kind of care or assistance to get for an older relative,
or choosing a place to vacation. Discussion of factors such as time, money,
energy, and more help a child see the reality of some limits.

Lord, help us show children that big decisions are made carefully.

#149

Walking with God and
family living means . . .   encouraging children to tell
"the reason why."

"The Lord God is a sun and a shield; the Lord will give grace and glory; no good thing will be withheld from them that walk uprightly." (Ps 84:11 KJV)

Children like the chance to practice presenting their own reasons and their own thinking. Children also need to be able to understand the reasons they like or dislike something, and to understand that reasons can be analyzed. Understanding that there are reasons for events and activities also helps build empathy and compassion. The long-range goal is to encourage children to think for themselves, and to have some practice doing so. This is fun when practice in thinking is done on non-essential issues, perhaps in a car or in a waiting room, and provides an interesting insight into how children think.

Parents can ask a child to tell three reasons why he or she should watch a certain television show. One child said, "because I get to see the inside of the police car and the policeman's belt and his gun." The parent determined that all this could be seen in just five minutes of viewing this fairly unacceptable television show, and the child was happy to see the things described.

A parent can notice if a child gains skill in giving reasons. Do the reasons children give increase in number and variety? Do they smile as they gain this skill? A parent should be sure to listen to and respect the child's views. Occasionally the parent may say, "I have a different opinion (or view) on this subject." Then the child learns an adult way to disagree or to see things differently. It is important to learn to see two sides, such as "pro" and "con," or even more than two sides to a issue, and thus come to a deeper understanding of decision making and its complexity.

Lord, help us build compassion and empathy in children and help us to listen to and respect a child's views.

#150

**Walking with God and
family living means . . .**   helping young people see decision making
as something to learn as a lifelong skill.

"May the Lord direct your hearts into God's love and Christ's perseverance."
(2 Thes 3:5 NIV)

Focusing and thinking through new ideas and plans, in a family helps a family group move into the information or knowledge age more smoothly and with prosperity. Making a conscious effort to relate to others and involve others, whether at home or at work, in this age when time is spent so often one-to-one with a machine (like a computer) pays great dividends. Working and deciding together builds on the strength of information-providing machines. Combined with the spiritual energy, initiative, and motivation of people linked together and working together in a family, this develops children from the "inside out," not just children at the mercy of numerous outside forces, especially the media, or raised from the "outside in." Children need to develop strong inner structures so they can handle outside pressures later.

An example of an inner structure that I have reflected upon from 1959 when I was just finished college and applying for a job as a department store buyer in the store's buyer training program is a small demonstration. At one point I proudly said I was engaged. The man interviewing me said "Oh, then we won't hire you because you'll just get married and get pregnant and all our training will be wasted." I thought it was a bit abrupt and unfair at the time, but only later realized it could have been called blatant gender discrimination. Young women today will not face anything that overt but sometimes a door will be shut. My thought for the result of that time is "this is the way, walk in it." This comes to mind because later, after having four children I became a college professor.

Lord, help our children become children of God and find their way in your world.

#151

Walking with God and
family living means . . .   keeping our eyes and our thinking open,
                                         when making decisions.

"When they call to me, I will answer them; I will be with them in trouble, I will rescue them and honor them." (Ps 91:15 NRSV)

Decision research over the last twenty years has shown that people in a wide variety of fields tend to make the same kinds of mistakes in decision making. Ten of the most common errors for adults and teens include the following:

1. *Plunging in*—Gathering information and reaching conclusions before taking time to think through the crux of the issue and to think through how you believe this type of decision should be made.
2. *"Frame" Blindness*—Trying to solve the wrong problem because the mental framework that you hold has allowed you to overlook some of the best options or some important objectives. Framing decisions is important.
3. *Lack of "Frame" Control*—Failing to consciously define the problem in several ways (always more than one), or being influenced by the mental framework created and held by others (such as family members or teenage peers). *Your* framing of decisions is important.
4. *Overconfidence in One's Own Judgment*—Not collecting key facts and looking at the evidence, because one is too sure of one's own opinions and assumptions. (Parents of more than one child need to be wary of this one.)
5. Taking *Short Cuts for the Short Run*—Relying on "yardsticks" or "rules of thumb" or trusting too much in information that's easily and readily available and convenient. Coming to conclusions requires looking at mid-term and long-term goals too.
6. *Winging It and Shooting from the Hip*—Thinking one can keep all the information in one's head and rushing ahead, rather than using a systematic procedure for making a final choice. Information gathering is important.

Lord, help me to remember that the intelligence of God is available to me.

#152

Walking with God and
family living means . . .   seeing two or more sides to complex
questions.

"I am about to do a new thing; now it springs forth, do you not perceive it?"
(Is 43:19 NRSV)

More areas or "frames" to check in family, or any, decision making include:

7. *Failing to Manage the Group Decision-Making Process* – Assuming that family members will (or will not) make good choices without using information and a method to arrive at this desired result can be costly.
8. *Inaccurate Interpretation of Feedback* – Not interpreting feedback for what it really says—whether one is protecting one's own ego or the egos of others, or because of being "tricked" by hindsight (e.g. "It seemed to work last time."). Learning from feedback is important.
9. *Not Keeping Track* – Failing to keep track of results of past decisions and to analyze these results in ways that reveal their key lessons.
10. *Failing to Review the Decision Process* – Failing to develop an organized approach to understanding one's own decision making, leaves one exposed to mistakes numbers 1 to 9. To begin to do this, list the frames and "yardsticks" or "rules of thumb" you usually use and your preferred strategies for arriving at conclusions. Ask which phase of the decision process is the hardest for you? Which of these areas can you improve on by becoming more aware of them, and which require formal steps? These might include changing how you make estimates, formalizing processes, analyzing learning after making major decisions (perhaps in a group), or keeping better records. List the steps you should take. Think what your present frames emphasize and minimize. How do you measure success? Frequency of problems? Sense of partnership? Usefulness of other people's input?

Lord, help our "frames" in decision making to be yours,
not ours, causing our own blindness.

#153

Walking with God and
family living means . . .   taking the risk of new challenges.

"Call to me, and I will answer you, and I will tell you great and mighty things which you do not know." (Jer 33:3 NASB)

Decision making, as opposed to problem solving, is usually future oriented and concerned with future consequences and the probability of success. Peter Drucker, a famous management writer, saw problem solving as often looking back. That is, when a problem is solved, a decision is no longer needed as things are restored to "normal." Decisions, however, lead to change and changed circumstances, so that problem solving is again needed. The "information age" has created some new challenges that need new solutions. As families see change as an opportunity, and practice problem solving techniques alone and with other family members, ahead of time, or on small problems, they become better equipped to make decisions that focus on a better future for the family.

Problems in families or with individuals are often a group of subproblems or even activities. Furthermore most problems have more than one right answer and more than one solution. Breaking down these problems into parts can be helpful, but a person also needs a feel for the total situation as it is often an opportunity for improvement. A problem can be the difference between the family's current state and its desired situation. A problem can result from new knowledge, new thinking, or new awareness. Defining where a family is and where a family wants to be helps them think over various solutions and paths open to them. They have thus defined the problem and the decisions that need to be made, and now can aim toward the goal. This hope can produce problems because there is recognition of a present imperfect situation and a belief in the possibilities of a better future. There is now a challenge, and challenge is another word for problem. But a problem identified is half solved, and now family members know where the family wants to go.

Lord, help us to press on toward the upward call of Christ Jesus.

#154

***Walking with God and
family living means . . .***   sharing decision making.

"For as many as are led by the Spirit of God, are children of God."
(Rom 8:14 NRSV)

Decision making depends on the decision maker's beliefs and values. Teens may see a decision as important in the eyes of their peers, while an adult might see this consequence as trivial. Helping young people become better decision makers can include seeing decision making as a *learned* skill and a life skill. If a young person learns step-by-step decision making early in life, these steps can become a habit over time.

Providing opportunities for young people to make decisions is possible in the family and in social settings. Starting young is important, for by ages thirteen or fourteen young people can learn to make decisions that take advantage of their ability to think more abstractly. Adolescence is a critical decision-making time in an individual's life. Adults can partner with teens in decision making, allowing them decisions with parental guidance. Young people have a right and a responsibility to participate in decisions affecting them. Knowing that learning to make good decisions will sometimes result in mistakes—is a part of the learning process—and helps parents in trying not to overreact. Modeling good processes shows the capacity to share in participatory decision making.

Lord, help us to help children learn to make good decisions.

#155

Walking with God and
family living means . . .   trying out different ways to state a problem.

"Yes, the Lord hears the good people when they call to him for help, and saves them out of all their troubles." (Ps 34:17 NRSV)

It is helpful to state a problem in as open-ended a way as possible. Then a selection can be made from any or all problem solving techniques appropriate. Children benefit from learning to solve problems, to re-define problems, and to use words to express their anger or frustration.

In creative problem solving, whether done by an individual or a family, redefinition of the problem may be needed. There are many ways to redefine a problem, and questioning is one of them. For example in a discussion of a child's playroom or a family room: What would happen if the room was larger? If it was smaller so it would be more compact? What would happen if we turned it upside down? (that is, put it on the top floor instead of the bottom floor?) Rearrange it in another way? What would happen if we made it sunnier—maybe with a skylight—so it would be more useful?

Stating the problem, and then restating it in entirely different words to get away from unseen boundaries and assumptions, can be fun and interesting. Then restating the problem in an even broader way allows the problem to be *seen* in an even broader sense. What would happen if we made the patio or the porch a family room?

Lord, help us practice fun decision making and creative thinking with our children.

#156

**Walking with God and
family living means . . .**   agreeing on guidance for mistaken
behavior.

"Call upon me in the day of trouble; I shall rescue you, and you will honor me."
(Ps 50:15 NASB)

Compare the difference: "Will this two-and-a-half year old always say no
and be rude? Will she be rude when she's older? Will she be rude as an adult?"
as one young parent asked. No, this child will become socialized just as other
children are, as they grow up. Or one could describe a child as exhibiting
mistaken behavior and misbehaving—such as screeching in a store " . . . toy".
Parents need to discuss and agree on guidance as a team, because parents want
children to grow up well and not be exhibiting mistaken behavior into adulthood.
It's well to know that if you say yes one time but not another the child thinks
"this time it might work" and tries harder.

General guidelines for problem solving can serve as a checklist for families.
Some additional problem solving techniques that help families with idea
generation and evaluating possibilities, even with two-and-a-half-year-olds, as
they relate to goals are the following:

1) Understanding the problem and clarifying it;
2) Obtaining any needed information about child development and
   developmental appropriateness;
3) Discussing the problem with someone else. (Is this really a problem to
   stop, or prevent? Or to mop up—treat, tolerate, or redirect? Is it under
   the parent's control? Is time important? Is change?) Ask a series of
   "why" questions. Look at the problem from different viewpoints.
4) Putting the problem in context: What is the history of the problem?
   What is the problem environment? What are the constraints?
5) Then generate ideas for possible solutions and list some: Use questioning
   and brainstorming. Then select an idea and evaluate the possibilities,
   and choose solution(s).

*Lord, help us understand that social and emotional development
and behavior is a slow unfolding, just like physical
development or a rose.*

#157

Walking with God and family living means . . .   restating the problem.

"He is a rewarder of them that diligently seek him." (Heb 11:6 KJV)

Restating the problem with a child with key beginning phrases can be helpful and fun: "What would you do if you had three wishes?" "You could also define the problem as . . . " one three-year-old child said, "The problem is this truck is a piece of junk." "The main point of the problem is . . ." "The problem put in another way is like . . ." "Another, even stranger way of looking at it, is . . ." "The worst thing that could happen is . . ."

Another question approach that is also creative is the "List ten ways this can be done" approach. Or ten ways this might *look.* One can also ask "How is it done in nature?" An example might be: If a mighty oak grows from a little acorn, maybe a strong, able person will grow from this "little acorn" of a child, or an idea might grow into a large business. Children can come up with amazing analogies when asked, "How is it done in nature?"

Lord, help us to have insight to see many sides to a choice or a problem.

Maddy

#158

***Walking with God and
family living means . . .***   trying out new words.

"Commit your way to the Lord, trust also in him, and he will do it."
(Ps 37:5 NASB)

A problem-solving technique that can be useful for individual parents and families to yield new insights and possibilities is first writing out the problem. Then underline nouns, verbs, and adjectives. Now, maybe with a dictionary, find two or three substitutes for each word underlined. One can now see new ways to define a problem, and this can lead to additional and new solutions. An example for a family shows how this can be used: Mr. and Mrs. Smith don't spend time (lunch? dinner? attention to?) to sharing their views (arguing? agreeing? using e-mail?) on children's guidance (mistaken behavior? pet behavior? personal behavior?). Solutions that show up from finding other words and renaming issues might include the use of time, new uses of time and using new ways to communicate.

Lord, lead us to new solutions.

#159

**Walking with God and
family living means . . .**   visualizing good outcomes.

"This is the confidence which we have before him, that, if we ask anything according to his will, he hears us." (John 5:14 NASB)

Wishful thinking, another creative technique, can make a valuable contribution to problem solving needs. To get started, try completing the sentence: "If I could ignore all restraints, I would . . ." For example, in budgeting, the advice is always given to design an ideal budget for what is really needed and wanted, and then work backward to what can be afforded, rather than to start with the present dollar amount available. Obviously this advice can be used for family budgets or personal budgets. Knowing a goal, or a possible goal, always helps any family group or individual move toward it better with more success. Visualizing and thinking through what this might look like and what would be involved can be enormously helpful for a family.

Allowing children to explore the implications of various alternatives in decision making and the responsibilities that will be involved is a valuable "thinking skill" and teaching that goes on in families. The classic example is that of a child that wants a pet as mentioned earlier. Discussing the responsibilities involved in caring for various kinds of pets: pony, puppy, kitty, bird, or goldfish follows. It may turn out that the last on the list, the goldfish, is the choice at the moment!

Lord, help us to visualize what we want for our family.

#160

***Walking with God and
family living means . . .***   keeping a wish list.

"Again I say to you, if two of you shall agree on earth about anything they ask, it will be done for them by my father in heaven." (Matt 18:19 NRSV)

A simple example of a family keeping a wish list occurred when one family posted a long sheet of paper inside the kitchen door. As family members had good ideas, they jotted them on this "wish list." When vacation or college planning time came, they checked the "wish" list to find if any topics matched. A new house, computer camp for one or two children, a new "weed whacker" for Dad, a pony for the eight-year-old were some of the things on the list. Since the yard was not large enough to accommodate a pony, that item was dealt with quickly, but the eight-year-old was honored to have it discussed (at all). An individual thinking alone, and this happens more frequently, might wish for an advanced degree, a new car, other material goods, or more friends in the community.

Many kinds of restraints can be ignored in wishful thinking. The size of the home, the salary of adults, or the budget for education are only a few examples. This approach sets up new thinking patterns. The next phase is to return to the practical, with statements such as "I can't really do that, but I can . . ." Looking into scholarships, starting a home business, planning a home addition are a few that come to mind. Focusing and thinking through new ideas and plans in a family helps a family group handle change. Making an effort to involve the whole family helps families in dealing with expected or unexpected change.

*Lord, we know that a problem identified is half solved.
Help us to identify our problems and seek your guidance.*

#161

***Walking with God and
family living means . . .***   finding divine ideas available to you.

"Thy blessing be upon thy people." (Ps 3:8 NASB)

Devices often found in childhood storybooks, analogies, and metaphors can also be used in "management" in families. An analogy is a direct comparison with a similar thing, object, or idea. In contrast, a metaphor is a reference to one thing, object, or idea to suggest a reference to another such as "the ship of state" or referring to an old age as "the evening of life." Both are useful in problem solving to generate information and to produce ideas or solutions about a problem. Metaphors are more powerful because they demand a greater change of perspective, but both help thinkers see new connections and principles. For example, in the evening (as in the "evening of life"), the light softens, the birds sing, and things quiet down. Other metaphors include "quiet leadership," "bear hug," "reengineering the business process" or even "brainstorming," and many of the words attached to computers such as "Internet explorer" or "your obedient servant" once a name for an Internet search engine. In a family one can say to a teenager "just because the hole in this boat (or in your thinking) is in your end of the boat doesn't mean it doesn't affect the whole boat," which unfortunately is a negative example, but is an example of analogy.

Lord, help us to remember that we have divine ideas available to us.

#162

Walking with God and
family living means . . .   creative problem solving.

"Then you will call, and the Lord will answer; you will cry, and he will say, 'Here am I.'" (Is 58:9 NASB).

Analytical techniques, such as creating a checklist, or listing pros and cons can be done effectively in a family group. Decision techniques can be individual or done in groups. Just addressing the questions *"What is the problem? Who needs to involved? What more do we need to know? What would an ideal solution be? What would be the first step?"* begins to get answers from a family group discussion that "break open" the problem. The ideas can be written out for all to see. One family group was making a "Before Supper" chart of who would do what: walk the dog, start supper, set the table, bring in the mail, etc. Another chart listed "After Supper" cleanup jobs. A week later the parent followed up with praise and a comment about how better to clean the stove top—"please don't spread out the parts of the stove top on the family room rug—keep them on the tile floor." (A true story!) Other examples might be how to spend the holidays, planning for get-togethers, planning for care of a disabled grandparent, or a new family member (such as a new baby).

Creative techniques include brainstorming. Brainstorming produces a large number of ideas but not necessarily a deep level of new insights. However, it is fun for children and good practice in families for generating alternatives.

Lord, help us to see more alternatives when we have a decision to make.

#163

***Walking with God and
family living means . . .***   generating many positive alternatives.

"Therefore I say to you, all things for which you pray and ask, believe that you have received them, and they shall be granted you." (Mk 11:24 NASB)

Brainstorming works best when there has been some sort of warm-up, whether at a family meeting on a certain topic, or with something to read, and it can just be a description of the issues to be considered. The questions *("What is the problem? etc.")* listed previously provide a family group warm-up for many problems and are a shortened version of a checklist. The group then can begin brainstorming possible first steps. Another warm-up that is individual is to ask each person to write down three or more ideas on the topic or possible solutions, before the family group time begins, such as "why is watching too much TV bad?"

Brainstorming is divided into two parts. The idea-generation part is first, and there are some rules: (1) that all ideas are given equal respect, (2) there is no criticism of any suggestion no matter how wild, and (3) that all ideas are written out for all to see. This allows the family to see the ideas and build on other family members' suggestions. Reverse brainstorming can be used also, as in "What are all the possibilities of what could go wrong?" (or whatever the reverse side of the question might be). Then contingency plans could be made for these possibilities. For instance, "If it rains, we could go inside."

Writing the ideas also sets the stage for the second part of brainstorming when the ideas are ranked or given priority. One approach to the ranking is to give every family member three to five votes (depending on the total number of ideas that will be ranked). Allowing three to five votes rather than just one demonstrates greater variations within a solution. As voting occurs, a natural ranking appears.

Lord, help us to withhold judgment on ideas until we have heard from all the family members.

#164

Walking with God and
family living means . . .   coming together.

"It shall come to pass that before they call, I will answer; and while they are yet speaking, I will hear." (Is 65:24 KJV)

Regular family meetings are "safe" opportunities in which everyone is free to say what they think and feel as they cooperate in making decisions and solving problems. It's a time for recognizing good things happening in the family, setting up rules, distributing (or redistributing) tasks fairly, and settling conflicts. Setting aside time together, and planning and having fun together are a foundation for looking together at what is working and what is not working in the family. As soon as children can use words, they can participate. Ten to twenty minutes fit the needs of young children and still provide a special time. As children grow older they can help decide on the agenda, the refreshments, and the time needed. One family took time to discuss and decide the benefits of good and bad television. Celebrating happy times and discussing not more than one or, at the most two, problems per meeting helps issues from becoming unwieldy. Nine practical steps for successful family meetings include the following: Meet at regularly scheduled times, rotate who plans the meetings, encourage all family members to participate, discuss one topic and solve one problem at a time, use I-messages (not you-messages) and problem solving strategies, summarize the discussion to keep the family on track and to focus on one issue at a time. Then make a decision by consensus and remember what is decided this way and post it on the refrigerator if necessary.

If things get hot, take a break. Food is always a good break. End with something fun to do that affirms family members. The key to successful family meetings is to be flexible and to use what works in THIS family to handle the ups and downs of family living. This helps when risk taking is needed. Families that know how to adapt well to inevitable change tend to have higher marriage and family satisfaction levels.

Lord, help us to include you in all our decision making.

#165

**Walking with God and
family living means . . .**   creating an excellent family sharing
recognition, self-esteem, growth, and a
sense of the worth of the work with family
members.

"Christ in you, the hope of glory" (Col 1:27b)

"They . . . are children of God, being children of the resurrection."
(Luke 20:36 NRSV)

The best families of all kinds agree on one thing: family members support what they help to create. This includes the understanding and building of vision, goals, and plans. When people, including children, are involved in thinking through the vision, the goals, and the plans for a family, a plan for a clear task is more likely to result that will capitalize on the natural motivation inherent in each person. Everyone is motivated all the time by something, so the parent's task is to set a supportive climate with high goals, to try to access this natural motivation. This will promote a self-fulfilling prophecy that this is an excellent family where wonderful people live, love, grow, teach, and go to work or school. By encouraging people, especially children, to take responsibility and by constantly checking one's own assumptions about people, being wary of gender role stereotyping, a parent is well on the way to having a family in which family members often motivate themselves toward goals appropriate for their ages. Many motivator factors are an inherent part of growing up in a positive family, such as self-esteem, recognition, achievement, growth, and learning, and a sense of the worth of the tasks or work. These all can be also be a part of a philosophy or vision statement.

Lord, help us develop goals for our family together and Lord, help me to see the sacredness and creativity of each member of my family.

#166

**Walking with God and
family living means . . .** helping children grow up in a positive
family.

"We walk by faith, not by sight." (2 Cor 5:7 NRSV)

Two types of factors are needed to motivate individual family members according to some theorists. The first type of factors are the dissatisfaction factors. "Dissatisfiers" is a useful concept in describing dealings with teenagers or disgruntled family members. This concept clarifies why some efforts may bring those "dissatisfied" up to "neutral," but it takes more to "motivate" them. These first 'satisfier' factors include rules, surroundings, allowances, and interpersonal relations. The second type of factors are called *motivator factors*. Many motivator factors are an inherent part of growing up in a positive family, such as self-esteem, recognition, achievement, growth and learning, and a sense of the worth of the tasks or work. These all can also be a part of family tasks and "work." Having fun is always a motivator with children.

Lord, help us to seek motivators as well as satisfiers for our family.

Valerie + Lindsey

#167

Walking with God and
family living means . . .　　　is not losing heart.

"Do not grow weary in well-doing, in due time you shall reap, if you do not lose heart." (NRSV)

One set of the factors in motivation can be called the dissatisfaction factors, which really means the extrinsic or outside factors. If they are NOT present, people are "dissatisfied." These extrinsic or outside factors are the things in a family that parents often *can* do something about. They are group-oriented factors that are all around a person at home, and set an atmosphere. Included are living conditions, interpersonal relations, allowances, rules, time together, status of individual family members, and security. One measure of high quality parenting, according to researchers, can be observed by whether the parent follows children around too closely and is nosy, or whether the parent trusts the children. Trust is a major component of empowerment for children. The dissatisfaction factors are those usually chosen for improvement when a parent wants to strengthen motivation in a family. However, it has been found that even if all of these factors are excellent, this excellence *will merely prevent family members from being dissatisfied,* bringing *the family member from a minus position up to a zero or neutral position.* He or she may not complain as much now but the individual (think teenager for an easy example) is still not motivated to do his or her best work or give a best effort.

Many families think that when they want to motivate children, they should increase their allowance, improve their time together, have more family parties, or improve some of the other outside factors. In a family, improving interpersonal relations and security are always important. However, in numerous studies, it has been found that all that improving the dissatisfaction or external factors does is to keep human beings/family members from being dissatisfied. It is important not to ignore the external factors, however, because if a person is too dissatisfied, he or she will not even be interested in the motivating factors or in considering changes. In any family, one or two of the external factors may be beyond the parents' control. In some families, the hours of parents' work and their wages are controlled by outside factors, but a two-factor group theory of motivation is particularly applicable in families as most or *all* of the *motivator* factors can be developed, and these cost nothing or very little.

Lord, help us to build recognition, self-esteem, and value for all our family members.

#168

Walking with God and
family living means . . .   appealing to the best in people to motivate
                                      family members.

"For nothing will be impossible with God." (Luke 1:37 NRSV)

The second category of factors needed in families are the motivator factors. In order to motivate family members, parents and leaders of all types need to build motivators that are really internal, it has been found. Feelings of satisfaction and motivation are more likely to come from the growth and achievement possible. These include a sense of achievement, a sense of responsibility, and a sense of the worth of the effort itself. In many families, there is a tremendous benefit gained from this factor because what people are doing is inherently worthwhile. For instance people involved in raising families will have a part in shaping the future. It is important to remind all family members of this, and to say, "Thank you: this is *important* work. You are enhancing your own and other people's lives when you help the family and when you help around the house."

In many families, this factor of the importance of working with each other and helping each other to develop is a built-in motivator, and there is an understanding that this is inherent in the family work or task itself. In contrast, people who work in factories, turning three bolts all day long, or inserting three computer chips every day, will have to be turned to other motivators as the work itself will never be as inherently important and as far reaching as working with family members and helping people who are improving their lives.

Lord, help us to build a sense of responsibility and a sense of the worth
of the effort and work, for all our family.

#169

***Walking with God and
family living means . . .***   feeling a sense of satisfaction in a family.

"You will have courage because you will have hope." (Job 11:18 LB)

The motivators are some of the things that can be developed by any parent, so that children and other family members feel a real sense of satisfaction in their family life and tasks, not just an absence of dissatisfaction. Other motivators include building self-esteem, encouraging children to grow and learn, giving them opportunities for growth and development, and giving children some autonomy. Giving children autonomy means allowing them to do projects on their own that are appropriate for their developmental age level. Studies have found that people will stay at a task longer, if it really satisfies (or motivates) them, even though it doesn't reward them well.

Recognition is another important motivator for all ages, adults or children. Everyone likes to be recognized for something: for a bright smile, for a job well done, for having the most of something, for bringing up a new idea or for their own unique qualities whether family related or not. These motivating factors are important and really cause people to be motivated and happy. External factors are important and lead to family commitment. The external factors actually build family commitment. But if the motivating factors are also present, it leads to family and lifelong commitment. Loving and lifelong commitment is commitment to the goal of this particular family, which may be supporting the children to the best of their ability, or even of having the best family possible. Most families have some overriding goals beyond just keeping the family barely going. The goal might be for the children to have a sense of pride in being part of such a fine family. However, all of the family needs to be committed to the family's overriding goal of being the best possible, or whatever goal is selected. Developing these motivator factors within the family environment really helps to secure this needed commitment of family members. It is interesting to take the list of motivators and brainstorm ways that more motivators can be written into the daily life of a family. List the factors from #166 and then try for new insights into what would motivate family members.

Lord, help us to allow our children enough autonomy to build self confidence.

#170

Walking with God and
family living means . . .   recognizing and rewarding efforts of family
members.

"Christ in you the hope of glory." (Col 1:27 KJV)

There are many ways to give awards for achievement and recognition, a known motivator in families.

1. Feature a "Family Member of the Month" on a bulletin Board or on the refrigerator; tell about hobbies, interests, favorite jokes, and school or work achievements; list compliments given this person and have other family members add these.
2. Give a certificate(s) with a gold seal on it, at a family supper for a child's first contribution to a difficult family project.
3. Mention names of those who have helped in a letter written to grandparents or other relatives.
4. Give "thank you" notes at the end of a project to those who have helped in extra ways. This also promotes *the children's* writing of thank-you notes.
5. Acknowledge and implement family member's ideas whenever possible. Affirm and validate their input at family gatherings for solutions that are useful.
6. Praise the child in front of the rest of the family. Reinforce and complement children's positive interactions with each other.
7. Involve children in writing or dictating paragraphs for the holiday newsletter or for thank-you notes.

Lord, help us to see you in all the members of our family.

#171

Walking with God and family living means . . .   emphasizing the worth of the work in helping the family.

"Be strong, and let your heart take courage, all you who hope in the Lord." (Ps 31:24 NASB)

More "motivators" can be seen in ways to emphasize the worth of the work in families.

1. Send "happygram" notes to children for their efforts. Include comments on the benefit of how their efforts are helping improve and enhance the family.
2. Share good ideas on what other families are doing about projects similar to this one, or for trip ideas, or for vacations.
3. Reinforce and comment on the value and worth of the family *to you* and *to them*, regularly.

Lord, help me to tell *my children how proud I am of them.*

#172

Walking with God and
family living means . . .   planning and acknowledging projects
completed.

"I know whom I have believed, and am persuaded that he is able to keep that which I have committed unto him." (2 Tim 1:12 KJV)

There are a variety of ways to delegate and reward responsibility in families.

1. Encourage projects that a child can plan and execute by himself or herself such as a picnic or a flower garden.
2. Encourage family members to do simple "intact" projects that help: to make gifts or decorations for the home, to plan a schedule, or to organize a drawer or closet. Try to use or acknowledge each.
3. Encourage children to look at responsibilities in all their roles: family, household, student, and extracurricular activities such as sports or music or collect their ideas which can include being in charge of cleanup for their own room plus one other, or more; doing their own laundry after age ten, or whatever. Teach children discipline as learning responsibility and making some of these decisions on their own after considering the implications and consequences.

Lord, help us to help children see the consequences
of their decisions and make mature decisions.

#173

***Walking with God and
family living means . . .***   encouraging children to learn to think for
themselves.

"For this God is our God forever and ever: He will be our guide even unto
death." (Ps 48:14 KJV)

There are a lot of ways to encourage autonomy and respect in families.

1) Discuss patiently the implications of two or three alternatives in a
decision a child wants to make, such as which team to join, or which
activity to do.
2) Respect the child's choices whenever possible in situations in which
the parent has no preference such as which shirt to wear? Which book
to read? etc. Practice in decision making begins early with respect and
(some) autonomy.
3) Show respect for a child by giving the child a chance to tell a parent the
story from a book or DVD or video he or she liked. As a high schooler
one child's career goals included becoming a veterinarian for exotic
animals, after building cages and discussing the DVD of "The Lion
King" at age three.

Lord, help us to really listen to little children, even the youngest.

#174

Walking with God and
family living means . . . helping those in the family to grow and learn.

"And hope does not disappoint, because the love of God has been poured out within our hearts through the Holy Spirit who was given to us." (Rom 5:5 NASB)

Some ideas for ways to provide for advancement and growth in families include the following:

1. Sharing information about resources in the community.
2. Encouraging children to read library books on different fiction and nonfiction topics, and later at suppertime, vote on which books to give their "seal of approval." This is especially good for books on different countries as the books can inspire new thinking and insights. Have a family library shelf for books that need to be returned.
3. Invite interesting guests and students from other countries for a meal. It is important to be thinking about how to get more motivators into the family setting, because, by and large, these motivators are free, or at least easily affordable. One goal is family enrichment. The payoff in commitment and motivation is to get good results for the "family" and to get the "maximum effort" at least some of the time. The end goal is to help family members develop responsibility and build up to their own full potential.

If there is a child who is very creative, give him or her more opportunity to use that talent of creativity in a way that helps him or her to grow. The family has an obligation to recognize the potential in family members, and this leads to great return for the family over the long term. Many families are losing out in talent today because they do not know or use these motivators that also build trust and lifelong commitment. The outside, extrinsic, external satisfier factors can recharge a family member, but with internal motivator factors he or she becomes his or her own generator. The importance of building a child's self-esteem, and of helping a child to reach for his or her full potential, is good theory about people and can apply to any age or stage of life. Adults and children respond to those who believe in them and who recognize their potential, just as students do in school. Adults as well as children like to be helped to create and achieve, to be responsible, and to grow. The more a family can help close that gap of what a child is capable of, versus their everyday life, the more of a sense of commitment it will build toward family goals.

Lord, help us to recognize talents in our own family members.

#175

**Walking with God and
family living means . . .**   learning to handle responsibility in a
supportive environment.

"If you are willing and obedient, you will eat the best from the land."
(Is 1:19 NIV)

Adults and children need to be *trained* to handle more *responsibility*, however, and they have to find satisfaction in it. Children and adults need to build competence and confidence, and have a sense of being able to grow. It is not wise to just require a lot of extra responsibility and expect children (or adults) to be happy and fulfilled, especially if authority is harsh and not shared, along with the responsibility.

Ways to train children in responsibility might include giving a small section of a task at first, on a regular basis, and with something specific to do. This builds a *sense of achievement* into a child's task and also some responsibility. Or delegate another child to train the first child as in "Please show Jane how to sweep the front steps."

Children accept the authority of a parent based on the relationship with the parent, not the role, research shows. When the children see the parent as an attractive model and feel valued and respected, more authority for the parent emerges. However it has to be merged with the child's sense of fairness and justice to be effective. One important aspect of authority is to transfer it as the child becomes more capable of self-direction. Essentially, authority based on power is given up in favor of children's autonomy and self-control as they grow older. As children become more and more able to make their own decisions about rules, choices, and social activities, that is, exercise personal jurisdiction, and these are tied to responsibility, they increase in the ability to take responsibility.

Lord, help us to help children learn to make wise decisions.

#176

***Walking with God and
family living means . . .***   emphasizing the value of the work.

"Train up a child in the way he should go and he (or she) will not depart from it."
(Prov 22:6)

Emphasizing the *value* of the work itself is one of the easiest things to reinforce in a family, but it is often not done. Parents can remind people of the family's philosophy or vision/mission statement regularly: in notes, in e-mail, or letters if they're away, or on a bulletin board or the refrigerator at home. Say, "We believe in having an excellent family," reminding children that they can use the power of their minds to make their lives better, or whatever simply stated goals the family may have. These goals can be fresh every year, to keep interest in them high.

Recognition is also easy for a parent or schools to give, and free of cost. Anything that gives the child or the family a lift, just naturally helps them to be nicer to each other whether outside or inside the home. Gold stars on a chart of tasks also give recognition.

Lord, help us to give children the recognition freely, which they crave.

#177

***Walking with God and
family living means . . .***   reaching out to the broader community.

"You shall love the Lord your God with all your heart . . . you shall love your neighbor as yourself." (Mk 12:30-31 NRSV)

Growth also includes new goals as families see that "the family is an end in itself." It has become a vehicle through which family members can effectively contribute to the well-being of others through church and community activities as well as for developing themselves. As families move from the areas of stability and survival, where the primary goals and mental energy focus are on problem solving and paying the bills, into a new focus beyond food and shelter and getting out of debt, by creating goals and visions and purposes that transcend the family itself, these might include: What kinds of education do we want for our children? What would we like our finances to look like five to ten years from now? What can we do—as a family—to contribute to our church or community? The major focus grows into creating positive things that were not there before: new goals, new options, new alternatives, and being "opportunity-minded" rather than "problem-minded." This helps the family bring new things into existence that were not there before. At this point we learn to live in the solution, not dwell in the problem.

Learning becomes much easier, and children "hear" what is being taught when they see good models or examples, feel loved, and have good experiences. Parents should give *themselves* a gold star (perhaps on the calendar?) when teaching has occurred beyond routine help and support. Parents modeling attractive and warm, friendly behavior also helps children be more accepted and popular with their peers it has been found, as they model that friendly behavior.

Lord, help us to be patient with ourselves as we practice being good models.

#178

**Walking with God and
family living means . . .**   helping people feel good about themselves.

"If it is possible, so far as it depends on you, live peaceably with all."
(Rom 12:18 NRSV)

People, children or adults, like to feel good about themselves. It is a real human need. Helping people feel good about themselves is something that is not very hard to do. There is a tendency that when a parent feels discouraged, he or she thinks, "How come *they* get to feel good about themselves when I've got this XXX (budget) problem?" However this is dead-end reasoning. If parents can give children something such as recognition, self-esteem, or a sense of the worth of the work, it is likely that the fruits of this will eventually cheer up the parent too. These concepts can also help families to understand themselves and each other better.

*Lord, help us to understand ourselves and each other, better.
Thank you for the blessing of children who are even happy
to help us find our noses.*

Valerie

#179

Walking with God and
family living means . . .   speaking kindly to yourself as well as to
                                         others.

"Let the word of Christ dwell in you richly; teach and admonish one another in all wisdom." (Col 3:16 NRSV)

Teenagers tend to be down on themselves. The "external" or satisfier factors such as living conditions and getting along with others, are those that are easy to complain about and, when rated at 100 percent, still only keep people from being dissatisfied. The "motivator" areas of praise, growth, and recognition are much more important for lasting success and an optimistic future outlook for a child. Readers can ask themselves questions as a "self-management" exercise to see if they need to praise themselves more or reward themselves for the efforts they make. They can ask "does my 'self-talk' (conversation with myself) only include the *shoulds*?" As in "I 'should' diet more" or "I 'should' exercise more," or "I 'should' clear the clutter more." Being kindly in speech to one's self will help one to be kinder to children and to other families.

Lord, help me to love myself as well as I love others.

#180

Walking with God and
family living means . . .   feeding the hungry.

"You know these things—now do them! That is the path of blessing."
(John 13:17 LB)

Abraham Maslow (1970) is quite well known in the field of psychology, and his work on the hierarchy of human needs is also used in management. His theory states that the bottom level of needs in a vertical listing must be met before an individual can or would want to move on to the next level. A person therefore is motivated by one factor: whether his or her needs on his or her level are met or not. The theory, in terms of motivation, assumes that meeting the person's needs on his/her level will *motivate* the person to go on to the next level. When the need is filled, the person is satisfied and ready to move on. Maslow's theory of motivation looks at individuals, whereas other theories look at motivation within groups. Maslow's theory is based on the assumption that those things absent will satisfy when they are present in this order: Maslow's Hierarchy of Needs

Self-actualization
Self-esteem needs: promotion, achievement, status
Love and affection needs: belonging
Anxiety, safety, and security needs
Physiological needs: Food, air, water, sleep, sex

Humans tend to concentrate on meeting physiological needs before being concerned with higher level needs. When the needs at this level are partially satisfied, other needs emerge, for example once teenagers gets name brand clothes they might want to go to a theme park. The classic example of this lacking is of the early missionaries attempting to preach to people that were starving. Starving people have to eat before they can hear any message being brought to them. Sleep deficit from a long commute and/or long working hours also shows up at the physiological level. Fast-growing teenagers may be affected by both these needs, which can block what an adult is trying to say to them a teacher or a parent.

Lord, help us to look at basic needs that may be beneath the needs we see.

#181

Walking with God and
family living means . . .   helping people to move forward.

"May your unfailing love rest upon us, O Lord, even as we put our hope in you."
(Ps 33:22 NIV)

One can see the effect safety and security needs, and anxiety have on a personality by observing people who worry about being robbed, and have many locks on their doors at home, often in cities. This fear and worry (need) is so great, and with good cause, that the higher level needs such as having friends or being famous, concern them less. If a job requires a public transportation ride and a long commute into the inner city to work (due to expensive or inadequate parking), some people are definitely reluctant to work late after closing. An individual may also experience this "security" need after a traumatic experience such as an auto accident. The person might be quite fearful and worried about safety while driving or riding in a car for several months or years following the accident. It is important to "meet people where they are."

Lord, help us to meet people, especially children, where they are, and understand them better.

#182

Walking with God and
family living means . . .   encouraging people where they are.

"I can do all things through God who strengthens me." (Phil 4:13 NASB)

Encouraging people to be active in their place of worship, community group, or the family group helps meet the very human need for love and "belongingness." This can be seen in adult workers that seek companionship at work to fill this need. Some theorists think that most of America is at this level. If a person has a feeling of being cared about, is not really feeling unsafe, is not really hungry or in need of rest, then that person would not mind being Chair of an activity or something similar, or in gaining self-esteem in some way including through a promotion. This is considered a "self-esteem" need, which implies that a person with pressing needs in another area doesn't need or want status responsibilities on top of their other worries.

Some researchers say that to motivate people, one needs to meet them on the level where they are and help move them forward to the next level, and this can work in families. Of course it is difficult to be certain of estimating the level of need correctly.

Lord, give us the insight to see the needs of others.

#183

**Walking with God and
family living means ...**　　　enjoying the moment.

"One thing I do: Forgetting what is behind and straining toward what is ahead, I press on toward the upward call of Christ Jesus." (Phil 3:13-14 NRSV)

The highest level needs for development and self-actualization are satisfied only after needs at the four lower levels have been met according to some researchers. At this high level, the individual is concerned with the development of his or her potential. This person has peak experiences of insight or understanding. The person at this stage, which many people never reach, has a better perception of reality, accepts herself or himself and others, is more creative, and is better able to become completely human in the realization and development of his or her full potential. Truth, goodness, beauty, and meaningfulness are recognized and enjoyed by this person. Some writers say that only older people can be at this level, people like Winston Churchill or Eleanor Roosevelt. This writer has found many positive people in churches, in the helping professions and in other "learning organizations" who have, periodically, tremendous moments of feeling really good about their work with individuals of all ages. It is important to take time to value the positive feeling when you can see that something has really helped someone. This is a "payoff" of a kind for the effort expended. One might take a moment to think: "I worked hard on that, and it really seems to be clicking!" Similarly, people must value the insights that come to them about what they might do next. One can write down these insights and review them until one is ready to put them on to a goals list—either long-range or short-range goals.

Lord, help us to live in the moment with appreciation for our own or others' efforts that are well done.

#184

**Walking with God and
family living means . . .**   learning throughout life.

"We rejoice in the glory of God." (Rom 5:2 NIV)

In the book *First Things First* by Stephen Covey, motivating one's self is discussed in the context of considering what *are* the "first things" in one's life, and putting them into time blocks in a weekly calendar *before* it gets filled up with work and community commitments. Such things as family, health and fitness, social/emotional refreshers, and keeping one's skills and knowledge base current need to have a "reserved" time slot. Since people live longer lives, with more career and job changes than their parents had, "continuous maintenance" checkups for more health and education are a must. After all, car owners do this for their cars! "One-stop shopping" for education ending in the years of the early twenties just doesn't last a lifetime anymore. Going back to school and taking courses has become important at all income and age levels.

Lord, help us to be lifelong learners in this wonderful world of yours.

Lindsey & Megan

#185

Walking with God and
family living means . . .   being willing to learn.

"Let us not grow weary in doing good, for at the proper time we will reap a harvest if we do not give up." (Gal 6:9 NIV)

An adult who seems motivated and willing to learn could be reacting to any of the five levels of needs on Maslow's hierarchy.

Think what would cause an adult to be willing to learn and motivated on the physiological level: (1) Hunger/need to keep a job; (2) Saving time and energy at work, allowing technology to do the work. What could cause an adult to be willing to learn and motivated because of safety and security concerns, fear or anxiety? (1) Best way to keep a job or get a new one (learn more technology); (2) former boss or workplace was oppressive, with frequent power threats or job threats; (3) high bills, poor credit, or other unstable situation at home; 4) to keep self and family secure.

What could cause an adult to be willing to learn and motivated because of love and belongingness needs? (1) Group activities and making new friends, (2) being able to talk about new learning in social situations, and more.

What could cause an adult to be willing to learn and motivated because of self-actualization needs? (1) Enjoy the joy of creating new ideas; (2) creative work in writing, art, or music; 3) creative activities with children.

From these questions one can see that adults (and children too) might act the same way for different reasons. For example, one person came to work and was suddenly anxious to learn more computer skills. It turned out this person's brother had just gotten a fancy new computer, and this turned out to be a "belonging" need—or sibling rivalry by another description.

Lord, help us to be willing to learn new ways and ideas for whatever reason.

#186

Walking with God and
family living means . . .   meeting a child's needs.

"Always give yourselves fully to the work of the Lord, because you know that your labor in the Lord is not in vain." (1 Cor 15:58 NIV)

The same meeting-needs concepts for motivating adults can also be used with children. The first step in motivating children is to think of different behaviors or problems a child might show based on each level. For instance, a child who is a discipline problem could be exhibiting any of the five levels of needs on the hierarchy. What physiological needs might cause a child to be a discipline problem? Hunger (no breakfast); lack of sleep; diet (junk food), too much sugar; illness. What safety concerns, fears, or anxieties might result in a discipline problem? Afraid of dogs; is hit a lot (abused); broken home (fear other parent will leave); newborn in the home or parent in the hospital; siblings or friends bully or "pick on" the child. What love, affection, and belonging needs could cause a child to be a discipline problem? Whining and clinging; insecurity; attention getting behaviors; deprived of love or self-respect.

One idea for motivating children who exhibit love, affection, and belonging needs is to implement a "Child of the Week" poster idea similar to those under "recognition" mentioned before. A family could send the poster to a grandparent after posting it on their own refrigerator for a month. This is self-worth and self-esteem building in action. A "King" or "Queen" for the day can also build self-esteem. (Have two or three crowns on hand for emergencies.) Even adults respond to such esteem-building activities.

What self-esteem needs would cause a child to be a discipline problem? Very well coordinated physically; acts like a superhero and leaps off furniture; acts rude to adults to impress peer group; has high IQ and is bored; brags about being on a sports team.

Lord, help us to recognize the needs of children AND adults.

#187

***Walking with God and
family living means . . .***   helping children develop to their full
potential.

"Thou will keep him in perfect peace, whose mind is stayed on thee."
(Is 26:3 KJV)

One can see that children (or adults) might act the same way for many different reasons. The parents' analysis of what level the child is on needs to be on target. For the parent, seeking out more training can be helpful in sharpening one's analysis of levels, as selecting the correct level is hard to do. One looks at a child who is lethargic and unmotivated, for instance, and thinks "I'll get to you in a moment." But if that person—child or adult—is really exhausted or hungry, more attention will not help him or her much. Parents can use this concept when analyzing their own or other children's behavior.

If a child or adult really needs something, solutions based on another level of need will not be effective motivators. In another example, a parent who had grown up in a large family, had never had a room of her own, was having problems over sharing space. By encouraging the family to each have spaces of their own, in which she could keep her things separate, a need of hers of having her "stuff" protected, having her own space, was met. This solution met this adult's need better than giving her a book on human relations or some other solution based on a different level of need.

A parent can think about each child, decide if they have a pressing need, identify it, and then try to work with that level. Adults can be operating on the level of physiological need also: going to work without breakfast, getting too little sleep, or having a problem with alcohol or other substance abuse.

Other problems or needs that lead to applications of Maslow's theory to understand more about the level that an adult might be on, in addition to the *physiological level* mentioned above, might be the following: *Anxiety level*: worried about a health problem, worried about financial problems, spouse lost job, sudden divorce, spouse abuse. *Love and affection level*: single parent, conflict with spouse. *Esteem level:* loss of job or spouse. *Self-Actualization level*: not enough opportunities to use talents, skills, and abilities.

Lord, help us not to rush to judgment as some have heavy burdens.

#188

***Walking with God and
family living means . . .***   encouraging others to do their best.

"Surely God is my help; the Lord is the one who sustains me." (Ps 54:4 NIV)

Encouraging other adults to be supportive and kindly to parents also builds a positive climate for children in all environments.

Maslow's one-factor theory encourages one to look carefully at an individual, try to identify their level (and one's own) correctly, and try to work toward solutions based on this level. It is helpful to brainstorm (even alone) some of the possible causes for an adult or child's behavior at each level of need: physiological, security, love and affection, self-esteem, or self-actualizing. Look carefully at the adult or child to help prevent identifying the wrong level and then pursuing a dead end.

Encouraging parents and families to do their best, to reach for their full potential, and to feel good about themselves is valuable whether in a family or in a life's work. This encouragement will reap tremendous returns to the family and to the persons who encourage it. As with seeds that when planted, which are slow to germinate, one must wait and perhaps not even see the harvest.

Help us wait patiently to the results of our efforts and yours.

#189

Walking with God and
family living means . . .   taking other viewpoints.

"Give me discernment that I may understand . . . O Lord." (Ps 119:125 NIV)

Assuming the viewpoints of others can help find solutions to parenting problems. Many parents have poor morale and help their children less than they could. It is helpful to write down the identities of three people who are ordinarily associated with a problem, say a poor parenting morale problem. An example might look like this:

Problem Statement: Many parents have poor morale and help their children less than they could.

I.   Identities of three kinds of people possibly involved:

       1.   Parents and Spouses,
       2.   Teachers and helping professionals,
       3.   School and Agency heads.

II.   Next, describe the problem from their points of view:

       1.   Parents and Spouses think the Schools or the wife/husband (other) should "do more."
       2.   Teachers and helping professionals think parents should do more (and not do it "wrong").
       3.   Schools and Agency heads think parents should do more, but "they can't do much because they have 'budget problems'."

III. After studying the identities of these three categories of people and their differing perspectives, think of suggestions and solutions for ways to share information, such as parenting information to use to solve some of the problems.

Lord, help me to walk in others' shoes.

#190

Walking with God and
family living means . . .   making a team effort in the family.

"The heart of the discerning acquires knowledge; the ears of the wise seek it out." (Prov 18:15)

Families actually are functioning small groups. These groups need a "supportive climate" rather than a "defensive climate," which allows for the openness, caring, and good morale so needed for all adults and children and, therefore, obviously needed in families. In supportive, strong families there is empathy and a realistic concern for the self-esteem of all children and adults involved. Spontaneity, creativity, and a willingness to try new things (risk taking) are valued in children and adults. Equality of all concerned to take part in problem solving regardless of status, with allowances for age level, is another hallmark of the family climate needed in an open, caring family of any size.

The family climate needs to be focused on problems to be solved rather than interpersonal faultfinding, and on use of expertise and teaching to solve issues. The focus is on how to do it better, with concern for mutual learning and strategies to do it better. In short, a supportive climate would be descriptive (of behavior), solution oriented, vision driven (the family vision can be restated, often), empathetic, friendly (friendship among family members), and experimental. It is helpful to involve many family members in the planning and implementation of programs or plans for the family. This is an effective approach for families and groups and the approach that leads to strong families.

Lord, help us to develop a strong, caring, and supportive family.

#191

Walking with God and family living means . . .   understanding infants and toddlers.

"The children of the promise are counted as offspring." (Rom 9:8 ESV)

Often a child at the infant-toddler age will move on to a new stage, perhaps even before the parent can figure out what to do. The "smile of mastery" is a wonderful thing on a baby's or a child's face. A six-month-old smiles as he or she masters the upper arm muscles and flaps his or her arms. Parents can (and should) watch for these smiles. In every description of stages, whether physical, intellectual, social, or emotional, add plus or minus three to six months to stages read about for a particular child. The sequence is often more important than the exact chronological age of the child, and even the sequence may vary. There are milestones for development and the Gesell Institute has a book series with good descriptions that have been validated and revalidated over many years. Since the weeks and months of babyhood are well covered in many sources, they are not further described here.

An infant or toddler is developing motor skills: the developmental sequence goes from head to toe and from the inner body to the outer body or fingertips for an infant. Thus arm movements precede leg movements as can be seen in a six—to nine-month-old learning to crawl by dragging the body along by the arms. Fingertip control comes long after upper arm and then lower arm control. Ages four, five, and six months are still working on eye-hand coordination. Leg control follows arm control. A toddler is very much into large muscle coordination, having finally graduated from crawling, then cruising (around the furniture) to that all-important first step and a new view of the world. Infants and toddlers' special needs include a need for love, affection, and cuddling from parents; time, patience, and understanding from adults; simple, regular routines; and they need the opportunity for interaction and language development with adults: talking, singing songs, and hearing others talk.

Lord, thank you for creating these beings to be so cute and adorable.

#192

***Walking with God and
family living means . . .***   seeing the miracle of a child learning
to talk.

"Yes, Lord I'm listening." (1 Samuel 3:9 LB)

Infants and toddlers are developing language by listening all the time. Around one year they watch an adult's mouth as the adult speaks and even try to touch the adult's mouth. Reading briefly to a child from picture books (if the adult can get him or her to sit still) is priceless at these ages. This age is showing some baby teeth though on a varying schedule. In twins at the same age of seven months, one may have two teeth and the other six teeth in fraternal twins. Many or most are gradually acquiring some skill in feeding themselves, holding the bottle until it's given up for a cup, and picking up finger food of all kinds to eat from the high chair tray, for babies. Even more skill is evident for toddlers.

Characteristic behavior might include playing alone, with little awareness of others; loving toys that hide the item when dropped through a slot, and then it reappears; and large muscle toys are especially popular. Other behavior includes imitating syllables and then language; being constantly active with an attention span of thirty to sixty seconds; and showing tiredness by becoming restless and irritable. Babies and toddlers are gradually learning what is acceptable and what is not (such as electric plugs and safety issues like steps). More repetition is required the younger the child. This age seems to have a need to explore. Parents might remember that brightly colored toys are cheaper than TV remote controls and other "adult" toys like car keys (which are unsanitary).

With questions about discipline, it is useful to spell out predictable behaviors that children might learn and repeat, with various strategies parents use in dealing with children in everyday situations. By looking at what seems to be a random process or sequence, parents get a better long-range idea of the long-term benefits of handling certain annoyances (or behaviors) in constructive ways that teach what they *do* want the child to learn.

For example, for infants and toddlers, when Mom initiates a phone call, and the child fusses, if Mom gives the child a cookie or a treat—the child will be quiet for a while—but learns to fuss during phone calls to get rewards. With Pre-Schoolers, Mom can interrupt the call and put the child in a crib or in another room with something to do such as look at a book, and the child is less likely to fuss next time.

Lord, help us to teach children what we DO want them to learn.

#193

Walking with God and family living means . . . understanding two-year-olds.

"Make (these things) known to your children and your children's children."
(Deut 4:19 ESV)

Every child is different, as every parent knows. Still, it is helpful to know what other children might be doing developmentally at a particular age. If a child doesn't fit this particular age group, read ahead for some discussion on older children, or read other materials about younger children. By exploring and keeping in mind the general stages of child development, a parent may be able to better understand a child's everyday behavior as well as his or her occasional behavior.

Ask other parents and yourself if you or they knew that the *parent* is the child's most important teacher. Research has shown this over and over, and research also shows that the most important thing for a child's success and development is for an adult to think he or she is wonderful. These two points cannot be emphasized too strongly. Points that will help can include learning the following about the two-year-old year.

Two-year-olds demonstrate unevenly developed motor skills. Large muscle coordination is good (the child can walk and climb), but small muscles and eye-hand coordination are still not well-developed. The age group between two and four goes through rapid language development. Vocabulary increases from a few words or short sentences to up to two thousand words by age four. These early preschoolers (twos) and preschoolers (threes and fours) gradually acquire skills in dressing and feeding themselves. By three or four these skills are in place. They go through changes in sleep patterns. A two-year-old or three-year-old is gradually giving up daytime naps but still needs a rest period and about twelve hours of sleep at night. At two a child has almost a complete set of baby teeth. Furthermore, these children often have begun to establish toilet habits and usually will be able to handle their own needs by age four.

Lord, help us to be patient with these ages and stages, which are gone so quickly.

#194

**Walking with God and
family living means . . .**   observing the joy of "parallel play" and
repeating what is important.

"May you see your children's children!" (Ps 128:6 ESV)

Characteristic behaviors for a two-year-old include playing alone, or beside, but not with, others (parallel play); not sharing or taking turns too well; and often saying no, but gradually becoming able to accept adult limits. Twos want adult approval and like to be close to Mother and Daddy. Twos help around the home and are beginning to understand their surroundings and the demands of daily life. They like to feel familiar with things and have a sense of security. They imitate language, manners, and habits; and they are constantly active and show tiredness by becoming irritable or restless, just like younger toddlers do. Twos, especially, seem to have an urgent need to explore. They are gradually learning what is acceptable and what is not. Much repetition is important. They demonstrate great curiosity and want to try almost everything.

Special needs at two, three, and four include a need for love and affection from parents. Grandparents can often see again what their child looked like at age two. Preschoolers and twos also need guidance and a consistent pattern of behavior to follow. They need time, patience, understanding, and genuine interest from adults and simple, clear routines and limited choices. Throughout the preschool years there is a need for opportunities to learn sharing and taking turns, and to learn to play cooperatively with other children. At three and four, learning give and take and having opportunities for play with other children and for a wider scope of activity become even more important, as children move from solitary play to parallel play to cooperative play.

Lord, help us to learn the joys and routines of two-year-olds.

#195

***Walking with God and
family living means . . .***   understanding three-year-olds.

"For you are all children of the light, children of the day." (1 Thes 5:5 ESV)

Three-year-olds demonstrate motor skills that are still unevenly developed. Large muscle coordination is still much better than small muscle and eye-hand coordination. Threes have a full set of baby teeth. They show an awareness of the sequence of steps and the probable outcomes of their activities. The three-year-old begins to plan ahead. This child continues to develop language ability at full speed. The most important and amazing verbal development occurs this year. He or she acquires more skills in feeding and dressing him—or herself and again goes through changes in sleep patterns but still needs a daytime nap or rest period and nearly twelve hours of sleep at night. A three-year-old may get tired easily. Three cheers! Toilet habits are getting better.

Characteristic behaviors at three include showing more interest in playing with other children. He or she still needs to play alone some and is not ready to share or take turns too often. At three a child wants adult approval and likes to cuddle. The three-year-old may reject the adult but still needs him or her. They become even more interested in helping around the home and like to imitate language, manners, and habits. As at four, they like to experiment and explore within adult limits, but are gradually learning what is acceptable behavior and what is not. Threes enjoy looking at picture and storybooks, and have a better understanding of words. A three-year-old shows great curiosity and asks many questions and is often a lighthearted, happy child.

Lord, help us to be lighthearted with our three-year-old.

#196

Walking with God and
family living means . . .   understanding four-year-olds.

"Then the children were brought to him that he might lay his hands on them and pray." (Matt 19:13 ESV)

Four-year-olds are much different than three-year-olds, as every parent knows. Again, readers are encouraged to add or subtract six months to a child's age, if that makes the developmental sequence a better fit for a child. Four-year-olds seem to have the desire to run, not walk, and the desire to yell, not talk as mentioned at the beginning of the chapter. However, a four-year-old still wants adult approval. Motor development is still better, especially in terms of large muscles rather than small muscles or eye-hand coordination, and rapid language development continues up to, and past, two thousand words. Fours learn many new words and ask many questions.

At four a child becomes quite skillful in feeding and dressing himself or herself but may need occasional help. Fours develop sleep patterns that still need to incorporate up to twelve hours of sleep each night. Toilet habits are established by this age period. The four-year-old child usually takes care of his or her own needs.

Characteristic behaviors of a four-year-old include showing more independence and reliability; having more interests in many things, including an interest in people and the way they act; and playing with real purpose. These children engage in much more imaginative play. They begin to pretend to be other people or animals, and they understand the environment better and enjoy trips. They can ask searching questions about people and their relationships to others. At four a child is more able to accept necessary limits and restraints from adults but still likes to be close to Mommy and Daddy. Fours are constantly active and like to help around the home, and to imitate language and habits. Now this child is becoming more capable of longer stretches of quiet activity as he or she approaches five. Four-year-olds need love and affection from parents, guidance, and a pattern of behavior they can imitate. They need to feel valued. They need to build trust in their parents' words and a negative pattern of whining can be built up as shown if this need is ignored as shown by a "Mommy, buy meee . . ." "Whining Sequence," when a child doesn't believe a toy will be bought, because Mom said yes last time and didn't buy it. This continues through future store trips, because THIS time it might work! Research has shown that humans and animals persevere harder when the answer varies.

Lord, help us be truthful with children and build trust.

"Mommy buy meee . . ." Whining Sequence Chart

Mom and child go to the store	Child fusses for a toy. "Please, please . . ."	Mom says, "OK, I'll buy it"—but doesn't mean to (just wants a little quiet).	Child is quiet.	Mom checks out of store without toy. Child fusses.	During the next store trip, child asks for a toy again and Mom says yes again.	Child doesn't *believe* Mom and asks again every five minutes all through the store. Child is NOT quiet. (Trust has been broken and "yes" doesn't mean "yes.")	Child repeats this behavior on all future store trips. If Mom occasionally buys the toy, the child fusses more in the future—because THIS time it might work.

A toy made by children in Tanzania.

#197

***Walking with God and
family living means . . .***   learning at all ages.

" . . . and apply your mind to my teaching." (Prov 22:17 RSV)

When I was four years old we lived in Florida near my great aunt and my Mother decided I should go to Preschool. We drove a long way (it seemed) to a nice house with other children and she left me for the morning. We had "art" which meant the children sat in a row and the teacher showed us how to draw a house. Later we all drew our own. First the teacher drew a tree, then a house behind and beside the tree, and then she added windows and doors. To this day I still can draw it and still draw houses that way. I never went back to the preschool as my Mother decided it was just too far away to manage with my brothers ages one and six to cope with in the car at the same time.

I later learned that most three and four-year-olds draw a house on top of a horizontal line in the center of the page. Some even do "X-ray" painting so you can see all the people in the house from the front. I also learned that allowing a young child the freedom to draw their own houses without prior instruction is the preferred teaching approach! It is also interesting! My house drawings are always viewed as unusual, though.

Lord, help us to realize how much young children learn and retain.

#198

Walking with God and
family living means . . .   understanding kindergarteners who are five-
year-olds.

"But the steadfast love of the Lord is from everlasting to everlasting on those
who fear him, and his righteousness to children's children." (Ps 103:17 ESV)

Five-year-olds are considered to be in a "balanced" age, which generally
means that their aspirations match their abilities fairly well. They are a "perfect
little kid" and do not yet pine to play baseball or go to the mall or to a popular
music concert. Their motor skills are much better developed than at four, and
their eye-hand coordination and fine motor skills are developing rapidly. These
are the years in which the world widens out beyond the family with kindergarten,
if it has not already done so, with child care and preschool programs.

Their speech matures and its functions become different as well. The early
types of speech are egocentric and social. Egocentric speech (talking to oneself)
is not designed for communication but may be used for entertainment or wish
fulfillment or even thinking out loud—or "talking to think." Social speech, for
communication, develops throughout early childhood. Children think first and
talk later, as can be seen with a fifteen-month-old who knows what he or she
wants but can't say it so may fuss. By the age of four or five, the act of talking
helps the child think. A curious child within a sensitive, warm environment that
encourages exploration and creativity will respond well in school.

Lord, help us to enjoy the "balanced" ages when they come.

#199

***Walking with God and
family living means . . .***   seeing cooperative play develop.

"And now, little children, abide in him." (1 John 2:28 ESV)

A five-year-old's characteristic behavior includes more independence, reliability, and follow through; more interest in the outside world; and playing with real purpose and learning through play and other learning situations in many ways. Fives enjoy interactive play with children their age. They have a better understanding of the environment and an enjoyment of trips, just as fours do, and they are still able to accept necessary limits and restraints from adults. They still like to be close to parents and at this age are more capable of longer stretches of great activity.

Parents like knowing that a five-year-old has motor development that continues to improve with large muscles still better developed than small muscles, but tying shoes or using colors and pencils are much more possible. Two children out of every thirty still may not have chosen right—or left-handedness yet and use both hands. Rapid language development continues both for egocentric and social communication. Fives now have the ability to feed and dress themselves with occasional help with difficult items, and have sleep patterns that still benefit from twelve hours at night, since naps are mostly gone. They continue to need the security of love and affection from parents, adult direction, and pattern of behavior to follow and a need to feel valued (just as all children do). In addition to needing time, patience, and understanding and a genuine interest from adults, they need a wider scope of activity and limited freedom to move away from home surroundings and opportunities to do things for themselves and for others.

Some five-year-olds think they are supposed to know how to read before they start kindergarten. They can be reassured that the teachers are very good at teaching this, but parents can (and do) start at home with imitation STOP signs and any large letters that are easy to read. Five is an ideal time to do games with numbers.

*Lord, give us the time, patience, and understanding
that these little ones need.*

#200

Walking with God and
family living means . . .   understanding six-, seven-, and eight-year-
olds.

"It shall be said of them, 'children of the living God.'" (Hosea 1:10 ESV)

Six is not as "easy" or balanced an age as five, and the "breaking up" of this age, as a child revamps for being seven, eight, nine, and ten is somewhat aggravated by six hours or more of first grade. A first grader will be tired and need to go to bed on time. One child said, "I had to sit there six hours! It cuts into my day." These children are "antsy" and frequently stand with one knee on their chair to eat their meals (which, of course, causes spilling of food on the chair). Parents are greatly reassured to know that most six-year-olds do this. When one asks a parent if their child does this, they say "How did you know?"

Emotions are not as calm as they were at five, and more fears appear. The best way to help children overcome fears is to help them find their own practical way of dealing with them. Giving a child a flashlight to shine in the closet or under the bed is one practical tip, which children love. First graders also begin to tell time by the end of the year and are fascinated by watches. Watching the minute hand move from one number to another, or a digital clock change five minutes, is a good "time-out chair" activity when "time out" discipline and a "break" is needed. In talking about what "you need" to tell time, one child said, "First you need an arm" (then a watch and so forth).

Some five-year-olds think they are supposed to know more than they do or to know a lot before they start kindergarten. They can be reassured that the teachers are very good at teaching, but parents can (and do) start at home with playing age appropriate games, especially those that are simple to handle. Five and six are an ideal time to do games with numbers, including adding and subtracting numbers under ten and counting to 100 by tens, a skill needed for telling time.

Lord, help us to learn about the basic, concrete thinking approach that six-, seven-, and eight-year-olds have.

#201

Walking with God and
family living means . . .   seeing your child go to first grade.

"It is evident who are the children of God." (Hos 1:10 ESV)

A six-year-old has much better vision and continued language development as he or she learns to read. Motor development continues to improve, especially for small muscle development as children learn to hold pencils more effectively, and learn to print and write. Large muscle development is good, and outdoor play is a must for the active, antsy six-year-old. Poor nutrition leads to less activity and slower growth. At six, seven, and eight, children have the ability to take care of their own needs in feeding and dressing themselves. Room cleanup is possible and expected, but occasional help may be needed. Backsliding occurs with such tasks as making the bed, as a six-year-old is not as cooperative as a five-year-old. Sleep patterns still require enough sleep at night (eleven to twelve hours) so that the child is not tired and cranky, as no nap is possible in first grade.

A six-year-old's characteristic behavior includes more independence, reliability, and follow through; more interest in the outside world; playing with real purpose; and learning through play and other learning situations. There is a better understanding of his or her environment and continued enjoyment of trips. Six is able to accept necessary limits and restraints from adults but still likes to be close to parents. Now there is a capability of longer stretches of great activity.

Families can encourage creativity and thinking skills. The six-year-old will value this encouragement, and this can lead to interesting "invented" games of their own. If five is a "balanced" age and six is a "breaking up" (of behavior patterns) age, then seven is an inward age that may say things like "nobody likes me." Eight is an outward, happier, expansive age, followed by nine, which has been described by Gesell as "the most nearly neurotic age there is."

Lord, help us to polish creativity and thinking skills,
which are gifts of the Lord.

#202

Walking with God and family living means . . .

understanding "middle childhood," ages nine to twelve.

"My child, be attentive to my words . . . Keep them within your heart."
(Prov 4:20-21 NRSV)

Each year bears a dynamic relationship to the years before and after it, for in development no year stands alone. The intense, taut-string quality of the nine-year-old is a necessary predecessor to the more relaxed, more organized ten-year-old.

The nine-year-old is more preoccupied, more self-critical, more striving, and earnest than the unself-conscious ten-year-old or the happy-go-lucky eight-year-old. Nine is less popular with his or her elders than ten is.

Nine is thus followed by ten, which again is a balanced, amiable, relaxed age. Ten-year-olds like their friends, their school—if it's "good," and likes to learn. He or she is not overly concerned about the teacher as long as the teacher is fair. Ten is an age that balances the resources already attained and demonstrates the generic traits of childhood. This is the peak of the decade of childhood and precedes the decade of adolescence that leads to "early adulthood" at twenty. Ten, like five, is a golden age of development (Gesell 1977). (Assuming that the reader or parent will make ample allowance for an individual child.) Again, readers are encouraged to remember that the sequence of development follows a pattern, even if it is six months or so ahead or behind for a specific child.

Middle childhood, as this period is called, is an extremely "safe" time of life for most children, with colds and respiratory infections being the most common illnesses. Major illnesses have usually already surfaced in a younger child. Nutrition and fitness have become important in this child's life, and outdoor exercise is a must for growing and developing muscles. Children lose their baby teeth, and permanent teeth appear. Vision is more focused, but some vision problems may still not have been detected.

Lord, help us enjoy the happy, balanced ages.

#203

**Walking with God and
family living means . . .**   building thinking skills.

"Yet wisdom is justified by all her children." (Luke 7:35 ESV)

Memory and language develop all through the school years, and there are many suggestions, ideas and products for starting early and enhancing a child's critical and creative thinking. Children, beginning between ages five and seven, enter a stage of intellectual development called "concrete operations" according to the researcher Piaget, which lasts until age twelve or thirteen and precedes "abstract thinking." The emphasis is that concrete means just that—this age has to see an object to understand what an adult is saying about it. For example, when my daughter was eleven, she was studying about what a fulcrum is in science in sixth grade. She asked me about it and I talked about a see-saw. Then I mentioned a hammer rolling to pull out a nail. She absolutely didn't get it until I got a hammer and *showed* her the "fulcrum" as the hammer rolled.

During these years children begin to understand the viewpoint of others, which improves their ability to communicate. They begin to be able to take all aspects of a situation into account when doing problem solving or decision making. Creativity that is developing, of course, helps with problem solving.

Creativity depends heavily on encouragement, education, and training from an early age. The valuing and usefulness of a created project enhances self-esteem and builds confidence for the next creative project. Using children's drawings and artwork for Mother's Day cards and all manner of greeting card exchanges are one example. The child later sees this (as highly valued) on grandmother's refrigerator or elsewhere. A photograph can be sent to the child of the display at a distant relative's home.

Lord, let us value the "memory banks" that are developing.

#204

***Walking with God and
family living means . . .***   understanding that ten years old is a
special age.

" . . . rejoicing in his inhabited world and delighting in the children of man."
(Prov 8:31 ESV)

Ten-year-old behavior includes sheer delight in physical activity, comradeship in groups, bursts of happiness and demonstrative affection, and a conscience that has to be informed to grow—it is in a relative state of immaturity. This age also has developed concrete thinking and static concepts that serve him or her well. There is less tension than at nine, but some nail-biting and playing with hair remain. There is now an unequal growth rate for boys and girls, and both are eating more than at eight or nine. Often they are not aware when they are tired and ready for bed; this age still needs to be reminded.

Ten, eleven, and twelve are more interested in the choice of clothes but are nearly finished with the money-mad state seen at eight and nine. Some ten-year-olds save nothing; others save everything. Fears are at a low ebb, although unmistakable anger can suddenly explode and anger is thought to be a subset of fear. Ten, eleven, and twelve have no great fondness for work.

Ten is a time for wide, expanding varieties of experience. This child wishes to try everything. Both boys and girls get along well with mother, but forerunners of eleven-year-old discord can show between daughters and mothers. Time management has improved so well that it is a great relief to everyone after seven, eight, and nine. This child can be nice, happy, casual, and sincere.

A nine—and ten-year-old needs facts, things related to here and now, not abstract concepts. They also need affection, love, and support from the family. A ten-year-old gets along better with siblings than at nine. Tens need patience and information as their conscience, and philosophic ideas and attitudes grow. Understanding that these concepts may proceed from the negative to the positive in terms of preoccupation with negative ideas and attitudes may help parents be less alarmed by them.

These ages need outdoor exercise for growing and developing muscles, and more food and adequate sleep. Ten is taller, bigger, and stronger than nine or eight.

Lord, help us to enjoy this ten-year-old child.

Walking with God and
family living means . . . knowing that ALL children are gifted.

"Behold, children are a heritage from the Lord, the fruit of the womb a reward."
(Ps 127:3 ESV)

Five and ten year-olds have calmer or "equilibrium" attributes in common, and two and a half, eleven, and fifteen have "disequilibrium" attributes in common. Readers are encouraged to look for these commonalities and see the pattern for themselves. A nine—to twelve-year-old is growing physically, emotionally, socially, and intellectually. Self-esteem at all ages cannot be underestimated. In a famous study, teachers were told that (average-testing) children in their class were gifted children. At the end of the year they were tested again and showed unusual gains in IQ. They really were in the gifted and talented range. Tone of voice, facial expressions, touch, posture—all can contribute to self-esteem. It was known that these teachers did not spend extra time with these children. Self-fulfilling prophecies and teacher-and-parent expectations, along with giving support, are very powerful influences.

Lord, help us to show our children how
gifted and talented they really are.

#206

**Walking with God and
family living means . . .**   understanding eleven- and twelve-year-olds.

"I have seen the business that God has given to the children of man to be busy with." (Eccl 3:10 ESV)

The calm, balanced, flexible nature of a ten-year-old, again plus or minus six months' adjustment for a particular child, gives way at eleven to a new growth force, eventually to be called adolescence—but now called preadolescence. Many tokens of the growing-up process begin to emerge. As with two and a half and age fifteen, a period of relative calm at ten, two, and fourteen is followed by instability, mood swings, lack of flexibility, and what is generally a stage of turmoil.

The emotions of an eleven-year-old rise with swift crescendos, and they have peaks of intensity. This may show up early at ten, however. Bursts of laughter, yelling, and rudeness can cause endless irritation. This age is in a state of change and is "breaking up" from the smoothness of childhood to allow room for growth into adulthood. In another decade this child will be at the edge of maturity. Parents often feel confused and frustrated by the intense behavior they see, so different from the year before even though the child might not *look* much different. Often the child does not understand it either and appreciates patience from parents (which, however, is rarely acknowledged).

Parents need to know about this shift into preadolescence. Eleven-year-old behavior includes incessant bodily activity and energy expenditure, and constant eating, talking, and sleeping, but often a growth spurt doesn't really show until the next year, for boys, especially. Girls have an earlier growth spurt in the ten to eleven to twelve age range. Some children have a "fat" period. Many eat steadily after school, take a break to eat dinner, and then continue their snacks. They have developing strength and the beginnings of sexual maturation; dissatisfaction with bedtime, regardless of its time—although needing sleep and peevish without it; an attitude of hating work and resisting doing it—and are good at making up excuses; and have "odd," vague, uncomfortable emotional feelings.

Lord, help us to understand that spiritual awakenings also develop at this age.

#207

Walking with God and
family living means . . .   being forewarned.

"And he will turn many of the children . . . to the Lord, their God."
(Luke 1:16 ESV)

It is not easy to understand the laws of growth and development at the particular stage of age eleven, and one parent said, "Why don't the schools warn us?" Eleven-year-olds need time, patience, and understanding like twelves. Parents who realize that this is less a personal rebellion than a reaction to complexities and uncertainties inside the child can learn not to take this behavior personally, or think it is due to family problems only (we just moved, grandmother is sick, and so forth).

Alert parents see that now there appears to be an ability more to challenge than to respond to parents positively, but still a willingness to be helpful, mostly "when he or she is in the mood." Nine through twelve doesn't want a parent to yell at him or her or be critical. "They can dish it out but not take it" as one parent said. There seems to be a lack of capability in answering parents' demands. Many get along better with one parent than the other, and most argue about everything, with strenuous self-assertiveness. They are not into abstract thinking yet—things have to be concrete for them to really understand them.

These ages need not-too-much lenience or too much sensitivity; an atmosphere conducive to good growth—but the child must do his or her own growing; a full refrigerator and adequate sleep; and good humor, fairness, affection, and interesting activities. Reassurance that "we'll get through this together" without probing inner depths, which the child doesn't understand either, is always a good idea.

Lord, help us to understand the complexities of this developing child.

#208

***Walking with God and
family living means . . .***   knowing twelve-year-olds can look big but
                                  are still very young.

"I have no greater joy than to hear that my children are walking in the truth."
(3 John 1:4 ESV)

The twelve-year-old becomes less insistent, more reasonable, and more companionable than the eleven year old. Maturity is not a uniform, steady process, but the behavior of the eleven-year-old is now leading into areas of new experience and thereby is preparing this child for increasing discernment and discretion. Twelve relies less on pressure and challenge than eleven, but tries instead to win approval from others. Twelve is basically a period that favors the integration of personality including reasonableness, tolerance, and humor. Gone are the belligerent, disagreeable, argumentative, and moody expressions of eleven, but they are not *entirely* gone. But good periods last longer and longer.

In spite of extremes, twelve shows a smoothing out of earlier behavior. Anger is still not under control, though it is moving in that direction. A younger or older sibling may arouse this anger, and it may include hitting, chasing, saying mean things, or throwing something. An increasing number, but still the minority of twelves withdraw, respond in silence, and go off by themselves to think it over. But twelve no longer argues just for the sake of argument, the way he or she did at eleven.

Eleven was searching for self. Twelve is beginning to take responsibility for more of his or her life, not only in the home and family, but also in the outside world. If twelve has an outstanding characteristic, it is enthusiasm. This can be so strong at times that he or she may be carried away by it. Empathy and insight are developing also, and these traits combine to make an outgoing, sociable young person.

Lord, help us not to miss this fun but brief stage.

#209

Walking with God and
family living means . . .   admiring endless energy.

"The light shines in the darkness, and the darkness has not overcome it."
(John 1:5 NRSV)

Twelve-year-old behavior includes enthusiasm that depends on a fund of energy that is always available to heighten any like or dislike, as in "I *hate* this food," "I *love* that movie!" However, saturation and sudden collapse in fatigue is possible. They have an increase in conceptual thinking and use of ideas but also periods of extreme tiredness that can occur when he or she hates everything and everybody that demands anything of them. Another characteristic is that they are not bored too often because they don't have time to do all the things they want to do. Colds are most likely to develop when a twelve-year-old has overtaxed him—or herself, but twelves also have the good sense to rest. These ages are eating as if their stomach was a "bottomless pit," and many (boys *and* girls) are gaining a lot of competence in cooking and making superb snacks. By now there is less fighting about bedtime, but some still sleep with a flashlight by their side (although they don't mention fear of the dark or of being alone).

Lord, help us to see this twelve-year-old as
the light shining on a grown-up future.

#210

***Walking with God and
family living means . . .***　　knowing that beginnings can be better than
endings.

"Do not provoke your children, lest they become discouraged." (Col 3:21 ESV)

During the ages nine to twelve, beginnings are better than endings. By twelve a child is spending more time on fixing up his or her room than keeping it in order, but clothes and collections still clutter up the room, and a bulletin board becomes a must for bits and pieces. By twelve they are being clever about saving money out of their own budgets, but a few are reckless squanderers with a burning desire to spend whatever money they have on hand. Earning money motivates a twelve-year-old, and there is less automatic resistance to work, but a twelve-year-old may need reminders to pitch in and may not volunteer to help.

This age is an opportunity for passing along a healthy attitude toward money and the ability to manage it. The challenge for any parent today is to teach restraint and responsibility in a society that alternates between valuing and not appearing to put much value on those traits. Tell these children that the advertising industry spends $50 billion a year to sell them things. Purely discretionary spending for such things as entertainment, trendy clothes, food, or a car does nothing for charity or saving for the future.

Lord, help us to help these children as they are learning about grown-up things, financial literacy, responsibilities and requirements.

#211

**Walking with God and
family living means . . .**   showing a genuine interest in the
in-between ages.

"David said further to his son Solomon, 'Be strong and of good courage, and
act. Do not be afraid or dismayed; for the Lord God, my God, is with you.'"
(1 Chr 28:20 NRSV)

The ages nine to twelve are not immune to having their feelings hurt, but
they try not to show it. By twelve there is little jealousy or envy except where
siblings are concerned, and they are delightfully open and uninhibited in the
classroom as well as at home. Twelve starts being especially aware of his or her
appearance, more so as he or she approaches thirteen. They arrive at decisions
and the choice of right and wrong almost spontaneously by how they feel, by
common sense, or by the inner dictates of conscience. Increasingly the choice
of right and wrong is thought of as a deliberately weighed process. There is a
very real religious concern by twelve, and he or she is wondering about it and
has been wondering, off and on, for the past year as abstract thinking abilities are
developing. Every year brings an increment of maturity, and these ages also need
time, patience, and understanding; an atmosphere encouraging good growth;
and (very important) his or her own alarm clock, calendar, and front door key.
Nine—to twelve-year-olds need adults who pick up on their interests and help
to facilitate their goals. This might include helping a child get to the store to buy
parts for a science project, or whatever. They need people who see and emphasize
their high points of achievement because these truly express the child's optimal
potential for future growth. The low points still exist however.

All of the ages nine to twelve continue to need a full refrigerator with access
to snacking, patience, adequate sleep, good humor, love, fairness, affection,
interesting activities, and a genuine interest and support from adults.

*Lord, help us to teach our children to be strong
and of good courage as they deal with their peers.*

#212

Walking with God and
family living means . . .   understanding adolescents.

"In the fear of the Lord one has strong confidence, and his children will have a refuge." (Prov 14:26 ESV)

Early adolescence, ages thirteen to fifteen, leads to many new phases of behavior that begin to emerge in the thirteen-year-old during this inward or internalized year. Thirteen-year-olds worry a lot, and then "I worry about worrying." One thirteen-year-old was reassured to have this read to him from a book and said, "I do that!" If it was "in a book it must be OK" was the subtext. This worrying is usually a normal sign of growth and leads to self-insight. Because so much happens for the first time during this year, time for internal processing is a need. He or she is not really withdrawing but is probing into reality more deeply by turning things over in his or her mind. A thirteen-year-old may look sullen and glum without being either. A thirteen-year-old is reflective but more cooperative than at twelve. He or she may be less spontaneous or outgoing. There is less conversation or humor. Sometimes a response is just a shrug. However, a thirteen-year-old is a tremendous self-critic.

Parents can observe thirteen-year-old behavior that includes getting along with siblings better than at eleven or twelve, except those siblings between six and eleven—as one mother said "I'm sorry—that's all we have in this family." There is a constant expenditure of newfound energy on private projects; voracious reading as one way to satisfy an inner urge for new ideas and thoughts; and extreme busyness that leaves little time for all he or she wants to do, much less time for household duties. Parents can remind themselves that this is not a plan just to annoy parents—many early adolescents are like that at this age.

Lord, help me to have confidence and be a refuge for my children.

#213

Walking with God and
family living means . . .   an exciting time with teens around.

"The Lord looks down from heaven; he sees all the children of man(kind)."
(Ps 33:13 ESV)

At thirteen a child may be friendly, but not communicative or spontaneous, but he or she is better able to control anger than at eleven or twelve. Thirteen-, fourteen-, and fifteen year-old young people all have a well-established appetite, and for some it is still as large as the twelve-year-old appetite. They are going to bed earlier but needing parents to remind them to turn off the lights, computer, TV, or radio. They are caring for their hair more than their fingernails and toenails and are more sure of likes and dislikes. Now they are capable of buying all but major purchases. Their rooms are still cluttered, not only with clothes and books, but also with papers and dishes from leftover snacks on the floor. However, these ages are capable of carrying through with chores with a certain amount of willingness and enjoy cooking, possibly breakfast on the weekend or deserts from mixes, while their skills continue to develop.

Thirteen is beginning to see him or herself more clearly. He or she has good insight and understands what another person means. The thirteen-year-old needs parents that understand when he or she says "I'm not too good-natured." They need parents that don't mind not knowing how to approach him or her when he or she snaps back with one-word answers. They also need parents that leave him or her alone to allow time for ruminating or cogitating on the day's events or whatever. They all need love and affection, but not in public, as thirteen is often embarrassed by his or her mother or father, and they need a parent that is tactful and reasonable with him or her, in a grown-up way, staying on the surface especially in front of their friends. Thirteens don't understand their own depths too well. They also need parents that support a wide range of hobbies, activities, and interests. The happy result is less time spent in front of the computer or television screen.

Lord, help me to enjoy this time and the enthusiasm that is developing.

#214

Walking with God and
family living means . . .   understanding the fourteen-year-old.

"Little children, let us not love in word or talk but in deed and in truth."
(1 John 3:18 ESV)

At fourteen, the withdrawal, shyness, and touchiness of the thirteen-year-old give way to an open, expansive personality phase with more laughter, noise, and singing in the home. A fourteen-year-old is better oriented to both him—or herself and to the surrounding environment. Fourteen enjoys life and feels the pressures of mounting energy. A fourteen-year-old has a more mature attitude toward adults in general and to his or her family in particular but still can be hypercritical. However, he or she is much less subjective than at thirteen, and has more friends.

Fourteen-year-old behavior includes a new developing capacity to understand how other people feel, fighting with siblings verbally rather than physically, being sensitive to group standards with friends, devotion to a group that may go to extremes and may be in competition with concrete demands of home and school. This outgoing age is eager and tireless in communication with friends, especially on cell phones and text messaging and in many ways. He or she has energy, expansiveness, and exuberance but may become swamped with undertakings and activities. There is a tendency to be realistic and objective, with a willingness to look at two sides of a question as they are beginning to use their minds in new ways, as abstract thinking continues to develop.

Fourteens tend to be happy and self-reliant, but also are self-critical, using new powers of reasoning. They now have crossed over toward more physical maturity, with rapid height growth for boys, and the body form of a young woman for girls. They have a continuing enjoyment of eating, but eating disorders may develop, especially in girls, at these ages. Other characteristics include having a loud voice; knowing enough to go to bed; hanging up his or her clothes—most of the time; being very aware of outward appearance, especially his or her complexion; being more of a spendthrift than in the past; having a changed attitude toward work; being easygoing, but getting moody; and worrying less than at thirteen, but still having pet worries.

Lord, help us to understand that communicating with friends carries a great thrill at this age.

#215

Walking with God and
family living means . . .   means preparing for tomorrow's world.

"They are to do good, to be rich in good works, generous, and ready to share, thus storing up for themselves the treasure of a good foundation for the future, so that they may take hold of the life that is really life." (1 Tim 6:18-19 NRSV)

No longer pathetically edgy and touchy, the fourteen-year-old seems to be coming into his or her own as a person. His or her maturity level is somewhere between elementary school and senior high school (a good reason for the name "Middle School"). Emotionally, the fourteen-year-old is not as precarious as last year, and has loosened up from the tight, withdrawn ways of the thirteen-year-old. A fourteen-year-old, with all his or her qualities of expansiveness, capacity for leadership, and readiness for change, is thinking about the kind of world he or she would like to live in: a world with unity and peace, a better world in general, with a better chance for people to grow up. Indeed if everyone followed the vision they had at fourteen, the world might be a different place. In fact, career planning consultants encourage people to think back to their dreams and ideas of the thirteen or fourteen year-old age. It helps to remember that fourteen-year-olds need to be helped to bring full realization to their promising potentials. This means parents that understand the fuller impact of how much it costs to raise a child; parents who accept his or her apology after a sharp word is spoken; parents who help in understanding how their activities relate to their whole lives (i.e., a parent can say, "You'll probably enjoy ice skating your whole life," etc.); and love, affection, and understanding perhaps expressed only by a hand on the arm or shoulder, if in public.

Lord, help us to see these children as you see them,
not as humans see them.

#216

Walking with God and
family living means . . .   understanding the fifteen-year-old.

"May mercy, peace, and love be yours in abundance." (Jude 1:2 NRSV)

It may seem that the expansive fourteen-year-old will get better and better as he or she turns fifteen, but the growth cycle hands out another inward cycle at fifteen. He or she may seem apathetic and sleepy, if not actually lazy. This seeming appearance, however, covers inner thinking about new experiences and inner states of feelings. A new capacity to focus on details of thought and feeling characterizes the fifteen-year-old. Many make a noticeable effort to find just the right words to express themselves correctly. Concern with the minute and for precision replaces the expansiveness of fourteen and precedes the integration that comes at sixteen. He or she has a thoughtful, quiet, serious side that is in evidence.

The behavior of a fifteen-year-old includes showing new sensibilities, irritations, resistances, aversions, and suspicions, but showing a new self-awareness and perceptiveness. By now fifteens stop omitting or skimping on greetings to family members and resisting restraints or restrictions, no matter how reasonable. However, they may be engaging parents in a cold war, which varies in degree, despite feelings of loyalty, and can include slamming the door when leaving, especially when going out at night, and following an urge for independence. By now, if this hasn't happened already, they are being affected by the pressures of the group and are gregarious and like groups, except those at home; wanting to outgrow parental control, but feeling conflicted about this. By now there are better relations with siblings, with the young person seeing an improvement in the siblings, but there is a feeling of gnawing anguish if parents do not get along with each other. Fifteens can sink into a slump when the effort required to define thoughts and feelings is too great; unfortunately such slumps can lead to school dropout. They are revealing new interests and hidden talents in reactions to specialized courses and activities at school and are neither antischool nor antihome—"just needs time to mull things over" and organize him—or herself internally. They may need to maintain an apartness, by withdrawing internally or going to the bedroom, becoming secretive, defensive, not wanting parents to know about his or her activities (no matter how reasonable). They are calming down on the subject of clothes and are finding that relaxation and sleeping mean a lot to them. Fifteens want to think that parents "don't really have the upper hand" and may not be the easiest person to teach in school but learn quickly in new fields.

Lord, help us to take the "long view" and appreciate the positives in a fifteen-year-old.

#217

Walking with God and
family living means . . .   is fulfilling.

"And God is able to provide you with every blessing in abundance, so that by always having enough of everything, you may share abundantly in every good work." (2 Cor 9:8)

A fifteen-year-old wants to define his or her thoughts, philosophy, and place in life. There is a constant cry for liberty and independence (even though he or she may have had these!). He or she is expert at stalling in answers to questions and ends up telling the questioner as little as possible. They begin to show an ability to identify with other people and situations but love an argument and a dispute for its own sake. Parents need to be warned that fifteens have a low threshold for all sorts of stimuli (e.g., everything bothers him or her) and have emotions like the weather, sunny and gloomy. They have times of feeling very tired, discouraged, and mixed up but are not getting as mad as often as they used to. They reminisce about the fears they used to have, and about other earlier stages of development.

Better yet and more amusing for parents, he or she may reminisce at sixteen about being fifteen. Security is important to the fifteen-year-old, and he or she wishes it for him—or herself, the family, and the whole world. They are down to earth in their thinking, revisiting concepts from ages nine and ten. Since fifteens have a tendency to rebel against authority, even though confused and floundering themselves; how authority treats them becomes very important. Remind yourself and other parents that some of the most annoying comments need to be ignored.

Real leaders often emerge at fifteen. A fifteen-year-old needs time to become receptive to requests and questions, so his or her answers may come slowly. They need parents that are aware that they may be arguing for "fun," but also to get their point across. Some maintain a closed mind. They need not to be idle; they would rather be rushed than do nothing, and they need to have parents and teachers who understand that they are uncertain and searching, with much turmoil and depth to this inner disquietude. They need parents that understand there are times when they *want* their feelings to be known; one doesn't have to be a genius to figure out the meaning of the cold stare, the shuffled walk, the apathy, and quietness; and they need love, patience, and kindness to carry them through this inner cycle to the greater integration that emerges at sixteen.

Lord, help us help these young people see the leaders
they are becoming and thank you for sustaining us.

#218

Walking with God and
family living means . . .　　　previewing later adolescence, ages sixteen
　　　　　　　　　　　　　　　to eighteen.

"Until now you have not asked for anything in my name."
(John 16:24 NRSV)

While this walk or journey in family living with God's help is primarily focused on parenting in the earlier years, a few words on issues parents of teens often ask about such things as driving, jobs, and college applications are in order. There are many more issues, of course, and other resource materials will be needed. Sixteen is an age of integration and is greatly helped by the adult world recognizing this. A few topics that cause frequent questions are the following:

Driver's licenses and allowing a young person to get a driver's license in this age period (according to the laws of different states) is one form of acknowledgment of this coming adulthood. Teens getting a driver's license, of course, make parents nervous. The graduated privileges type of driver's license developing in some states is a good idea. Driver's Education and careful parental supervision are also required.

Jobs are desired by many young people who are anxious to earn money as soon as getting a job seems possible. This is good in small doses, but today's competent young person may be pressured into working later and longer hours than is wise for schoolwork, health, and other activities. Helping the older teen to understand that the boss at the job is not the arbiter of his or her time may be necessary. One high school junior, washing dishes in a restaurant to save money for a school trip, reported that the owner locked the door, so no one could leave before 11:00 p.m. when the dishes were all washed. Practices serving the commercial world may not serve these young people and may even be unlawful. The young man in question had to be at school each day at 7:15 a.m. When he reached his target dollar amount for a school trip, he was able to resign, fortunately.

Lord, help us help young people understand that the real world can be less than
interested in their well-being.

#219

***Walking with God and
family living means . . .***   giving young people wings.

"Strive for the greater gifts." (1 Cor 12:31 NRSV)

College applications and applying for college are always a big hurdle for seniors in high school, and a few helpful hints from successful college applicants are included here.

* The summer before senior year, request on the Internet or write postcards requesting college catalogs and applications, with addresses taken from resource books listing colleges. This can be done online for most institutions. These books and Web sites tell all the attributes of the institution of higher education. Relying on advertising brochures that come in the mail is insufficient as these are often from expensive and mediocre quality institutions of higher education.
* Fill out the first one or two applications carefully and keep copies of them to use for ideas for the next ones. Keep copies of all applications.
* Apply to a variety of choices of institutions that teach the subject matter in which the student is interested: one large, one small, one near, one farther away, one difficult to be admitted to, and one easier to be admitted to such as a local state supported institution. Apply for scholarship aid as needed, and review ROTC opportunities and non-institution related financial aid possibilities, including the guaranteed student government loan program (see www.salliemae.com). If possible, mail all applications before Thanksgiving of the Senior year in high school, as many schools have a rolling admission, and January or February mail-ins are too late for wide consideration.

*Lord, it is fortunate we are not meant to go it alone.
Remind us that we are happiest when helping one another.*

#220

Walking with God and family living means . . .   reviewing new learnings.

"Above all clothe yourselves with love, which binds everything together in perfect harmony." (Col 3:14 NRSV)

To summarize the description of the characteristic behavior of different ages and stages for children, it is the *order* and *sequence* of these stages following close upon each other that is more important than the actual given age for any particular child. Just as in nature there is a predictable *sequence* for a caterpillar becoming a cocoon and then a butterfly, or the unfolding of flowers, shrubs, and trees in spring, we're not sure if spring will be early or late, or at the beginning or end of which month. But the sequence of crocuses, then daffodils and forsythia, then tulips, azaleas, and dogwood coming later is followed year after year in a particular latitude.

In the description of the age levels, the same general things seem to happen over and over. This distinctive sequence can be seen between two and five years, then again between five and ten, and once again from 10 to 16. Understanding this pattern is very helpful to parents. Two, five, and ten are smooth points, in "equilibrium." Then the smooth periods are followed by a period that seems troubled, disturbed, and "broken up" usually at two and a half, five and a half to six and near or at age eleven. The child seems "at odds" with his or her environment and with him or herself. Relatively calm period returns at three and a half, six and a half, and twelve followed by "inward" periods when the child seems to withdraw and mull over experiences and impressions. This quieter "inner" period often has disturbing side effects such as whining, emotional instability and tears, fears, poor orientation in space and stumbling, and even stuttering.

The seven—and thirteen-year-old, coming out of this inward stage, can be touchy, sensitive, withdrawn, and moody, and generally pessimistic about life. "Nobody likes me" is a comment heard even from a popular child. Thirteen-year-olds "worry a lot and 'worry about worrying'." Almost-four-year-olds may seem to be in harmony and at peace with themselves at this stage, even while their behavior is disturbing to others around them, which can be seen in their whining a lot.

Next follows "expansive" ages of four, eight, and fourteen when the child is outgoing and energetic. These are happy, peppy children usually, barring some trauma or family crisis. Younger children may actually get lost outside, and a fourteen-year-old may tangle in multiple and conflicting social commitments, as they "expand" their horizons.

Again there is a turn to the quiet side at four and a half, nine, and fifteen, but the periods still have similarities. Nine and fifteen have been called the "most nearly neurotic ages" even though they are normal stages of growth. They are followed by the relative stability of five, ten, and sixteen.

Lord, wherever your love is shared, there is harmony.

#221

Walking with God and
family living means . . .   recognizing patterns.

"I trust in the steadfast love of God forever and ever." (Ps 52:8 NRSV)

      Encouraging yourself to recognize the rhythms of growth and alternations between the stable and the inward periods in children's development immediately helps in predicting what words or approaches might be more successful in interactions with the children. These interactions will vary somewhat by the culture, gender, and age of the child and of the parent. But recognizing that each new age of a child brings changes for the better as well as for the worse, while their child grows up, helps any parent discover and enjoy the good while smoothing over the less desirable. Many parents are greatly helped by knowing there _is_ a pattern that makes the behavior of a child somewhat predictable over the long range, even while they are dealing with one age at a time. Parents will be evaluating their own child's development and their own understanding and reactions to this behavior, along with learnings, readings, and new ideas. This can lead to revised opinions that develop from having information on child development.

Lord, help us to understand children at the age and stage they are in at the moment.

#222

Walking with God and
family living means . . .   working together as a small group or team.

"I will give them one heart, and one way, that they may be (in awe) of me forever, for the good of them and their children after them." (Jer 32:39 KJV)

Small groups provide a source of satisfaction to family members that is of great importance. What goes on in small groups is a vital factor to any leader. With siblings this can change in alternating years with different children in the family being a "friendship groups." It is good to understand some of the processes that go on in small groups (or teams) in order to help develop family stability, family health, and family effectiveness. Internal dynamics and factors within a family can make it more or less productive. A small group is usually considered to be less than twenty and is often less than twelve. A family of three to eleven is definitely a "small group," and many of the dynamics seen working in families, which comprises just one "small group," are important and can be productive and one can learn from the dynamics known about small groups.

Lord, help us to have a family that works together.

#223

Walking with God and
family living means . . .   building a team.

"Children are a heritage of the Lord." (Ps 127:3 (KJV)

Small groups provide their members with social support and a feeling of personal worth. In a family one would add love and moral support to these benefits. The foundations for mature social exchange are established early in life through child-child and child-adult interactions that are favorable, thus demonstrating acceptance and approval. Acceptance and approval continue to be important in adult life.

It has long been found that small groups or teams will be more effective if they contain "friendship groups," that is, if they take into account the small groups that exist in the "informal organization." Do two children get along with each other this year better than with other siblings? (It may be different next year.) Individuals like to be surrounded by people who like them, even if it is a small number. Sometimes the attitudes and opinions of others are the only basis on which a child or adult can evaluate his or her own opinions and attitudes. People like to have a feeling of certainty about their beliefs, opinions, and attitudes and gain affirmation through shared values in a small group. Using a consultative style when introducing new information or new approaches to the family helps to preserve this positive feeling of support from the small family group around an individual.

Lord, help us build up, support, and teach children to work as a team.

#224

***Walking with God and
family living means . . .***   building up not giving up.

"In the fear of the Lord is strong confidence; and his children shall have refuge."
(Prov 14:26 KJV)

A negative aspect affecting teams, small groups, and families is that people
with low self-esteem tend to find frustrating conditions MORE frustrating than
those with higher self-esteem. Those with very low self-esteem may give up
in a situation in which a person with higher self-esteem might stay. This may
be a clue in a family as to why teenagers get frustrated by small things. Many
are so ill at ease with their own bodies and themselves, and so criticized by
school friends, that any additional pressures may be too much. Time cures this
as adaptations are made to self and at school, but it helps if parents understand
these forces and try not to "nag" too much.

Lord, help us to remember that small stuff **is** *small stuff.*

Big kids like to play with little kids but need careful supervision. An older
child can encourage a younger child.

#225

**Walking with God and
family living means . . .**   working out how we will work together.

"You shall rejoice in all the good which the Lord your God has given you and your household." (Deut 26:11 NASB)

In any family or group, especially a newly combined family, there are three observable stages: "forming," "storming," and "norming." Norming is defined as creating a social norm for the family. A "norm" can be a standard of behavior expected of family members. These three stages can be observed during the planning of a family project (especially if it is an extended family project like a family reunion), or even on a long-range plan. In a nuclear family, these "group standards" are usually clearer. The *forming* stage occurs as the group gets going, and a status hierarchy develops in the group. Status can be based on a child's age or a person's performance skills, interpersonal skills, or the job he or she has been asked to do. An example is "Suzy is 'creative,' can she help with the nametags?" Emergence of different roles can be seen in the group during this stage: the tough leader, the friendly helper, and the clear thinker. Clear expectations help speed this process, for example, by having an appointed leader, tasks move forward more quickly. An example for raking the yard would be "Johnny, you be in charge of the leaf pile." Sometimes the leader is just the person who has the rake or the pencil and paper or some other needed "resource."

The *storming* stage can cause tensions and occurs when one or more family members think the leader of the group is going in a direction with which they disagree. An example of this occurred during a family activity, a visit to an aunt, for which discipline of the children had never been discussed. One parent started off with a strong statement about her views favoring a fairly harsh philosophy of no eating in this room, no drinking, no moving of chairs or rearranging furniture in that room, etc. Another parent said, "Now, *wait* a minute." It should be noted that this is an "unclear task" according to the definitions given later, which contributed to the rough start of this group activity. Continued discussion clarified expectations of both parents for the children, before the activity (this visit to an aunt) had progressed too far. The third stage or _norming_ stage follows quickly and is based on shared beliefs and opinions in at least some areas. Family members need to feel that their objectives are worthy of attainment. They develop expectations about how people should feel about certain issues. There is usually some agreement about what is relevant and what is not. Interestingly enough, if family members perceive a difference in one area, they will talk *more* about it rather than less, perhaps trying to persuade the others to their point of view.

Lord, help us to continue discussion until we get it together.

#226

Walking with God and
family living means . . .   establishing everyday expectations.

"You must obey these laws that I will give you today, so that all will be well with you and your children." (Deut 4:40 LB)

Rules or norms can help family group or family team effectiveness and make the family team fairer for all. They reduce the need for decisions on routine matters and also reduce the need for the use of personal power. Rules like "No pushing, no shoving" are common in most families.

Early establishment of trust and acceptance; agreement about goals, procedures, and timing; and the exchange of information all helps family teamwork. The elements, which are not necessarily chronological, are orientation, trust building, goal/role clarification, commitment, implementation, high performance, and renewal and return to orientation and explaining things. An "awareness of the high cost of coercion" that sets back the whole interaction helps people avoid this approach. A very harsh approach can ruin a cooperative spirit.

Also there are specialized roles in family work groups. These different roles in a family permit the rapid achievement of assigned tasks. In a family this can sometimes be seen when the wife does most of the cooking for the first fifteen or twenty years in the marriage, and the husband does most of the cooking for the second fifteen to twenty years (or after retirement—this really does happen!)

Lord, help us to explain things and build trust in our family.

#227

Walking with God and
family living means . . .   learning to predict and plan for the family
"team" to be successful and effective.

"The father of the righteous will greatly rejoice, and he who begets a wise (child) will be glad." (Prov 23:24 NRSV)

Predicting how well a family will work together has been found to have three main variables within a situation: (1) how well they got along; (2) clearness of task (e.g. can it be written down?). This variable's importance explains why family goals and projects should be enunciated clearly, if not actually written down. This is the easiest variable with which to work; and (3) parental leader power. The clear task variable can be further defined as showing four ways a task might be clear or unclear: (1) If a decision could be shown to be correct or verified (such as in baking a cake—did you get a cake?). This is called decision verifiability. (2) If the family members understood the requirements of the task? (3) If more than one procedure can be used to accomplish the task (such as different ways to prepare a Thanksgiving dinner). (4) Does the problem has more than one correct solution? The goals or tasks of most families are not clear tasks—there are several right ways to do them and several correct solutions to most problems. Anything that adds clearness will be a help.

Lord, help us to be clear with our requests.

#228

Walking with God and
family living means . . .   being clear about tasks that need to be done.

"Children, obey your parents in all things; for this is well pleasing to the Lord." (Col 3:20 KJV)

It has been found that any group that has two out of three of the major factors (getting along, clear task, parent leader power) would probably be effective. If one looks at families and sees the tasks as unclear, one can see that getting along together, and parent leader power become essential. Conversely, anything that can be done to make the task clear such as written goal statements, project plans or descriptions, checklists, travel brochures, college brochures, or anything that is written, will help a family to be more effective.

A clear leader, good relationships and clear—and often discussed—family goals and planning for them will help any family function more smoothly. The "clear task" with talk about goals and plans helps family members to see progress. This approach can be used whether the goal is to increase the savings plan, help Daddy or Mom get ahead on the job, or help the children to be what they hope to be in adult life.

Lord, help us to see your way clearly for our family.

#229

Walking with God and
family living means . . .   people acting together as a group that can
accomplish things that no individual acting
alone could ever hope to bring about.

"Now to him who is able to do exceedingly abundantly beyond all that we ask or think, according to the power that works within us." (Eph 3:20 NASB)

The impact of the three variables, clear task, parental leadership and getting along, is transparent when seen in families. For instance an unclear task quite often in a family might be raising a child or children. There are many right ways to do this and many varieties of right results. Furthermore one of the best results is to have the child "develop to his or her own full potential" and not even the child knows what that might be. Therefore anything that adds clearness to discussions between parents, and with the child, helps. If the family does not enunciate goals or discuss future possibilities and horizons, if both parents work full time with no clear leader in family matters (even alternating leadership in different areas is better than no leader), but they do get along fine, they may manage, but the children may show no ambition or goal setting of their own. If this family gets along poorly, then all three of the characteristics would be weak, predicting a lack of success for the family as a group, and for the children.

Lord, help us to work together to see the way clearly.

#230

**Walking with God and
family living means . . .** coming together as a beginning, helping together as progress, and working together yields success.

"If two of you shall agree on earth as touching anything that they shall ask, it shall be done for them in heaven." (Matt 18:19 KJV)

The old-fashioned autocratic father who made it absolutely clear what children were to do and how, may not have been well liked (sometimes known as not getting along) but sometimes the results were more favorable than in an example with no parental leadership and both parents working long hours. Two of three variables needed, at least were present in the autocratic father example: a *Clear Task* and *Parent Leader Power. Positive parent-child relations* were missing, but two of three factors were present. However if parent-child relations are really bad, then children may leave home as soon as possible.

The reverse of the model above may do less emotional damage and is certainly easier to maintain with family members getting along well together plus clear goals and tasks, but no clear leader position power between the two parents. Here again two of the three variables needed are positive and present, but in a much more sustainable way for *family relationships with getting along* and *a clear task* being the two out of three factors present. Parent Leader Power may be missing or less important but with the other two factors strong these still lead to success for the family.

Lord, help us to get along and work together.

#231

Walking with God and
family living means . . .   knowing that a group can do more than an
individual can do.

"Truly, truly I say to you, the one who believes in me, the works that I do shall he do also; and greater works than these shall he do; because I go to the Father." (John 14:12 NASB)

Families can build "team spirit" in a number of ways. One family had "Family tee shirts" and wore them on vacation and when a family member was in the hospital.

A group exists when two or more people have a unifying relationship, such as common goals or physical proximity. When physical proximity is missing with a child at college or a parent on travel, team building is even more important and frequent telephone, e-mail, and text communications become a must. Utilizing the characteristics of groups is an important skill of leadership and understanding their dynamics can help a family.

Teamwork is necessary in families no matter how loosely connected the team is. While different teams will evolve and have an ebb and flow, the family unit needs to stay strong, as a working team. This is true for all families. All three factors need to be present as often as possible: parent leader power, clear (or structured) tasks, and getting-along-together relationships. Since the task often will not be clear (for instance, in raising children), it is well to be aware of these dynamics and put in the extra effort that is needed. Any activities that clarify the task will help. Any lists, check lists, or schedules, especially with stars for jobs well done, bring this clarity. In the home, regular "family council" meetings to restate goals and hear from family members about their goals and concerns is important.

Lord, help us to do the greater work you would have us to do.

#232

***Walking with God and
family living means . . .***　　　developing thinking skills and imagination.

"May the God of steadfastness and encouragement grant you to live in harmony with one another in accordance with Jesus Christ." (Rom 15:5 NRSV)

The family is the first and most important learning organization in which people find themselves, and it deserves attention. Families and children learning together not only build bonds; they have fun and enjoy quality time activities while building harmony. Adults never cease to be amazed at the creative and inventive answers children produce for what seem to be routine questions.

Creative thinking skills are valuable to children and adults. As children are growing up and asking questions, and as one learns more about the children at different age levels, creative thinking skills are valued more and more. A creative person has the confidence to express himself or herself and ask questions. A creative person is purposeful and courageous. Children that practice thinking skills move to the valuable "thinking on their own" so necessary in adult life. Creativity is important in all fields of endeavors, whether in designing a new part for an electronic receiver, which an almost four-year-old who asked "Who put in the mud?" did later as an electrical engineer, or in the field of cooking or the arts. Creativity can even be applied to designing a new financial product for a financial institution, which a creative thinking child did as an adult. Topics that are important in creativity include Creativity, Memory Stretching and Observing; Comparing, Classifying, and Imagining; Cause and Effect and Summarizing; Looking for Assumptions and Telling the Reason Why; Problem Solving and Decision Making; and Understanding and Organizing.

Lord, help us to grow children who are purposeful and courageous.

#233

Walking with God and
family living means . . .   developing creativity and asking why?

"Do not be conformed to this world, but be transformed by the renewing of your minds." (Rom 12:2 NRSV)

No person need ever pass out of the stage of asking why. There are no more exciting words to hear from a child or an adult than "I've got an idea!" Encouraging creative thinking is essential for the workplace and the home, and thinking at home, with children, is a continuing and rewarding surprise for families. In an easier-to-harder sequence, a short list of thinking skills listed before as topics, might include Observing, Comparing, Classifying, Imagining, Cause and Effect, Summarizing, Looking for Assumptions and Hypothesizing, Telling the Reason Why, Decision Making, Problem Solving, Understanding and Empathizing, and Organizing.

Trying questions with children, maybe on a weekend morning, leads to quality parenting that can take only five to ten minutes. One doesn't even have to be very alert or look good to enjoy this activity. And even five minutes a *week* in conversation with a parent can benefit IQ scores for three-year-olds, a large research study for 215 children showed. This rise in IQ was due to the children developing vocabulary and coming up with more ideas of things to do. Interaction builds vocabulary, which is measured on many tests. Memory stretching and imagination building can be enjoyable first steps. For memory development, parents can ask their children questions like these, which are good for memory stretching: "Does your back door swing in or out?" "What did you have for dinner yesterday? lunch? breakfast? the day before?" You can explain if necessary that Mom may have been the cook, but she probably has forgotten. Another memory question is "What did your teacher wear yesterday?"

Lord, help us keep curiosity alive and fresh.

#234

**Walking with God and
family living means . . .**   developing imagination.

"Happy are those who trust in the Lord." (Prov 16:20 NRSV)

For imagination building one can ask: "What would you do if it snowed green snow?" One answer from a five-year-old was "I'd get a green snow suit and green sled, and Mom couldn't find me!" "What would be funnier if it were bigger?" "What would work better if it were smaller?" "What would make cars better?" One answer from a child age ten was "Put swimming pools on the roofs of cars to make them better. Then we could swim at stoplights and in traffic jams." What would be prettier if it had more colors? If these sample questions are fun for families to do with children, then more questions from the suggestions on each thinking skill might also be something to try. A few minutes at a time is better for a child's attention span and is usually better for the adult's available time.

Lord, help us fit fun into a child's attention span and an adult's available time.

#235

Walking with God and family living means . . . observing and asking questions.

"For, in fact, the kingdom of God is among you." (Luke 17:21 NRSV)

The way to build observation skills is to encourage a young child to notice things in more detail. Parents can ask the child to look around a room and tell him or her everything that he or she sees. (This is especially good for waiting rooms.) Ask the child to describe what a friend is wearing. What is the friend doing? Look at magazine pictures and describe the people in the pictures. The child's list at first may be short, but as you encourage him or her, it will get longer. Encourage yourself to watch for this. For Comparing, another thinking skill, even young children can begin to understand varieties within a category such as apples and oranges are both fruits. Comparing is a basic thinking skill that will be needed for early math and early reading. By comparing many kinds of things within a category, children begin to see likeness and differences. Parents can ask, for instance, what is alike and what is different between the following: A brick wall and a plaster or wallboard wall? A bird and an airplane? Bread and apples? Sunny days and rainy days? What happens on them? Summer clothes and winter clothes? Compare the main character in two stories, for example, the wolf in *Red Riding Hood* and Father Bear in *Goldilocks*.

There are many right answers. Using pictures, books, magazine pictures, and audio CDs, comparing likes and differences helps parents help children. Next move on to comparing what people, or animals, do or don't do differently. Do they both cry with tears? Beginning science skills are developed with comparing. What happens when a dish of water is put outside on a freezing day? On a hot day? Or when it is put in the freezer? What happens when we cook eggs? Vegetables?

> *Lord, help us to enjoy children's answers as we ask questions that are for fun and also build thinking skills.*

#236

***Walking with God and
family living means . . .*** building on observing and comparing
to develop classifying skills.

"The new self which is being renewed in knowledge . . ." (Col 3:10 NRSV)

As children build on observing and comparing skills, parents can move on to classifying skills. Children become aware of many categories: birds, animals, clothes, foods, adults, and children. A young child of two or three may use one word, like "doggie" to mean everything with four legs. As language skills develop, the child becomes aware of many things in one category. A cow, a horse, and a dog can then all be in the category of animals.

Now, children can begin enjoying defining their own categories. In sorting buttons they can choose to sort by color, by size, or by the number of holes in the button. The concept of choosing their own categories is a valuable basic thinking skill. Books can be sorted by those the child likes or by those he or she doesn't like, which is more abstract than just by color or size. Foods or clothes can also be sorted by color, size, and personal preferences. Older children can become aware that larger concepts can be classified. The whole world or one room can be handled with North, South, East and West.

Parents can talk about the oceans on a globe and about seeing the ocean, a beach, or other water near them such as a river or lake, on a map. If it can be located on a map, parents can then talk about North, South, East and West and which way the water flows or the lake extends.

While reading stories or doing other activities, parents can see if children start asking *classifying questions* such as "Are cows always black and white?" "Are dogs always large?" "Are fish always small?"

Parents can notice whether a child's conversation with friends begins to reflect categories. "I have five dresses. But I think Roger only has three dresses." This from a girl, age three, with one sister who wore pants to preschool just like Roger did. She got the number and the category classification right, but missed the gender issue! Watch and see if the children begin to see more variety within a category. For example, bread, milk, meat, and fruit are all food, but are different food groups and each can be its own classification category.

Lord, help us teach children new ways to think.

#237

***Walking with God and
family living means . . .***   building imagination.

"The light of the eyes rejoices the heart, and good news refreshes the body."
(Prov 15:30 NRSV)

Many of the questions already listed in the beginning of this group of readings focused on Thinking Skills and build imagination and more thinking skills. While it may seem that children don't need any help with this, extending their thinking and affirming and encouraging their imagination is always good for brain development.

More questions for parents to ask children include "What you would do if you had three wishes." "What would you make larger so it would be more exciting?" "What would you make go backward in order to improve it?" "What would you make round so it would be more comfortable? A pillow? A bed?"

"What would you make smaller so it would be nicer?" These ideas and questions can go on and on with almost any two adjectives. Some of the answers will surprise parents. Imagination is vital in the business and career world. This can be seen (in hindsight) from this story by a seven-year-old boy:

"Once there was a little tiger who lived in a house. He was playing on the front porch. Then he went in the house; and then the house began to fly."

There was more to this story printed laboriously by a seven-year-old. The parent thought it was creative at the time. The writer of the story is the same child who as an adult invented a new product for a large corporation. However, one might never have linked these two examples of creativity except with the statement "I've got an idea!"

Lord, help us help children build imagination for a better world.

#238

Walking with God and
family living means . . .   practicing summarizing with children.

"I trust in the steadfast love of God forever and ever." (Ps 52:8 NRSV)

Like this summarizing statement from Psalm 52, the title of a story can be a summary of its meaning. It's fun to practice thinking up new titles for stories with children, and this also builds language and stretches imagination. Titles or names of toys and games can also be used for summarizing examples for parents and children to try out new thinking skills.

This builds confidence and a sense of enjoyment for a child to think of a title or to think ahead and tell his or her own end of a story. Parents can make a note of new titles or new endings children think up, so that if the children prefer them, they can try to use them again. In reading a story, parents can stop at a different place and have the child make up what will happen next. Mom or Dad can "prime the pump" with suggestions for new titles. A few examples are "Goldilocks Eats Cereal," or "Goldilocks Finds a New Bed" or "Little Red Riding Hood Goes for a Walk."

Lord, help us help children learn the meaning of summarizing.

Books are fun at any age.

#239

Walking with God and
family living means . . .   understanding cause and effect.

"Let me have this benefit from you in the Lord! Refresh my heart in Christ."
(Philem 1:20 NRSV)

Developing thinking skills at home with children is a continuing and rewarding surprise especially as the earlier skills of observing, comparing, classifying, and summarizing are practiced. These developing skills also build language skills.

Cause and effect occur every day, but learning to choose the desired effect and back up to the cause is a powerful learning at any age. A child gains confidence and feels powerful as he or she learns that one can make choices with a predictable effect. One can even make the choices according to the effect desired. A parent's job is to provide opportunities for the child to be a cause that the parent wants to hear such as choosing blue and red paint (or food coloring in water) to make purple rather than choosing to scream to get a cookie. Planting seeds, and making cookies (or other food products) show other examples of cause and effect taking place.

Parents can talk about the weather in discussing cause and effect. Ask what kind of clothes we wear when it rains? When it is hot? Ask how does this weather affect children's play?

Planting seeds in a garden or indoors in a paper cup is a wonderful observation and cause-and-effect activity. If possible, first parents show the child a picture of beans or zinnias or another easy-to-plant choice. Then let the child choose which to plant or even which seed packet to buy. Prepare the dirt together, read the seed packet out loud, and let the child drop the seeds in several places. Many of these plants have a sprout within a week to ten days, and do so in nice rows that are noticeable if they've been planted outside. Discuss this effect from the cause of planting seeds.

Parents can notice if their child starts talking about expected effects. For example, "I expect Susie will play with me today." They can notice if he or she comments when things turn out differently than expected. Do their children talk about how they will change things with toys or colors? Do children begin to build confidence in their choices and decisions, as outcomes become predictable? Do children talk about some effects that outside causes have on them, such as, "It was hot, so I took off my sweater!" "It was snowy, so I wore boots!" Many children's books describe cause and effect, and their titles may summarize this and the story.

Lord, help us appreciate the wonderful exhilaration of new ideas.

#240

**Walking with God and
family living means . . .** practicing looking for assumptions and
guessing.

"Teach me your way, O Lord, that I may walk in your truth." (Ps 86:11 NRSV)

Guessing is an important thinking skill and is often called estimating by adults. It is closely tied with hypothesizing, which means guessing into the future: what does one *think* will happen? Children at home can be invited to guess (or hypothesize) where an adult might have put things, such as the car keys, a book, or certain papers. One can say "where might I have put my papers?" Practice in this helps children become thinkers who collect evidence to support their opinions. They learn to *trust* their own opinions and intuitions, and to say things like "I think your paper is there because *last time* you put your paper there." This is historical evidence or precedent. It may not be true this time but it's a start. Guessing or hypothesizing is essential in thinking, but it's often discouraged. Adults can help to build this skill.

Developing thinking skills at home is a continuing and rewarding surprise, especially as earlier skills, plus those of cause and effect and summarizing, are practiced. This development also builds language skills and ability.

Lord, help us encourage estimating and guessing about the future with our children.

#241

**Walking with God and
family living means . . .**   becoming media literate.

"All the paths of the Lord are steadfast love and faithfulness." (Ps 25:10 NRSV)

Looking for assumptions becomes more and more important especially as the need to become media literate increases. Parents can show a child a picture and ask him or her to guess what is happening and tell what is really happening. Then do this with TV shows: look at the picture without the sound; then turn the sound up. Is the picture of mountains really a car advertisement? Talk about what is *really* happening versus what you assumed. Look at a picture in a newspaper or magazine together then read aloud what is happening. Did you both assume something different? Show the good side of a piece of fruit with a rotten spot on the back. Parents can ask, "Can you eat this?" Then turn it around. This shows the child that he or she has to know both sides of the question. It helps to make opportunities available for your child to learn what is real and what is not real or true. It also helps children to see choices in what is offered on television and in other media.

Lord, help us to develop our own media literacy along with our children.

#242

**Walking with God and
family living means . . .**   building children's self image at school.

"The unfolding of your words gives light; it gives understanding to the simple."
(Ps 119:130 NRSV)

When I was just finishing first grade in Massachusetts my family moved to Washington, D.C. At my elementary school there, the class had learned to print but not to write in cursive, as I had. The other children learned that I could write my own name and *theirs* in cursive, so they lined up three and four deep for me to write out each of their names. They realized that even they would be able to do this soon if another child could do it. What a boost it was for a new girl!

The curriculum guidelines were just different in different states. I learned this more as we moved with my father, who was an Army doctor. We lived in Virginia next, then Denver and I finished sixth grade in El Paso, Texas. I learned Texas history and later Missouri history! Sometimes I was ahead of the class and sometimes behind. In Denver I even skipped a grade as I had done all the fifth grade work in my last school. So even though I didn't start first grade until six and a half, I finished high school at 17 and started college.

When I was accepted at a well known eastern university another girl told me "You can't go there, you're not first in the class." I was 17th, not first but also not last of the 350 in the class. It was not "the last shall be first" but I did attend that university and had a wonderful time.

Lord, help us realize that unavoidable changes may have other benefits for our children.

#243

Walking with God and
family living means . . .   learning helpful problem solving.

"I will strengthen you, I will help you, I will uphold you with my victorious right hand." (Is 41:10 NRSV)

Children need to be aware that *they* can help solve a problem. Additionally, they need to see that problems can have more than one solution, but that one solution may be better than others. Furthermore, thinking through a problem before acting on it, then hypothesizing or predicting different results usually contributes to a better solution.

Parents can encourage and ask children what they would do in certain situations. All children of any age in the household should plan what they would do in case of fire. Discuss several different ways to get out of the home. Some families even have a fire drill. For problem solving practice with easier problems, ask what they would do if they had just settled down to do homework or to do a task for Mom or Dad, and a friend called to come over. Talk about other hypothetical situations.

Children of all ages can discuss problems. One four-year-old talking about a wheel broken off a truck started with "Actually the problem is . . . . this was not a very good truck," which is also looking for an assumption that it *was* a good truck. Later, as a grown-up engineer, this skill served him well. Ask for children's input into solutions: how to smooth up dishwashing chores (have teams? use paper plates? divide tasks by age?), hanging up clothes or coats, yard work such as raking or mowing, and sharing use of the computer. As is true in the organizational management, solutions that children have a stake in are more likely to work over the long term. Ask children what they think problems at home are, and carefully write down a list. Young teenagers love this and may have a long list. Then parents can brainstorm solutions with children for several items on the list. More solutions can be generated next week at another session with the child or children along with follow-up on this week's solutions. Be aware that tempers may fray if such a session is too long and the thinking skill practice gets sidetracked.

As children develop a sense of mastery and confidence in their own solutions, they will be more sure of themselves in considering their own or other people's problems. Parents can then discuss problems and solutions in retrospect also: How else could we have done it? What should be done differently next time?

Lord, we know your love will uphold us and sustain us and our children.

#244

Walking with God and
family living means ...   decision-making practice with children.

"Therefore be imitators of God, as beloved children and live in love, as Christ loved us and gave himself up for us." (Eph 5:1-2 NRSV)

When children can recognize a problem, it becomes easier to realize when a decision may be needed. Describing alternative solutions and predicting alternative results are good practice for human beings at any age, three to one hundred. Two-year-olds, also, can handle two choices occasionally, but aren't famous for being good at it. Choosing an alternative solution and being able to live with the choice is a good life skill for all ages. Parents can ask their child to put all his or her favorite books on the top shelf or the bottom shelf. This is an example of a decision that would be meaningful in his or her life and that the child could practice living with, and most parents are comfortable with any choice the child makes. The child is pleased to be asked.

Parents can help children have confidence that the decisions they have a part in are important. They can practice respecting the children's opinions and decisions and then ask the children to respect *their* parental opinions and decisions. Making sure this is two-way respect enhances the relationship with the child. Parents can share some adult concerns for adult decisions so that children can begin to understand the process adults go through when making up their minds such as: researching which car or TV to buy; considering what kind of care or assistance to get for an older relative; choosing a place to go on for vacation. Discuss factors of time, money, energy and so forth, to help the child see the reality of some limits.

Lord, in decisions small and large help us to offer decision-making practice to children.

#245

Walking with God and
family living means . . .   practicing planning.

"See, everything has become new!" (2 Cor 5:17 NRSV)

Planning goes hand in hand with decision making, and is also good practice. Parents can ask their child to plan how he or she would rearrange his or her room. Then for more practice, try planning for a new school, a new vacation, or a new way to spend the summer. Recognize and describe the possible outcomes. If this planning is written down, or it can be dictated by a young child, a parent can put a star by the points that will require a decision. Then play "what would you do if _____," if the books don't fit on that bookshelf? Ask for alternative paths that might be possible. Ask parents to notice if children can recognize and predict *more* possible outcomes, with practice. Notice if their child shows pride in having an opinion and volunteers it. Can the child give reasons for it? Are the children confident that their view or plan will be respected even if not accepted? Happier, more responsive children are a wonderful benefit of practicing these thinking skills, plus the child gains confidence that will last a lifetime. A child can even plan what questions to ask the doctor when going for a regular checkup.

Lord, help us plan ahead with children,
for fun and for important activities.

#246

***Walking with God and
family living means . . .***   understanding that all people have feelings.

"Let us then pursue what makes for peace and for mutual upbuilding."
(Rom 14:19 NRSV)

Children need to understand that all people have feelings and like to be understood. Furthermore, knowing something about a person or situation helps one to guess or to try to understand how people feel and why events occur. Knowing more about another culture, its history, geography, folk stories, and even its jokes is a very good way to understand the people from that culture. The world history and geography series or Home Learning Enablers called *Around the World in 180 Days* on the Web site www.homelearning.org/ helps children understand the global village we now live in.

Building empathy for other people whether friends and neighbors, or from distant cultures, can be developed. By looking at pictures of people laughing or crying, parents can then ask the child how this person feels and why as a start. Feelings and stages of development are universal across all cultures, and children can learn to identify this. For example, babies and young children from all cultures have many attributes in common: laughing, crying, wanting food, and wanting their mothers. Discuss some of the pictures from Tanzania, Africa at the end of this book.

Parents can notice if their child begins to show a greater concern for the feelings and problems of others. Then they can watch to see if the child guesses (or hypothesizes) about how people feel in movies or on TV shows. Parents can ask their child to say *why* he or she thinks this, to see if thinking skills are developing.

Lord, help us, young and old, to learn to live as one family of God.

#247

Walking with God and family living means . . .   practicing organizing.

"We have known and believe the love that God has for us. God is love and those who abide in love abide in God, and God abides in them." (1 John 4:16 NRSV)

Being in charge of planning and organizing, with some understanding of the feelings of others involved, helps a child feel independent and confident. Planning for an outing or a discussion about what he or she will need for a project can help a child be creative about gathering his or her own materials, and recover from the "nothing to do" doldrums.

Parents can talk with their child about two or three projects, and how to organize the items that are needed. Encourage children first to collect information (the research phase), if that is necessary. Read a book on how to build a puppet stage, or a cookbook for a baking project. What will be needed from the store? What is already available at home? Collect all the items or ingredients and then begin.

A younger child can gather a simple list of items, such as a doll or teddy bear, a blanket and some crackers for an indoor picnic. Parents can have fun noticing if the child plans out loud for some of his or her activities. Notice if he or she uses more words to describe what needs to be gathered before the project can start. Does he or she actually gather some materials, rather than expecting the parent to get them? As the child gets older, facilitate these projects with trips to the store or other helps that are needed. Notice if the child enjoys selecting activities he or she can organize without help. Other ideas include the following: What do you need for a backyard picnic? What do you need for a family picture album? What do you need for a birthday party? Does the child do this more and more often? Developing and practicing thinking skills at home with children can be a source of unending insight, surprise, and enjoyment for parents. As children practice estimating, predicting, giving reasons to support decision making, and doing problem solving, they build skills and confidence that will last a lifetime. This is a child becoming confident and competent.

Lord, help us pick up on our children's interests and projects as they get older.

#248

Walking with God and
family living means . . .   helping develop readiness to read and write.

"So Philip ran to him and heard him reading Isaiah the prophet and asked, 'Do you understand what you are reading?'" (Acts 8:30 ESV)

Reading builds on thinking. As a parent helps and if a child enjoys help, strategies such as the ones in this group of readings and in the next few meditations are able to make a child's school life much more enjoyable and successful. His or her reading enjoyment will last a lifetime; it is not just an early-years skill. Reading and talking together often develops a very satisfying relationship between parent and child, and children are delighted with the adult attention. Today it is thought that "writing to read" by practicing letters and inviting dictation helps children to read.

Brain growth and development now being charted in neuroscience by researchers show an extraordinary pattern of growth and definition. Before birth, the brain consists of 100 billion neurons (brain cells) connected by a circuitry of synapses through which impulses flow. In the first three years of life, the brain produces even more synapses, twice as many as it will eventually need. Up to 3 trillion connections can be built as the brain gets thicker and denser through the developmental years. During this time and throughout childhood, connections that receive repeated stimulation from speech, emotional experiences, touch, movement, sights, and sound (all the senses plus the emotions) are strengthened and protected. Unused connections are carved away as time goes by. Thus the brain is wired in a unique pattern for each human being by the interplay of genetic inheritance and early experience. This wiring becomes the foundation of intellect and emotion throughout life.

Lord, help us help children "break the code" for reading and understanding.

#249

***Walking with God and
family living means . . .***   seeing windows of opportunity.

"My purpose shall stand, and I will fulfill my intention." (Is 46:10 NRSV)

There are distinct windows of opportunity during the formation of different aspects of the intellect, scientists and researchers know. Speech development takes place over a long period of time as the recognition of speech begins at birth (or even before birth, as the fetus can hear the sounds of a particular language) and continues until about age ten. The acquisition of vocabulary begins in earnest at about fifteen to eighteen months and continues throughout life. Some aspects of vision, on the other hand, must be developed by age four, which means that early detection of deficits in vision is critical.

The windows of opportunity can also be windows for missed opportunity. Beginning at about two months of age, a child's brain begins to build the circuits that will handle emotions. During the next three years, children whose emotional needs are met develop brains that are wired to handle a range of complex emotions—joy, sadness, envy, empathy, pride and shame, to name a few. Children who experience neglect and abuse, or distress develop a different pattern of wiring, one which dampens happy feelings and diminishes the ability to form healthy attachments to others. It also produces heightened anxiety and stress responses.

With just a little extra attention to developmentally appropriate activities, parents can ensure that their child's brain develops as it should. The new recommendations are the same as the old: read and talk to your children. Hold them and be responsive to their needs. Parents can give their children opportunities to explore and play. Their brains do NOT come genetically determined at birth. They are growing and developing. Around age ten when the brain begins the final pruning of unused connections and the shape of the brain becomes more fixed, change is still possible but becomes more difficult and the chances for complete remediation are less.

Lord, help us be responsive to children in the early years.

#250

Walking with God and
family living means . . .   reading with young children.

"Let the little children come to me and do not stop them; for it is to such as these that the kingdom of heaven belongs." (Matt 19:14 NRSV)

     A family's goal can be to lead a child into reading more easily by exposing the child to reading readiness activities. Starting with reading and talking with the child and working up to some of the other activities described, this can give a child a leg-up in first grade. If a child does learn to read early, it's fine as research has shown that early-reading children maintain their reading achievement over the years. One founder of early reading was the nineteenth century Italian educator, Maria Montessori, whose teachings are popular in the U. S. She said the best time to learn to read and write is between the ages of four and six.

     Often readiness-to-read activities are just another way for parents and children to enjoy being together, very much like teaching children to play ball. The concept of sequence and easier-to-harder is an important component in all home activities and actually in all learning. Activities suggested in the next few readings provide a springboard for this sequential approach.

Lord, help us as we help children "break the code" to written language.

#251

***Walking with God and
family living means . . .***   reading and talking to young children.

"All my words that I shall speak to you receive in your heart." (Ez 3:10 NRSV)

Between the ages of two years and four years, a child will have rapid language development, from a few words to an average of two thousand. Adults can help enormously with this development by reading and talking to young children. By helping their children gain new words, parents smooth many of the frustrations felt by young children when they can't explain what they mean. A child has to learn to talk before learning to read. A child who is able to communicate frustration is ultimately a happier child. Parents can try fun questions such as "How would you describe xxx?" to help a child see and describe himself or herself, or his or her actions, or his or her world.

Young children receive their parents' words "in their hearts." Adults seek to do this, receive words in the heart, with God's words and with their children's words sometimes.

One of the best ways young children can learn new words is from parents reading out loud to them. A young two-year-old may be happy with a question-and-answer conversation about one or two of the pictures in a storybook. Reading two or three pages of a book and then discussing the story may be just right for a child who is almost three years old. The story line is not important at this age; identifying objects, enjoying time with Mom or Dad, and cuddling close are what is important. An older child may want the whole story.

Take a child to the library. Let the child pick out his or her own books. He or she may be ready for nonfiction books from that part of the children's section of the library. Books about rockets, Native Americans, the Coast Guard, railroads, or almost any subject are great and can be used for the pictures alone. Discussing the captions of the pictures will help your child learn more about his or her world. Ask the children's librarian for book suggestions.

*Lord, help us to remember that young children
receive our words in their hearts.*

#252

**Walking with God and
family living means . . .**   enjoying stories with young children.

"They read from the book, clearly, and they gave the sense, so that people understood the reading." (Neh 8:8 ESV)

To enjoy stories with young children, repeat a lot. When young children two—and three-years-old enjoy a story, they want to hear it over and over again and learn what it means. Help your children enjoy language by substituting new words for old ones and see if they catch you. Or skip a section of the story and see if they notice. Make up a new ending to the story and then encourage them to do the same. This will really show you that they understand the story.

Some simple how-to's include the following: When reading to young children, first discuss the picture on the first page and the title to set a basic understanding of what is to come. Then a parent can ask questions to help a child think: What does he or she think the book is about? What clues does the child have? Then use a lot of sound effects! Read enthusiastically and with drama. Encourage children to observe details, ask questions, guess what happens next, and discuss what's going on. For instance, "Why do you think the boy ran away?" Point out that the page numbers change as you turn the page.

Lord, remind us to enjoy young children's answers about reading and stories.

#253

Walking with God and
family living means . . .   discussing how to tell if a book is good.

"Let your light shine before others, so that they may see your good works and give glory." (Matt 5:16 NRSV)

A discussion with your child about how to tell if a book is good might include the following: Do you and the child enjoy the experience? Are there brightly colored, realistic pictures? Can the children tell what the pictures are? Is the story simple and easy to identify with? Since two-, three-, and four-year-olds are the center of their own worlds, they like stories in which they can see themselves. They particularly enjoy and identify with talking animals or machines. Is there a lot of repetition? A young child likes to know what to expect. This gives him or her a chance to join in the fun. Does it have clear language? Do the books show both men and women, and people of all races, doing a variety of things?

There are many benefits of reading to young children. Reading lets the child know that you think reading is important in the home, or wherever you are. According to research, it helps children do better in school. Reading together is a time for loving and warmth; it helps children associate this intellectual and stimulating experience with a warm and friendly time.

Lord, as we predict book endings with our children,
let us enjoy the books along with children.

#254

Walking with God and
family living means . . .   talking about reading with children.

"He grew strong in his faith being fully convinced that God was able to do what he had promised." (Rom 4:20-21 NRSV)

Talking activities for reading with young children can include asking children questions while reading aloud such as the following, but only ask three or four questions at any one time: What is happening? What has happened? What do you think will happen now? How did this happen? What caused this to happen?

Next: What took place before this happened? Where have you seen something like this happen? How could we make something like this happen? How does this compare with what we saw (or did)? How can we do this more easily? How can you do this more quickly?

Or ask: What kind of a thing is it? What is it called? Where is it found? What does it look like? Have you seen anything else like it? Where? When? Then: How is it like other things? How is it different from other things? How can you recognize or identify it? How did it get its name? What other names does it have? What can you do with it? What is it made of? How was it made? What is its purpose? How does it work or operate?

The best kinds of books for children include simple stories and animal stories, ABC books that are clever and different, counting books for beginners, Mother Goose rhymes, learning books, lullabies and bedtime/sleepy stories. Also include books about themselves and other people, and, of course, any book the parent thinks their child would enjoy.

Lord, remind us that the schools do a good job of teaching children to read—once they can talk!

#255

Walking with God and
family living means . . .   helping build eye-hand coordination.

"For God all things are possible." (Mk 10:27 NRSV)

A child needs to master complex visual and muscular skills before he or she can do simple tasks at school like drawing a square or reading an A. Some activities parents can try include the following:

Using a large chalkboard or even the sidewalk and oversized chalk, let children scribble and experiment. Then put two dots on the board at random, and ask the child to draw a straight line from dot to dot, one at a time. Start with short distances and large dots. As the child's skill grows, parents can increase the distances and the pace of the game. Use cardboard or a ruler if that helps. Now ask the child to try drawing different sized circles. Work up to a vertical line and then a horizontal line. This can all be done with chalk outside on the sidewalk.

Another idea is done with a large foam ball that can be suspended from a tree or a door jam inside with a string and tape and swung (gently) as a pendulum. Invite a young child to touch the ball as it passes. Next, try to hit it with a ping-pong-sized paddle. Work down to a smaller "bat," a wooden spoon, perhaps. Parents can tell the child to keep their eye on the ball. This builds eye-hand coordination. A child that has real trouble doing this may need an eye exam and glasses in the future because the eye must adjust rapidly to different distances as the ball swings.

Other coordination builders include doing jumping jacks (fast or slow), or lying flat on the floor and make "angels in the snow" (without snow) by raising hands over the head to touch, and legs apart and together, like a flat jumping jack. These can be done right side only, left side only, and then turn over and the child can do the angels on his or her stomach. Any variety or sequence will be fun for the child. Walking a balance beam, a two-by-four, or even a log also helps a child learn to balance and build coordination.

Lord, help me remember that my faith, and my faith
in this child build a limitless future for the child.

#256

Walking with God and
family living means . . .   playing shapes games with young children.

"Those who are attentive to a matter will prosper, and happy are those who trust in the Lord." (Prov 16:20 NRSV)

In order to read, a child has to be able to recognize shapes. Parents can point out shapes in daily life and in the community. Then move on to matching smaller and more intricate shapes, such as parts of alphabet letters or even whole letters. Then try three or five, then ten sets of large and small alphabet letters to match. Talk about the sounds these make with hard consonants like K,D,P, B, and T, which are good early choices. Next add in one vowel, such as *A* and make some words: *pat*, *tap*, and more rhymes. One can increase the sets of large and small letters to fifteen and then to twenty-six, as the child learns to match more and more.

Matching numbers, starting with one and moving up to a hundred, a thousand, and a million is also a form of matching shapes. Learning to count by twos and then by fives and tens can follow as the child matures.

As children learn new words, parents can make a train of these words, or print them on cardboard for the child to carry around. Reading pictures extends this beginning reading by looking carefully at drawings and photographs. Researchers have observed that children can learn and remember words that are important to them such as "Santa Claus" or "Grandma."

Lord, remind us that children's hearing is often better than their sight.

#257

**Walking with God and
family living means . . .**   keeping older children reading

"Lay aside immaturity, and live, and walk in the way of insight."
(Prov 9:16 NRSV)

Once a child learns to read, it's a temptation for adults to relax and let the schools take over. However reading is a skill, and early reading needs to grow and develop if it's to have continuing meaning in a person's life. Parents should not deceive themselves that their child's school is taking care of all of a child's reading needs. For one thing, school libraries are not open at times when children need them most—in evenings and on weekends. Parents can realize that any game that a child reads to figure out how to play is really a reading game.

Using the library gives more encouragement for older children in addition to using the Internet. Helping children WANT to read using the visual and listening activities mentioned in this section of *Walking with God* readings comes from children seeing that reading will give him or her pleasure and information. Thanks to many community libraries, which are open on weekends on Saturdays, if not all weekend, and in the evenings, families can make a weekly trip to the library. The nonfiction section of the children's library area is loaded with books on various topics with interesting pictures that can be good for discussion only if the reading level is too high. Parents can let their child browse in the library, to make book discoveries. If a book a child selects seems too hard, a parent can check out another book quietly that is just the right level, and bring it out later, after reading the ones the child has chosen together.

Furthermore, parents can find out the child's own interests and capitalize on them. This will stimulate curiosity and helps avoid imposing the adult's interests on a child, thus building the child's thinking and decision-making skills—in an area about which most parents don't have strong opinions.

Lord, help us all never to grow out of asking why.

#258

Walking with God and
family living means . . .   encouraging reading as a daily habit.

"Make a joyful noise to the Lord, all the earth; break forth in joyous song and sing praises." (Ps 98:4 ESV)

Parents can encourage children to take turns reading aloud to others. Instead of reading *to* beginning readers, read *with* them. Have the child read *to* you. Parents can take roles and act out dramatic stories, songs, or even poems with the child. If possible, they can record the reading or singing to be played later. It's fun to take turns reading every other page. Even sixth graders welcome this for interesting, but harder books.

Let younger children dictate stories and draw pictures to illustrate their words. Then they can read them back to you. A primary grade child, with eye-hand coordination that is still developing, appreciates being able to dictate a homework assignment to a parent, and then copying back his or her own words. This way if the child's thoughts get ahead of a hand that's gotten tired trying to write, at least the thoughts are captured.

Take books along on family outings such as picnics for reading aloud. Reading in the car is particularly good—especially when stuck in traffic. Newspapers can even be read for headlines during long stoplights, and reading time can turn commuting time into something useful and interesting.

Lord, help us encourage a growing maturity in reading habits.

#259

***Walking with God and
family living means . . .***   using more reading resources.

"But the word of the Lord, remains forever." (1 Pt 1:25 ESV)

Children's magazines, books, encyclopedias, computer software, and the Internet are all useful reading resources. Why bother to buy books when parents can go to the library and take them out? However, some books need to be around to be read over and over, especially the Bible and a children's Bible. Many parents have noticed that their children do read books over and over, and when they ask why; the answer is "I like them." That is a good reason to have some special books around the house. When buying books, discuss which books to buy with the child: What subjects? What are some favorite books? If relatives want to give books as presents, parents can make up a list and share it. Look carefully at school book fairs for recommended books also. Magazines are handled in the same way. What are the child's special interests? Magazines are fun because they come with new reading material once a month sometimes addressed to the child, without needing a trip to the library or store.

Encyclopedias are an important home research resource, but today, many CD-ROM and Internet encyclopedias are easy and inexpensive to use with a computer. They are quite extensive, and fun to browse. Many or most have sound effects—the lion roars, the waterfall in Peru sounds like falling water, and so forth. The hypertext aspect also adds to the usability with many offerings, as the child or parent can just click on a word and learn more about that subject. CD-ROMs and DVDs are particularly suitable for children as they are nearly unbreakable and standardized, handling in the same way as music CDs. Other CD-ROMs are also available such as dictionaries, thesauruses, and many "bookshelf" extras. DVDs widen the range of resources available.

Lord, thank you for the abundant resources available for reading.

#260

***Walking with God and
family living means . . .***   encouraging writing and communication.

"In the beginning was the word, and the word was with God and the word was God." (John 1:1 ESV)

Some people say that written language is a gift of God. Written language can be traced to 3,000 years BC in ancient China. Writing is a needed skill in communication, more so than ever today with e-mail requiring writing and keyboarding skills. Some simple games can help children get started and practice writing. Even a four—or five-year-old can have fun spelling out letters in a large font (16 pt. or larger) on a computer. Writing "morning messages," in which children leave notes on paper to each other, and receive surprises, also builds writing skills. Simple short words such as "I love you. See you soon." build reading skills, and parents can encourage a written response. The schools are allowing "invented spelling" to encourage first—and second-grade children to write out their thoughts, without worrying about the correct spelling until later grades. The concept of encouraging a child to express him or herself in written form is very much "in" and positive. Texting is fun, and immediate, but hard on spelling skills.

To get started in writing, pictures can be "worth 10,000 words." Parents can invite children to select a colorful picture, to look hard at it, observe the details of it, and figure out what's happening in the picture. Next talk about stories having a beginning, a middle, and an end. Invite the children to make up a story about the picture, and either dictate it to you or write it down themselves. Prime the pump with questions such as "What's happening? What do you think just happened before the picture was taken? How do you think it will all turn out?" Another version of this is to "storyboard" pictures by putting together several pictures in a sequence to tell a story the child makes up. Invite several children and even adults to tell a story about the pictures and notice the variations. Even preschoolers enjoy this, and if the order of the pictures changes, so do the stories. Now try writing down the stories, for the children who can write. Parents can help those who can't. Explain the basics of a story form again—that it has a beginning, a middle and an end. Practice understanding and talking about the beginning, middle, and end of familiar stories such as *The Three Bears* and *Goldilocks*.

Lord, help us provide all the positive inputs we can with children.

#261

***Walking with God and
family living means . . .***   practicing writing and developing stories
with plots.

"Whatever is true, honorable, just, pure, pleasing, and is commendable . . . . if
there is anything worthy of praise, think about these things." (Phil 4:8 NRSV)

Interesting story starters include "round-robin story telling," when each
participant adds another sentence or two. Or one person can tell most of a story
and have a child finish it. Some children even get into a "plot fight" with "she
didn't finish it the way I wanted her to." A "logical order" sequence story can
be a game made from paragraphs cut from a newspaper and then rearranged
into new order to tell a new story. Elementary children enjoy this game and
particularly like puzzling their parents. Small or short paragraphs work best.
Family photographs are another good source of ideas for developing a story.
Or parents can just invite children to think up new captions for photos—that is
writing, and is also practicing the skill of summarizing.

Older children really enjoy "developing an argument" or "making a case."
By nurturing children's natural instinctive ability to argue, they can be taught
to pull together their ideas and synthesize them into a point of view to make the
case. Parents can ask a child to write out "Five good reasons why," whatever the
issue of the moment is. Next ask children to argue the other side of the question,
"Five good reasons why not," and they learn to argue a point, pro and con,
and also practice understanding other points of view. Work up to encouraging
children to write a simple essay with three parts: (1) a subject, (2) a statement
about it, and (3) proof(s) for the statement. These skills will be invaluable when
writing assignments are handed out in school.

Lord, help us help children see two or more sides to a question.

#262

Walking with God and family living means . . . seeing children as people who can accomplish things.

"By this everyone will know . . . if you have love for one another." (John 13:35 NRSV)

Self-esteem is crucial for a child to feel like a do-er and to *be* a do-er, in all activities from learning to throw a ball to learning to read and write. All of the ideas in this section are keyed to the idea of helping all children see themselves as people who can accomplish things. The child who can read and write has an enormous advantage. He or she will be a success in first grade and will go on to mastering complementary skills in math, science, and to develop hobbies and pursue sports. It's up to the parents and teachers to make sure a child builds on his or her reading ability and moves beyond it to more challenging reading and writing. Climbing skills develop with practice in the same way.

Lord, help us to remind children that more practice in doing things makes things go better.

Brennan

#263

Walking with God and family living means . . . extending investigations about math, money, and science.

"Keep on doing the things you have learned and received and heard and seen in me, and the God of peace will be with you." (Phil 4:9 NRSV)

Every place can be a place to extend investigations in math and science, and in the use and awareness of money. Every kitchen, with its sink, stove, refrigerator, dishes, pots, cans, and boxes (some with prices on them) has the necessary ingredients to be a place for learning math and science. Learning to solve problems is the principal reason for studying mathematics. Problem solving is the process of applying previously acquired knowledge to new and unfamiliar situations, according to one definition. Problem-solving strategies involve posing questions, analyzing situations, translating results, illustrating results, drawing diagrams, and using trial and error. Many of these build on thinking skills. In solving problems, parents need to be able to help children apply the rules of logic that are necessary to arrive at valid conclusions. Children shouldn't be afraid to guess at tentative conclusions, and they must be able to subject their own conclusions to their own sharp review.

Parents can think about math activities that really use the home and community to supplement and not duplicate the math children get in school. They can aim to use everyday resources to reinforce books and lessons from school to prepare and to inspire children, to build children's skills and to enhance family life as well. For example, the concept that the whole can be divided into its parts and then reassembled back to the whole can be taught by cutting cupcakes. This is called "invariance of quantity" in math vocabulary. Every time a child pours the same amount of water or sand from one container into a different shaped container, the child is getting basic experience in the math understanding of "reversibility". Piaget, a famous researcher, found that children do not begin to see this concept, and the concept of conservation, until ages 7 to 11, and a three or four year old will argue fiercely that "the tall glass holds more than the short, fat glass." Reversibility is one of the most defining characteristics of age and intelligence, according to the researcher Piaget. If thought is reversible, it can follow a line of reasoning back to where it started.

Lord, help us build children's thinking skills.

#264

Walking with God and
family living means . . .   playing with math concepts at home.

"On the day I called, you answered me, you increased my strength of soul."
(Ps 138:3 NRSV)

Giving my best when doing things with young children can be seemingly simple. Just because these interactions are easy doesn't mean they aren't important to a child's learning. Math concepts can be shown by combining two parts of a cupcake, which *will* combine into a whole, and then combining a cupcake and an apple, which *will not* combine. This is called "combination and dysjunction," and a child who learns these words, or at least this concept (and maybe gets to eat the cupcake), will view it as an old friend when it comes up in math class. From dollars to bagels, from the kitchen to the store, from the bathtub to the car, math is all around the child.

Some activity ideas that are easy, take no money and little teaching time, and can be done at home such as:

* Paper towels or napkins can be folded into all kinds of fractions. Start with half and move to quarters, and eighths. Use a marker to label the parts.
* Find hidden numbers wherever you look in the home. On packages, newspapers, the television or the radio. Only the font size of the number will limit a child; young children have trouble seeing small letters and numbers even up through ages six or seven.
* Find shapes all over the kitchen: circles, squares, and triangles.
* Parents can have children count the settings when they set the table, measure ingredients in cooking, time cooking projects, and read the percentages of nutrition supplied by foods on the shelf. Cut recipes in half or double them for a child who is in fourth grade or above.
* Play store with a juice or milk carton and other boxes and cans. Real money can be used in multiples of pennies and nickels to teach that five pennies equals a nickel. Work up to dimes and quarters. Have the child price the item: How much for a carton of milk? a can of soup? a box of cereal? Then compare prices with the ads in the newspaper.
* Cut paper plates in half in an uneven way and put an addition or subtraction problem on one half and the answer on the other half. This makes a puzzle. Keep them together in a large envelope.

Lord, help us to remember that little things are learnings too.

#265

Walking with God and
family living means . . .   having more fun with math at home.

"Make a firm covenant in writing." (Neh 9:38 ESV)

Give a child a newspaper and have him or her circle all the foods that cost less than $1 and put a square around all the foods that cost more than $1. An older child can look for clothes under $20 or furniture under $50, or even a car (in the Classified Ads) under $3,000. Next do this with a catalog that comes in the mail. Ask the child to figure out the "best buys" at the stores. More ideas include the following:

* Encourage children to help clip coupons and take them to the store to match up with the items. Parents can split the coupon payoff with the child.
* Measure the living room with a yard stick, a tape measure, a string—almost anything can be used to measure. Measure a lamp. How wide is the room? How long is a table? Teachers call this "using a number line," and any early experience with numbers is invaluable. Parents can first have their child guess the measurements.
* Use the TV schedule to practice planning time and making selections about what and when to watch. Give the children a total time limit and have them make their choices to fill up an hour or two. Encouraging children to make the choices gives decision making practice and cuts down on their need to watch too much television. Talk about all the numbers in sports and on television.

Family finance assistance can be found in the home. Give a school age child a budget of a certain amount and ask them to plan a new wardrobe from a catalog. Pretend all their clothes were washed away in a hurricane or a flood, or some other similar catastrophe.

Lord, help us raise "financially literate" children.

#266

Walking with God and family living means . . .   playing math games with young children.

"Little children, let us love, not in word or speech, but in truth and action." (1 John 3:10 ESV)

Loving in action can mean widening a child's learning in simple around-the-house ways. Teach a young child his or her address and telephone number, perhaps to the tune of the Alphabet Song. Have the child print phone numbers of friends and relatives on a cardboard and keep it near the phone as the child's "phone book." In the bathroom, talk about weights with the family scale, and then weigh many different things—the trash basket, clothing, a glass of water. First, let the child guess what something will weigh, then do research and find out. Count the tiles in one part of the bathroom.

Young children love water play in the bathtub or sink. Provide plastic cups and containers. These might be free toys from grocery packaging that can be washed up and recycled. In the bedroom match laundry items. Watch the clock—estimate times: how long to match the socks? how long before the TV show starts? ("About as long as the TV show" is one answer—as many young children can understand this half hour unit of time). Every school age child should have his or her own alarm clock. Place a calendar in every child's room—use free calendars with big font numbers if possible. Check off the days until special events happen.

Use the child's allowance to teach number combinations. Start a personal savings account for the child, with additions to be made regularly. Practice addition and subtraction.

Lord, help us build "number memory" in children.

#267

***Walking with God and
family living means . . .***   playing math games with graphs and charts.

"God is our refuge and strength, a very present help in trouble." (Ps 46:1 NRSV)

Understanding, aided by graphs or a chart, can lead to peace and strength when complex situations present themselves. A graph or a chart illustrates quickly something that might take many words to explain. Try doing a chart or a spreadsheet or graph on a computer with the different heights of family members. Children think this is fun when done with varying lengths of toilet paper, even. Put a date on the paper chart or the computer, as next month or next year the chart will be different as the heights will be different. Do a pie chart of the family budget, and put in the slices for monthly expenditures for food, clothes, transportation, education, insurance, and entertainment. Parents can give children an understanding of this math essential by dividing up the "Family Finances Pie." Always ask children to think whether the results are "reasonable." For example, "Is a $8,000 hotel bill reasonable for three days?" Make up preposterous examples and play a game with this. When an exaggerated example presents itself in the media, point it out.

Lord, help us to help our children use clarity in their thinking.

#268

**Walking with God and
family living means . . .**   building money value awareness and
encouraging financial literacy.

"God blessed them, and God said to them, "Be fruitful and multiply, and fill
the earth." (Gen 1:27-28 NRSV)

Trying to pass along to children a healthy attitude toward money is a
challenge for any parent that wants to teach restraint and responsibility in a
society that has seemed not to value those traits. Many teens work after school
or on weekends for their own discretionary income for entertainment, trendy
clothes, or food. Saving for college and helping the family and charity may not
be in their plans.

In a recent survey, only 18 percent of teens and 37 percent of adults knew
that the annual percentage rate is the best factor to show the cost of a loan. In
learning to be a knowledgeable shopper, teens and adults need to learn about
percentage rates and credit cards. Furthermore, auto insurance can vary by 100
percent in the same regional area with the same driving record. Being financially
literate is as important as being media literate in the twenty-first century.

When children are given incentives and opportunities to learn about money,
they catch on quickly, it has been found. They save and shop around for bargains.
This also helps good decision-making and planning practice. Tell the child in
advance how much you plan to spend on clothes and let the child figure out
what to buy and help plan the spending. A solution to children thinking that
parents are rich and extravagant is setting a workable allowance plan. Parents
have about ten years to develop money wisdom in children, ages five to fifteen
approximately, and to resist peer pressure in money areas. All of this is good
math practice also.

Lord, help us to raise money-wise children.

#269

Walking with God and
family living means . . .   family leadership.

"Jesus said to him, 'If you are able!—all things can be done for the one who believes.'" (Mk 9:23 NRSV)

Family leadership can be like a long garden hose or a slow-to-warm-up shower. It seems to parents that it takes a long time for anything to get through to children, but even a trickle of input eventually gets through. If conscious efforts are made, more leadership of the family gets through faster. But if the "water" is turned off (giving up, or separation and divorce), eventually the person's leadership is turned off too. However, the time delay in results may fool a parent into adjusting too late or too much just like in a shower. When one is dealing with systems, including family systems, one must expect time delays and not expect to see the results of change immediately. A system maintains its existence and functions as a whole through the interaction of its parts, and the behavior of different systems and including family systems depends on how the parts are related, rather than on the parts themselves. This concept helps one to understand many different systems and to know that the dynamic complexity comes from the great number of possible connections between the parts—because each part may have a number of different states of being—think of a preschooler or a teenager, for instance, for different "states of being."

Even if parents forget to use positive encouragement and leadership, some positive results are still felt. This is called a "balancing" system because the level of results does not go down even though there is little effort made to raise it or it appears that no one is doing anything. However, with input and encouragement from Mom or Dad, the system becomes a "reinforcing" system and does even more than just maintaining the same level, helping a fuller "flow" of water in the hose, the "flowers to bloom," and/or the children to feel a more positive effect.

Lord, help us to build and develop family strength
and traditions that are long lasting.

#270

Walking with God and
family living means . . .   being gentle but firm with children.

"And he will give you the desires of your heart." (Ps 37:4 NRSV)

Family leadership in the family means respecting the child and the parent, and both are involved in new practices when setting new goals. This type of parenting or family leadership is linked to many aspects of competence in children, which shows up as children grow into adolescence. These positive aspects include high self-esteem, academic achievement and involvement in school learning, social and moral maturity, and level of educational attainment. Family leadership also includes authoritative, or the gentle but firm style of parenting, but extends further than that. This gentle but firm style of parenting is characterized by parents who make reasonable demands on their children based on their maturity, hold firm on these requests and set limits, and require obedience while also giving guidance. They also express warmth and affection. They listen patiently to their child's point of view and encourage participation in family decision making.

Lord, help us be clear with our children with warmth and affection.

#271

***Walking with God and
family living means . . .***   creating traditions, rituals, and memories.

"My purpose is that they may be encouraged in heart and united in love, so that they may have the full riches of complete understanding, in order that they may know the mystery of God." (Col 2:2-3 NIV)

Within the family, leadership continues like a long garden hose. Any parent of adult children can tell you of family "traditions" their children described as adults that were originally put into place and done for some other reason. "We always had to pick Daddy up"—we only had one car; "We watched that every Sunday night"—because nothing else acceptable was on television, are two examples. When more positive images and activities, plus listening and encouragement, are put into the hose or pipeline intentionally, the children come out with more. They come out with quite a lot even if a small amount or very little parent/family leadership and encouragement is consciously done. The love and care of parents, and their continuous support, do lay a foundation so that those they care for will have full and enriching lives. Therefore continuous support from the Lord is needed in helping the family. This becomes a "reinforcing system" and not just a minimal "balancing system." When the level of effort in parenting is low, the children's abilities may still tend to rise, but not as fast.

Lord, help us encourage our children and the children around us.

#272

**Walking with God and
family living means . . .**   trying new goals and new processes.

"Strive first for the kingdom of God and his righteousness, and all these things will be given to you as well." (Matt 6:33 NRSV)

Leadership for individual parents, families, and organizations means planning, and planning for change. Leadership behaviors are designed to accomplish change for the improvement of the family group, not just for change's sake. Managing behavior and responsibilities may reside in the same person in a family as leadership responsibilities, but these just keep things going: systems, practices, rules, car maintenance, and housework—these are the areas that fall under management and responsibility. Responsibility and management alone are not leadership. They are just using old practices to obtain old goals. Leadership would be using old practices to obtain new goals, or leadership would be using new practices to achieve old, ongoing goals, or even new practices to reach new goals for a family or an individual.

A new goal for a family might be to help children in school by becoming a "learning family." For example, to learn more about the world, perhaps through world history and geography, a new practice would be to try to learn new things about specific countries or areas using home-learning activities. An adult could try out some activities, maybe even read up and prepare some ideas or activities while on an airplane to or from another country for a meeting. For younger children folk stories and folk songs teach a lot about other countries and about other parts of our own country, such as cowboy songs for eastern children. Inviting guests from another country is another alternative.

Lord, help us to build on old practices and bring in new ones.

#273

***Walking with God and
family living means . . .***   holding the vision.

"I will strengthen you, I will help you, I will uphold you with my victorious right hand." (Is 41:10 NRSV)

A long-range example of family leadership can be seen in the example of a mother of four young children who was suddenly widowed when her husband was killed in the crash of a small airplane. She had to work to maintain her family, and eventually worked for a large university. All of her four children were able to attend and graduate from that university with her tuition benefits, tuition free. This had been an old goal of both parents achieved through new practices, when the family circumstances changed suddenly and new parent leadership was needed. Holding this vision clearly helped the *children* persevere toward graduation also. A similar example can be seen in a divorced mother whose four teenagers eventually went to college and graduate schools—but not at the same university, through a combination of loans, jobs, co-op jobs, and internships plus leadership and vision shared by the parent.

Other simple applications for families might be to have a new "Family Fitness Goal" for one year and actively try to plan hikes and a camping trip. (Or even practice fitness moves while cleaning together). An old goal for individuals is often "I should lose some weight," but what about a new "Body Plan" for a long life, that includes doctor's or clinic appointments and a "vision" for ages forty through ninety (or one hundred)? The "old process" of diet and exercise helps with this new (or old) goal also.

Lord, help us to persevere in your steadfast love.

#274

Walking with God and family living means . . .   balancing the positive.

"May our Lord Jesus Christ himself and God our Father, who loved us and by his grace gave us eternal encouragement and good hope, encourage your hearts and strengthen you in every good deed and word." (2 Thes 2:16-17 NIV)

The philosophy and approach of moving children toward goals without making power or status differentials obvious, helps bring success to families and to any group. This approach works well within families. Saying to a child "Because I said so" may be needed occasionally, but every time a power status differential ("I am the 'powerful' adult") is emphasized, there is usually a balancing act or a cost put forth by the child, certainly after ages nine or ten, (such as "You can't make me" or "Spank me—see if I care" as two examples). Autocratic parenting (harsh and bossy) and using coercive power has been called *authoritarian* parenting and builds costs and teaches as well as models defiance. Obviously the type of positive leadership that is part of what is called positive or *authoritative* parenting requires interpersonal interaction skills to persuade children, and these same skills apply to leading adults also.

Lord, help us be positive parents.

#275

***Walking with God and
family living means . . .***   having realistic expectations of children.

"I will instruct you and teach you in the way you should go," says the Lord.
(Ps 32:8 NIV)

There are different *sources* of power described in management theory and management in family leadership can be helped by combining two or three of these to strengthen parenting. Power is the *ability* to influence others and is granted from below. Sources of power are ways one can seek to influence another's behavior: *Reward Power* derives from the capacity of one person to reward another person in some way in exchange for their compliance with desired behavior. This compliance is expected to happen without supervision and works best when the results of the person accepting direction and providing effort that *can be seen*. As one three-year-old said, "We're playing 'character'. That's when I do what I'm supposed to even when Daddy isn't watching." If behavior has been reinforced at the time, then it can easily be referred to later when the father or the mother is giving the child a raise in allowance, or selecting a family member to be honored in some way such as taken to dinner or lunch or out to breakfast, in a one-to-one situation.

However the issue of compliance really relates to an accurate understanding of what children's abilities are at each age. So often problems arise because expectations aren't realistic. Expectations need to take into account the developmental age of the child. *Coercive Power* is harsh and bossy and is not just withholding rewards, but it is the capacity to actually inflict something negative on a person, child or adult. The outcome of the use of this kind of power is not good, and it tends to cause children in families, to cover up, to lie, to make false statements and in general to sabotage the goals of the family.

Expert guidance and legitimate, authoritative power can be built and come somewhat naturally with the parenting role unless there is a severe breach of trust.

Lord, help us to build trust and respect with our children.

#276

**Walking with God and
family living means . . .**   having faith in ourselves as parents.

"Show by your life that your good works are done with gentleness born of wisdom." (Jas 3:13 NRSV)

More kinds of "power" that can be increased include legitimate power and referent power. *Legitimate Power* is just that: the parent is the parent, so family members expect him or her to lead and ask them to do things. However, the efforts to initiate change made by the parent "leader" must appear to be "reasonable and correct" to the family group or else the leader will need to inform them of his or her point of view or have them understand more about his or her responsibility. Even young children have a sense of fairness and correctness. Letting people know about one's responsibilities is a good idea in families.

Referent Power is a source of power that describes a situation in which family members find the parent so attractive, competent, and understanding, that they want to identify with him or her. They want to please the parent by seeking to do as he or she asks. This is the kind of parent who inspires people and often they have no idea of the power that person even has over them. This is one of the most powerful sources of power and a valuable source for all parents. It is also "modeling" of the best kind. It is important for parents to be family leaders and to model ways to inspire the children in a family. It is a well-known saying, "people (and children) do as you do, not as you say."

Lord, help us to be a parent who inspires children.

#277

Walking with God and
family living means . . . helping children learn from positive
interactions.

"Your word is a lamp to my feet, O Lord, and a light for my path."
(Ps 119:105 NIV)

When a person, young or old, models his or her behavior after a parent, it allows the parent great influence over the young person. Children do things then because they like the parent and they want to do something the parent might like, and/or they want to be like the parent. Adults and teenagers will have different areas in their lives, or "groups of reference," which might each have a different referent person after whom they model, such as work or school life, social life, family life, or religious life. Younger children often have only the family from which to learn positive interactions.

> _Lord, help our children to learn positive interactions from us,_
> _even if they borrow Mom's costume jewelry._

Kerry

#278

**Walking with God and
family living means . . .** learning new paths.

"Show me your ways, Oh Lord, teach me your paths; guide me in your truth and teach me, for you are God, my savior, and my hope is in you all day long." (Ps 25:4-5 NIV)

Expert power is easy to acquire and *can* be acquired. This lies in the children's view that the parent has more knowledge and ability in a given area that is, is more expert in a particular area including parenting. This is an easy power source to add to, by updating one's knowledge with child development information and courses, keeping up with parenting reading—and talking about it—informally. Adults and children will provide support and follow directions without supervision in relationship to how expert they think the leader is. Children are affected by their developmental age in following directions, but children also value expertise in the adults around them in the family. Modeling lifelong learning as a parent to the children in a family gives them an invaluable gift. Putting in place family traditions, celebrations, and rituals are part of expert parenting in a purposeful family. Even habits, routines, and customs of service and of practicing, are valuable.

The strategies parent authority figures use to gain obedience will influence the likelihood of compliance or obedience and the types of noncompliance children will display. Early childhood parenting literature separates these strategies into three types: (1)negative control, (2)control, and (3)guidance. *Negative control*, like coercive power, conveys a negative feeling toward the child (e.g., anger, spanking, slapping, annoyance, criticism, threatening, and other punishments.) *Control* includes giving orders, offering no choice, and/or offering a reward contingent upon compliance, somewhat like reward power. *Guidance* leads to the results most parents want. Read more on this in the next reading.

Lord, help us to know what a difference we can make in a child's life.

#279

***Walking with God and
family living means . . .***   using positive guidance with children.

"Teach me to do your will, for you are my God; may your good Spirit lead me on level ground." (Ps 143:10 ESV)

Guidance is verbal or physical instruction that is nonintrusive and relates to the child's behavior, such as suggesting, persuading, "talking through," and sitting next to the child to show him or her something. This approach has different effects on the child in the long run than harsh approaches.

Since good and effective discipline and teaching are a form of family leadership, it is interesting to note that those researchers studying parental control strategies or uses of power found that reward power combined with guidance using expert power and legitimate power gained a higher frequency of obedience and compliance from children and that negative control or coercive power gained a higher frequency of defiance from children. They found that control, tempered by guidance, gives the child clear information about what is wanted while not being threatening. Since children are sorting out issues of autonomy and *self*-control throughout childhood, with more testing of limits at some ages than at others, it is encouraging to note that the child's willingness to cooperate with a parent or any caregiver can be enhanced by the parents' willingness to cooperate with the child. Making suggestions, requests, explanations, and using distraction and bargaining to thus allow the child to negotiate are all indirect parenting management styles that work, while building the child's verbal abilities. Direct strategies, on the other hand, using coercive power, correlate with direct defiance as the child is reflecting the parents' model. The parent is actually *teaching* the child defiance.

Lord, help us to lead by teaching.

#280

Walking with God and family living means . . .   helping children internalize rules and guidance.

"May the Lord direct your hearts to the love of God and to the steadfastness of Christ." (2 Thess 3:5 NRSV)

Parents' main job is working themselves out of a job with children as the children become eighteen to twenty-one or twenty-two years of age, according to a wise old saying. Being clear and consistent on what is expected and respecting the child's autonomy in the long run teaches a child how to internalize the rules, builds competence, and establishes a relationship of trust and flexibility with a parent. This allows for some negotiation. Overly harsh and bossy, and inconsistent parents, can work to reduce the incidence of temper tantrums caused by too much use of coercive power and can learn more effective authoritative parenting. Authoritative parenting would include setting standards, following up on rules while also recognizing the child's autonomy and self-respect in general, by using *guidance* and positive *control*. This will gain better results with any child than a harsh bossy approach.

Lord, help us to build our children's own internal guidance controls and decision-making skills.

#281

**Walking with God and
family living means . . .**   being strong and praising children.

"Be strong, be brave . . . the Lord your God is with you." (Josh 1:9 NRSV)

When dealing with children's ideas, work, or belongings, one should always maximize the child's self-esteem, young or old, and give credit at the end of a project when it is successful even if it's for somewhat routine cleaning of a room or preparing food. The person, child or adult, will be grateful to be saved from the embarrassment of criticism and will learn the value of praise and how to give praise and affirmation in return. A wonderful return is when your child encourages you back. One three-year-old said, "Be strong, Daddy" when he was washing dishes. She had learned the verse above in a song at Vacation Bible School.

*Lord, help us be strong and to know that you, the Lord,
will help us with our children.*

#282

***Walking with God and
family living means . . .***   keeping your word.

"I wait for you O Lord; you will answer, O Lord, My God." (Ps 38:15 NIV)

In a family a child is usually grateful for the years of feeding, clothing, and general caretaking, so the parent usually has a "plus balance for idiosyncrasies" as the source and provider of life and love. (Some children seem not to admit this until they are ages twenty-five to thirty or so however!) Starting from a neutral balance similar to a checking account, or from a positive balance in families, and this can be extremely important in stepfamilies and blended families, then (1) Everything the (family) leader says builds plus or minus credit; 2) The follow-up on what he or she says builds plus or minus credit—getting resources as promised, keeping promises; and 3) The reward or punishment for doing well or poorly toward family goals, builds plus or minus credit. If naughty or "mistaken" behavior is ignored, it is likely to be repeated until some comment is made.

In families, therefore, it builds future trouble if promises are freely given that are not meant to be kept. Children learn honesty and follow-up fairly early, and at worst children can become persistent "whiners" when promises are followed up sometimes but not others.

Lord, help us to be consistent with our promises to our children.

#283

Walking with God and
family living means . . .   helping the family to have goals.

"All who listen to my instructions and follow them are wise, like a man who built his house on solid rock." (Matt 7:24 LB)

Providing social support for family groups and family members can be a most important activity. This is a "causal or input variable" that a parent leader can control that leads to and can build good attitudes. Love and morale building in a family are irreplaceable supports. Also family leaders who are always clarifying the overall goals of the family and reminding children of their importance can be the most successful. Even children like to be reminded of their importance and clarifying tasks and steps to accomplish them for a family house cleaning morning, for example, helps. This is guidance combined with control.

Lord, help us to remind others of their importance, especially children.

#284

**Walking with God and
family living means . . .**   learning to be problem solvers.

"Blessed are those who keep justice, who practice righteousness at all times."
(Ps 106:3 NASB)

Good leaders of all kinds know what they are about. Taking parenting
courses, and reading books to keep up, helps parents to be problem solvers and
helps them teach and educate children in a "learning family." Learning about
child and adult development is important. While family leaders can be friendly
with their children, they don't use swear words or tell dirty jokes, go out and
party with their teenagers, or share details about their recent divorce. By being
sure to do the things that only a parent as a leader can do and not always being
tempted to *be* one of the teenagers, including not dressing like one, they can
serve their families better. This is not to say that they do not pitch in when a
child needs help, but it is important to reserve time for planning and keeping
up with parenting. Single parents also can remember not to lean on a young
son to "be the man of the family" or in some way load a child with a burden
too heavy to carry at a young age.

Lord, help us to be adult problem solvers for our children.

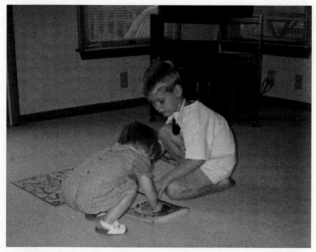

Brennan

#285

***Walking with God and
family living means ...***   abiding in his love.

"If you keep my commandments, you will abide in my love; just as I have kept my Father's commandments, and abide in his love." (John 15:10 NRSV)

Providing general supervision means not close and specific supervision, but watching over children in a *general* way. The idea here is that children are competent and are trusted to do a good job. General training and direction can be offered first and at family meetings. It was found that specific, close supervision makes people, children and adults, feel mistrusted. Even nosy praise can "hem them in." Children and adults who feel mistrusted immediately develop attitudes of disloyalty and nonsupport for the family goals. This is an important concept when teenagers are involved who are trying to be their own people and be somewhat separate from the family, anyway. Nosy praise or supervision annoys them even more when they are annoyed anyway.

*Lord, help us to understand the stages our children are in,
and to love them.*

#286

Walking with God and
family living means . . .   changing your attitude.

"'I will pour water on the thirsty land, and streams on the dry ground; I will pour out my spirit on your offspring, and my blessing on your descendants,' says the Lord." (Is 44:3 NIV)

Attitude changing for families can be viewed as having three sets of variables. If one wants to effect long-term change, one must have input into the first set, which then affects the second set, and then the third set. These variables as applied to the family might look as follows: First, *causal or input variables,* which the family has some control over include: values, love, interpersonal relations, money, rewards, rules, and times together, celebrations and traditions. Second, *intervening variables* that include perceptions, attitudes, and loyalty which build, based on the input variables. New attitudes for new times may be needed. These can be negative also and include antagonism and backbiting or criticism. Third, *end or action variables* that *result* from the attitudes and loyalty in a family and include as an end goal positive results, cooperation among family group members; or on the negative side, waste, lying, stealing, run away children, and/or children missing curfew or family activities. Remember the need to consider the *time* factor in the attitude-changing process. The time or family "organizational lag" needed is six months to two years between sets of variables to effect a change in the next set. In other words don't judge an effort until more than one or even two or three years have passed. Stepfamilies or foster families may need a full two years between sets of variables. This means two years of inputs and supportive loving family activities, two years for attitude changing and loyalty building, and maybe four to six years before positive results start to show, but these are well worth the wait.

Lord, help us to build happy, competent family members.

#287

Walking with God and
family living means . . .   going back to the beginning.

"Children's children are a crown to the aged, and parents are the pride of their children." (Prov 17:6 NIV)

If undesirable behaviors in the end variables are found when the concept mentioned in the last reading is applied to a specific family, plans can be made to start a change in the input or causal variables. In a family perhaps it is time to have the family as a group review and update a family practice. Long hours at work are a problem for some parents, but three-day weekend breaks, family leave, and telecommuting (or partial telecommuting) from home are some possible solutions.

An example of a simple change illustrating the effects of input or causal variables can be seen in the story of Sue, a financial vice president in a large bank with two small children. She was working eighty to ninety hours a week with her travel and felt this was just too detrimental to her young children. Her boss adjusted her schedule to three days a week, thus making it professional part-time work with a five-day per-week secretary, and now she probably works almost forty hours and travels one day in those three days, but she is still very productive for the bank, still traveling, and is home two additional days with her children.

Sue was very grateful (intervening variable) for this understanding attitude on the boss's part and was loyal to the organization and energetic and enthusiastic with the customers for the rest of the time she was employed there, which was several years. The children were pleased to have her at home and much happier, and the babysitter came four days instead of five so Sue could do errands one day. The sitter was happy with a day free. The time lag in this change in Sue's perception from feeling that this was just a career with long hours, to a feeling of gratitude and having happier children, occurred considerably faster than the usual minimum six months on the chart, but then this was a small change.

Lord, help us to wait patiently for results as we try
to follow your guidance and footsteps.

#288

Walking with God and
family living means . . .   building a participative family.

"Then they put their trust in God and would not forget his deeds but would keep his commands." (Ps 78:7 NIV)

In a family, saving money and working as a team to increase effectiveness and resources also requires understanding, cooperation, and teamwork. This benefit of a participative family, characterized by extensive, friendly interaction with productive problem solving, reflects the fact that the most valuable asset of a family is its members. When a parent gets "over-task oriented" (bossy), he or she is selling short his or her most valuable asset—the family members as people. In fact, when yelling "clean it up," "let's have less noise" or harsh and bossy dictator attitudes come in, the most able children slow down and even leave for other activities as soon as possible. In a participative family, parents know what children's hopes and dreams are and help them work toward them.

Some families do not have the vision to build toward a participative parenting approach, and fiercely put in place autocratic, short-term, and even budget-only oriented solutions to problems. The specifics of how a family applies participative parenting and authoritative parenting goals varies with the individual family. People, adults and children, have to be treated well in order to want to put any extra effort into attitude changes and family improvement.

Some families with undemanding and/or unresponsive parenting styles have essentially *no* family management or leadership and bored, nonparticipative children who have few, if any, goals of their own. Parent leaders need to respect each individual family member, within his or her *own* uniqueness, goals, and dreams. Families need love and supportive relationships plus high goals (that is, they need opportunities to do better) plus educational competence, and this will lead to a successful family.

Lord, help us to provide love and support in our family to build cooperation and teamwork.

#289

Walking with God and
family living means ...   understanding the "implementation lag."

"Do not be afraid. Stand firm and you will see the deliverance the Lord will bring to you." (Ex 14:13 NIV)

When one first starts to build new family attitudes, loyalty, and perceptions, seeing results may be slow in the first six months, because resources previously *all* were put into results or material goods. This has been called the "implementation lag." Some family members may have been "just waiting" to let you know their problems. This can happen in a family with teenagers, when a parent first tries an "active listening" approach. One parent noted down a long list from an upset teen, including his little brother "always messed up his room." Maybe storage with doors or covers was needed. Taking dictation about these concerns is an easy indicator of being seriously interested on the part of the parent—it's also interesting! But in this phase of "building attitudes" to survive, parents can listen, and (1) use up things on hand, (2) borrow, (3) cut back in other ways. In the long run, a child that feels *respected* will be much more willing to give the family his or her maximum effort. This leads to the family really becoming a great family. It also leads to children being proud of their family.

Lord, help us to respect our children and listen to their concerns.

#290

Walking with God and
family living means . . .   meeting together.

"Wait for it, it will surely come, it will not delay." (Hab 2:3b NRSV)

In a family the dynamic of "building attitudes" can be accomplished in a family get-together meeting or in one-to-one times with individual children. One can ask them what their concerns are, and then practice "active listening" and even list their concerns on a piece of paper. (This makes any human being feel *really* listened to.) Be patient in listening and then discuss the concerns with the child or children. The effect is that they feel "listened to" and relax a little, so that the child's cooperation picks up and improves. For example, in one family, the third son, who was nine years old, had a list that looked like this: "Joe yells too much; Susie gets into my stuff; no one listens to me; when I suggest a picnic, no one wants to go."

The list was posted on the bulletin board (with permission), and one night the father came in, read it, and said, "What's this about Joe yells too much?" This engendered more discussion, and solutions emerged. Meanwhile, the child was VERY impressed that an adult thought his concerns were important enough to write down on paper and post. Some children have a long list (especially teenagers), but they "lighten up" considerably when they get a chance to verbalize some of their concerns and "be heard." Listing and writing down the concerns patiently, discussing them, and then watching as cooperation picks up works at any age.

Lord, help us to hear what children are trying to tell us.

Dee Dee 1959

#291

**Walking with God and
family living means . . .**   envisioning where we want to go.

"He is a rewarder of them that diligently seek him." (Heb 11:6 KJV)

The family get-together at regular intervals is also important for the discussion of "what we are about" and "where we want to go." A vision can be very powerful, but the more it is spelled out with details from all the family members, the better hold the family group has on the idea. Research shows that this family visioning is what gives successful children the drive to succeed—more powerful than money, opportunity, or the quality of their schools. It is known to help individuals rise above their past in life and act on what is important to them.

Lord, help us to hold the vision.

#292

Walking with God and
family living means . . .   meeting together in love and patience.

"Be patient. Wait for the Lord, and he will come and save you." (Ps 27:14 LB)

Regular family meetings are "safe" opportunities in which everyone is free to say what they think and feel as they cooperate in making decisions and solving problems. It's a time for recognizing good things happening in the family, setting up rules, distributing (or redistributing) tasks fairly, and settling conflicts. Setting aside time together, and planning and having fun together are a foundation for having time to look at what is working and what is not working in the family. As soon as children can use words, they can participate. Ten—to twenty-minute gatherings fit the needs of young children and still provide a special time. As children grow older, they can help decide on the agenda, the food for a treat, and the amount of time needed. One family took time to discuss and decide the benefits of good and bad television as mentioned before. Celebrating happy times and discussing not more than one or, at the most two, problems per meeting helps issues from becoming unwieldy.

Nine practical steps for successful family meetings include the following: (1) Try to meet at regularly scheduled times. (2) Rotate who plans the meetings. (3) Encourage all family members to participate. (4) Discuss one topic and solve one problem at a time. (5) Use "I" messages (not "you" messages) and problem solving strategies. (6) Summarize the discussion to keep the family on track and to focus on one issue at a time. (7) Make a decision by consensus. Remember what is decided this way and post it on the refrigerator if necessary. (8) If things get hot, take a break. Food is always good. (9) End with something fun to do that affirms family members. The key to successful family get-togethers is to be flexible and to use what works in THIS family to handle the ups and downs of family living, and to maintain the family's resiliency and ability to bounce back after experiencing a negative or traumatic event. Families that know how to adapt well to inevitable change tend to have higher marriage and family satisfaction levels it has been found.

Lord, help us to grow together.

#293

***Walking with God and
family living means . . .***   sharing power so it will increase.

"Not by power, not by might but by my spirit says the Lord." (Zech 4:6b)

Sharing in a family has always been important. In fact power actually increases when you share or give it away. There are more ideas and more people involved. Some people think the more power they share or give away, the less they have—a few powerful autocratic fathers and bosses in the old days are good examples of this.

A small example of this can be seen in a family or in a car pool, when the riders are asked to vote on which way to go in a bad traffic jam if the driver has no preference. If the result goes awry, the group doesn't blame the *driver*, but says, "Oh, we should have gone the other way" (e.g., taken the other option). This works wonderfully well with fussy teenagers in a car. If they had a vote in which way to go, they too are stuck with the results in a traffic jam. This concept extends to getting group approval on things that need responsibility shared, especially with volunteers in a family or in a group.

Lord, help us to share the power and dilemmas of family life.

#294

***Walking with God and
family living means . . .***   recognizing abundance in many forms.

"And God is able to provide you with every blessing in abundance, so that by always having enough of everything, you may share abundantly in every good work." (2 Cor 9:8 NRSV)

Anytime the decision-making responsibility is spread over a larger group on important or long-range issues, or even in small issues such as a family car ride that may cause conflict later, the sharing creates a balancing element if things do not go as planned, or do not go well. In addition, much more power is released by combining the brainpower of several thinkers.

However, there *are* times when a leader in a family needs to take the lead and be "in charge." Two things determine whether or not taking charge or "power attempts" will work: (1) The potential costs and the potential consequences of the change or choice the family leader is initiating; and (2) the family's view of the leader's responsibility.

The parent/leader needs to consider the family's view and change it by giving them information about his or her responsibilities if necessary. This is a good time to discuss the budget or work schedules or in the car, the other traffic path, and to develop joint goals to solve the problems creating the need for changes. Working as a group to develop joint goals also implies that positive potential consequences of the change being initiated that include you as the parents, valuing the family's input and ideas. Naturally, this would help to offset a potential cost of the change being initiated—large or small—such as the rearranging of schedules or bedrooms.

Lord, help us build thinking skills and share decision making as we work together as a family.

#295

Walking with God and
family living means . . .   cooperating together.

"If they obey and serve him, they shall spend their days in prosperity, and their years in pleasures." (Job 36:11 KJV)

If a parent gets the family into cooperating in his or her favor, they will accept many more of the ideas suggested. To do this, the parent can talk individually with family members. Hopefully, this "cooperative coalition" would include the entire family, but if the majority or even a few, especially the spouse, understand the change and have had time to make suggestions informally, the "coalition concept" will help the parent-leader(s) reduce costs. Parents need to discuss and plan together to prevent the costs and possible argument involved with presenting an idea and having it rejected. Family dinners are a good time for discussions in any country, as this picture from France shows.

Lord, help us to think clearly and fairly as we work together.

#296

Walking with God and family living means . . . building trust slowly.

"Trust in the Lord with all your heart, and do not rely on your own understanding. In all your ways acknowledge him and he will make straight your paths." (Prov 3:5 KJV)

Our little peculiarities can also be called idiosyncrasies. Idiosyncrasy credit, sometimes called personality credit, develops slowly, over time. The term "idiosyncrasy credit" directly refers to the number of idiosyncrasies (or peculiarities) the new parent/leader (or new step-parent or foster parent), is allowed to have. The "credit' is the amount the family group sees as okay. This amount of credit grows with time.

A new or 'refreshed' parent or a new step-parent now a leader, may see lots of things he or she wants to change in a family. Experts advise new leaders to write all these good ideas in a journal or notebook to use later when their fresh perspective may have worn off and they cannot identify the needs as clearly. Then choose only two new ideas to begin implementing the first six months. The second six months he or she can choose two more. A letter "to the family" on a bulletin board or the refrigerator at home works in many families. The co-parent/leader includes a paragraph on two idiosyncrasies, plus thanks for each person's special efforts. The idea here is that he or she gets to have two idiosyncrasies—even if they are a little unusual—just because he or she *is* the family leader (the parent). This concept is especially important for new stepparents or even new foster parents. An example might be: "Dear Family, Please tell me when you'll be home when you go out and also please say 'excuse me' when you leave the dinner table.'"

Lord, be with stepfamilies as they build trust and develop a new third set of ground rules for a new home life which may be different from the previous two homes.

#297

Walking with God and
family living means . . .   sharing and setting goals with the family.

"If any of you is lacking in wisdom, ask God who gives generously and ungrudgingly, and it will be given you." (Jas 1:5 NRSV)

Having no plan or goal is like planning to go nowhere. If families put one-fourth or one-half of the thought and energy into thinking of family goals together, and informing and educating each other about them, as they do for goal setting in the workplace, more positive, intentional, and purposeful results in families might result. Informing family members' attitudes about individual and joint activities and goals can smooth many family discussions. Of course, this has to be done at an appropriate age level for the children. Concepts of developing a vision, goals, and teaching interactions for developing perceptions have been much more available in organizational literature than in family literature. These concepts are essential for the fast-moving information age to build strong families. To help families develop to their full potential, good planning is always needed.

The common topics of conflict between parents and young children include manners and politeness, taking turns and possession, destructiveness and dirt, hurting, aggression and unkindness, rules of the family, physical space, and independence or autonomy and self-control. Common topics of conflict for teens include regulating behavior, personal style, chores, academic behavior and achievement, interpersonal relations, and finances. Family leadership and becoming more expert in what to expect realistically, helps. Knowing that compliance every time is not the end goal, nor is the appearance of "being in control" to other adults important. The development of the child's autonomy, competence, and internal rules are more important. A mutual parent-child interaction process can be helped by parents becoming more expert in giving age-appropriate guidance and learning, with a variety of conflict resolution strategies. These are valuable end goals and build expert parenting effectiveness, parent leadership, and parent power.

Lord, help us help our children learn to set goals, plan,
and then to see progress toward them.

#298

***Walking with God and
family living means . . .*** helping children learn from missteps.

"For God gives those who please him wisdom, knowledge, and joy."
(Eccl 2:26 LB)

Children build high self-esteem and a strong self-concept at an early age.
They learn that they are desired, loved, and popular. This in turn helps them to
take risks and to make decisions. Because they are popular, they are asked to
make decisions or to take risks first.

But adults as well as children can learn to value the payoffs that result from
risk taking, such as asking a family to implement one change. Adults can learn
to accept failures that can also result from risk taking. By learning from their
mistakes, adults and children can say, "I won't make the same mistake twice"
or "I can usually do something to help correct a wrong decision." This is a
wonderful philosophy to model for children.

Lord, help us give wisdom, knowledge, and joy to our children.

#299

***Walking with God and
family living means . . .***   learning to read people.

"He will teach us his ways, and we will walk in his paths." (Is 2:3 KJV)

Some family leaders understand how others perceive them, and some do not. The ones who don't keep going out on a limb and getting no cooperation or support. To read perceptions, leaders have to read children's behavior, their slouches, for instance. They need to be sensitive and "read" people. If a family leader doesn't feel he or she has support, it is better not to take a stand but discuss the issue more and more ahead of time, informally, in one-to-one conversations. Stress can block some of this discussion, or perceptions, so a relaxed situation, over hot chocolate, coffee, or food of some kind, might be in order. This is especially effective with teenagers in a family setting. A dinner or just ice cream out with Mom or Dad *alone* can uncover all kinds of blocks and/or hidden dreams and aspirations. The important one-to-one relationship with every member of the family can be fostered by such outings.

Lord, help us to know when to have patience and when to move forward.

#300

Walking with God and
family living means . . . knowing what is realistic to expect.

"Peacemakers who sow in peace raise a harvest of righteousness." (Jas 3:18 NIV)

The more valuable the parent or leader is perceived as being, the greater the love and appreciation that parent receives. This can also be true of families, with more knowledge and parenting strategies bringing more effectiveness, and more children bringing more love and joy and hidden potential for the future to a family. Learning to use a "talking stick" approach with children so that no one talks when the other has a turn with their hand on the stick can be another help. Slowly their hands alternate up the stick.

Planning, decision making, and developing clear tasks and problem solving, to go with vision and goals, are all a part of this approach to positive parenting attitudes and family management.

Lord, help us to be realistic in of our expectations of our families, and to see the joy and blessings a family brings as we walk with you.

Author's Note

Child development is the same in all cultures as these seventeen ending pictures show of children growing up in Africa. Photo credits are to Deborah Washburn Burke for pictures taken on her travels in Africa. Photo credits throughout also are to Janet Heim Jones, Allison Jones Lundeen, and Margaret McLennan Jones.

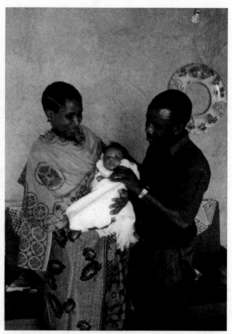

INDEX

A

C

D

E

F

G

H

I

N

P

R

S

T

Z